12/08

UNCOVERING HIDDEN RHETORICS

Dedicated to the past, present, and future faculty and graduate students
in the Department of Communication Studies
at the University of Texas at Austin,
a community of excellence.

UNCOVERING HIDDEN RHETORICS
Social Issues in Disguise

BARRY BRUMMETT
University of Texas at Austin

SAGE Publications
Los Angeles • London • New Delhi • Singapore

For information:

Sage Publications, Inc.
2455 Teller Road
Thousand Oaks, California 91320
E-mail: order@sagepub.com

Sage Publications India Pvt. Ltd.
B 1/I 1 Mohan Cooperative
  Industrial Area
Mathura Road, New Delhi 110 044
India

Sage Publications Ltd.
1 Oliver's Yard
55 City Road
London EC1Y 1SP
United Kingdom

Sage Publications Asia-Pacific Pte. Ltd.
33 Pekin Street #02-01
Far East Square
Singapore 048763

Printed in the United States of America

Library of Congress Cataloging-in-Publication Data

Uncovering hidden rhetorics : social issues in disguise / Barry Brummett, editor.
     p. cm.
Includes bibliographical references and index.
ISBN 978-1-4129-5691-8 (cloth)
ISBN 978-1-4129-5692-5 (pbk.)
     1. Rhetoric—Social aspects. I. Brummett, Barry, 1951-

P301.5.S63U96 20078
808′.042—dc22   2007023769

This book is printed on acid-free paper.

07   08   09   10   11   12   10   9   8   7   6   5   4   3   2   1

Acquisitions Editor:	Todd R. Armstrong
Editorial Assistant:	Katie Grim
Production Editor:	Astrid Virding
Copy Editor:	Jane McGraw
Typesetter:	C&M Digitals (P) Ltd.
Proofreader:	Dennis Webb
Indexer:	Nara Wood
Cover Designer:	Janet Foulger
Marketing Manager:	Carmel Withers

Contents

Politics in Disguise

Gender and Sexuality in Disguise

Acknowledgments

This book grew out of a research project into the rhetorical power of form that was begun with some graduate students at the University of Texas at Austin in the Department of Communication Studies. I am grateful to the dozens of graduate students and faculty in this department that have, over the years, made it a productive scholarly community. Thanks to Todd Armstrong, our creative and diligent editor at SAGE, who can see possibilities in unusual book proposals and to the reviewers of this proposal who provided helpful comments and suggestions: George N. Dionisopoulos (San Diego State University); Mark Meister (North Dakota State University); John M. Sloop (Vanderbilt University); and Patricia A. Sullivan (State University of New York at New Paltz). Thanks also to Roger Gatchet for his thorough and professional editing work on the manuscript.

Social Issues in Disguise

An Introduction to Sneaky Rhetoric

Barry Brummett

The words we hear or say, the images we make or see, usually have multiple meanings, connections, allusions, and resonances, yet we are rarely aware of all of those implications. Sometimes movies, television shows, political speeches, and hip hop music carry in disguise certain thoughts, attitudes, or political and social convictions. That is to say, a text or message may seem to be about one thing on the surface, but it is also about another thing, if we know how to unlock the text. For instance, some may argue that *The Lord of the Rings*, which appears to be about elves and hobbits and orcs, is *also* about World War II or the Cold War, but in disguise.

These disguises can cover a wide range of things, from innocuous social expressions ("I'm going to step in here for a minute" instead of "I have to go urinate") to more serious social and political issues. By social issues, we mean those conflicts, hopes, fears, and possibilities that have to do with how power is managed, how people live together or in opposition, how people construct their identities, communities, and lives. Social issues are issues on which we must make decisions with serious outcomes for ourselves and others. Yet sometimes social issues are managed in disguise, such that we are not fully aware of what is happening when we create or receive messages.

In the 1988 presidential election, Vice President George H. W. Bush repeatedly (and successfully) painted Democratic nominee Michael Dukakis as being soft on crime and punctuated this charge with ads infamously depicting Willie Horton. Horton was an African American in Massachusetts, Dukakis's home state, whose release from jail on a prison furlough program allowed him to commit crimes again on the street. It was widely charged on the left and among Democrats that Bush's appeal to fight "crime" was really speaking to racial fears, that it was "code" in some way for Scary Black People. The Willie Horton discourse, a number of people feared, was a disguise for racist discourse (D. Anderson). Bush could not, of course, explicitly articulate white people's racist fears, but he could disguise them in another discourse and, many charge, did so.

The Disney Corporation's film *The Lion King* met with complaints similar to the Horton ads in ways important to this book. Critics of the film, which on the surface seemed to be an innocent children's movie about animals in Africa, charged it with presenting disguised stereotypical caricatures of race and sexual identity. Animals with, arguably, the most African-humanoid features were also among the laziest, stupidest, most duplicitous characters in the movie. And the arch-villain lion Scar, so the charges went, displayed femmed-up, campy gay mannerisms of speech and gesture that were an affront to gay men. The rub was that all this pernicious antisocial work was done under the cover of a children's movie. Racial and sexual identity slurs, in other words, were given free rein in the film precisely because they were disguised as cartoon animal characteristics (Byrne and McQuillan; Giroux).

Author and social critic bell hooks describes another sense in which discourse may be hiding something. In her book *Where We Stand: Class Matters,* she argues that, although Americans are quite aware of socioeconomic class, we rarely talk about it in any focal way. Instead, she argues, we speak about race and gender, which become stand-ins for class issues. We may feel uncomfortable about another group of people and attribute our discomfort to *racial* differences when, in fact, were we to probe our feelings and our discourse, we might find that what we feel is discomfort about a *class* of people different from our own. People might discuss the problems of disadvantaged blacks as if their plight were mainly a racial issue when really the difficulties faced by that group of people come more from class than from race. We decry the challenges faced by "welfare mothers" as if they were problems of gender discrimination when what we mean is that they are problems of class. Often when we rehearse topics of race or gender, we are talking about class in disguise.

We frequently hear of social issues in disguise, hiding in plain sight in the garb of other kinds of discourses. Politicians speak of family, values, morals, and so forth and are accused of speaking "in code" the language of the religious right. Observers of the news may wonder why the issue of flag burning excites so much passion and suspect that the act of desecration as well as attempts to outlaw it are both hiding some deeper social conflict or anxiety. People complain when others speak in a language of "political correctness," and what is that but disguising the raw emotions of certain social issues in a bland and blameless language (R. Lakoff 86–117)?

To some extent, social issues are always disguised in the language we use and the texts that we consume. Our choice of topics and vocabulary will reveal, if closely examined, depths and implications of which we are often unaware. Language is a minefield of ethnic offense in disguise. If you complain of being "gypped," you are actually using an ethnic slur deriding the Gypsy or Romany group of people, taking them as synonymous with thievery and swindle. Ordinary language use in English is full of words that have disguised implications for gender equality. For instance, when we say, "If a person wants to succeed, ___ should study," what we put in the blank disguises stances and commitments on the subject of gender. If we say "he," we may seem to ignore women. In addressing women, we have the forced choice of speaking to them in ways that mark or do not mark their marital status (Ms., Mrs., Miss), whereas in addressing men, we have the forced lack of choice to mark marital status since the only term available is "Mr." And on and on. It is hard to speak, to see a television show, or to watch a film without the stuff of our discourse implicating and alluding to some wider social issue, a social issue that is thus at least partially in disguise. Language and images are unruly, sending tentacles out beyond their immediate locations, connecting to wide ranges of issues beyond the conscious intentions of creators and users of messages.

Social issues may be disguised in discourse for other reasons. There may be strong social pressures not to deal with certain issues openly, not to talk about some public problems, not to express ourselves freely. As we saw above, bell hooks argues that this happens when we speak about class in terms of race or gender. Race relations itself has been such a complicated, difficult, and painful issue for so many Americans for so long that free and open discussion of racial matters may be difficult for people. We may instead refer to "inner city" this or that when what we mean is "African American" this or that. We may pontificate on "the problems of the inner city" when what we mean is racial strife or the confluence of economic difficulties with particular races, exacerbated by other urban ills. I was recently in an electronics store and found a whole section of recorded music labeled "urban." In point of fact, nearly every artist on the CD covers appeared to be African American, and nearly all of the music was hip hop—but of course, the store could not have put up a sign saying "Black folks' music here" without incurring some social cost. Also, consider that for a long time sexual identities other than heterosexuality were not discussed openly—Oscar Wilde called homosexuality "the love that dare not speak its name"—so, in the past, instead of referring to someone as a "gay man" (or worse), one might disguise that fact by speaking of a "confirmed bachelor."

Disguising issues in discourse may be a cultural preference. Henry Louis Gates, Jr., has studied *signifyin(g)*, which he identifies as an African trope that became of importance to enslaved Africans in America and their descendants as a survival skill. Signifyin(g) is a preference for *indirection*. It was important to this group of people to be able to disguise some of what they were saying so as not to incur the displeasure of their oppressors. Gates argues that this preference for indirection, saying one thing and meaning another, continues as a way to disguise some issues in discourse even today. He gives the example of a woman who sees that her sister is obviously pregnant, so she remarks that her sister has been putting on weight—already a kind of indirection, since the first woman really means to call attention to the pregnancy. The pregnant woman blandly agrees that she has been putting on weight, at which point the first woman, exasperated but still disguising the issue, says, "Now look here, girl, we both standing here soaking wet and you still trying to tell me it ain't raining" (83). A preference for disguising certain issues in discourse is quite widespread and is no doubt a strategy across many different cultures.

Because it is important to know what we are doing if we engage social issues in talk, films, popular music, television, and so forth, understanding how social issues may be disguised in discourse is an important goal. If we need to disguise social issues, we should do so with awareness, and we should especially be aware of how those issues may be disguised in the messages we encounter. This book is a collection of essays that explore a wide range of ways in which social issues may be disguised in the public talk of leaders, news media, and ordinary people as well as in the texts of entertainment and popular culture. The goal of the book is to give its readers some tools for seeing the hidden social issues in those texts. Whether you intend to produce public messages or, as is the case for most of us, to consume them, knowing how to see through those disguises is important. This introduction will explain two general methodological concepts for doing just that: *metaphor* and *form*. The chapters that follow all show in more detail how we can detect social issues in disguise.

Metaphor

A *metaphor* is when we say that one thing is another; in the slightly different form of *simile*, we say that one thing is like another or acts as another does. If we say, "The center on their football team is a tank," or "She can throw that ball like a missile," we are using metaphor and simile, respectively. Metaphors create equations, and they link things together. It is hard to get through a couple of minutes of talk without running into metaphors. There, we just did it in that last sentence, treating "a couple of minutes of talk" as if that were some sort of physical substance that we must "get through" and in the midst of which we might "run into" some obstacle. Metaphors are all around us in our everyday speech, in the pronouncements of others, and in the media. George Lakoff and Mark Johnson's classic study of metaphor points out how important they are to guiding thoughts and actions.

Metaphors, of course, need to be interpreted, even if their meaning is immediately apparent. They are not literal—nobody would ever take the example above to mean that an actual military tank is on the opposing team—and so in an important sense a metaphor *is* the principle of disguise in discourse.

Metaphors can reveal great depths of meaning once we start to probe them, and these depths of meaning are often connected to social issues. But because those issues are expressed in the form of a metaphor rather than in an outright statement, the issues may be in disguise.

For instance, when President George W. Bush described North Korea, Iran, and Iraq as an "axis of evil" in his 2002 State of the Union Address, he used a metaphor going back at least to the Second World War when Germany, Italy, and Japan were known as the "Axis" powers. In picking that particular way to describe North Korea, Iran, and Iraq, the president used a metaphor that equated them with the villainous enemies of the United States in that war, countries currently treated by history (as written in the West) as unambiguously wrong. After its involvement in a series of morally ambiguous wars, beginning (in recent memory) in Vietnam, the United States may be yearning to be absolutely *right* in its geopolitical conflicts. Hardly anyone questions the idea that we were absolutely right in World War II. The president in an important sense was asking us (but in disguise) to see the current geopolitical struggle against terror as equivalent to the, from the U.S. perspective, morally pure struggle we engaged in during World War II.

Take another example: At this writing, Israel is militarily attacking the Islamic group Hezbollah in southern Lebanon. By the time you read this book, no doubt this ancient conflict will be under way in a slightly different circumstance somewhere else, with new messages delivering the same sad, old news. In reporting the current conflict, FOX News quotes Israeli UN ambassador Dan Gillerman as saying that Hezbollah is a cancer in the body of Lebanon ("Hezbollah Sharply Rejects Cease-Fire"). Remarkably, the *Meru Foundation Newsletter* has quoted an official of the Palestinian Authority as describing Israel as a cancer in the body of the Arab nation (Alexenberg). Rhetorical scholars Robert L. Ivie and Michael Osborn have, in several studies, called our attention to the importance of unpacking metaphors such as these. Would it be too much to say that both metaphors are metaphors of genocide, since the ideal solution to any cancer is to remove it entirely? How can one live happily in close proximity with cancer? Genocide, which one may not "safely" advocate openly, may thus be what is disguised in the discourse of these official spokespersons in the conflict (although we should not assume that everyone on both sides or on either side embraces that way of speaking).

Metaphor is a function of language that may be present even when there is not flowery or clearly figurative language in use. In fact, the philosopher I. A. Richards called metaphor "the omnipresent principle of language"—it is in all our talk (92). Any language that attempts to equate one thing with another, to link two entities together, may be working metaphorically, especially if the linkage is a kind of disguise for social issues. The earlier examples of coded or politically correct speech illustrate the principle of metaphor, as does our search for rhetorically acceptable ways to say that someone does not have the full use of some physical feature that others enjoy ("differently abled," "disabled," "handi-capped"). Racial descriptors work metaphorically. Over the last 50 or 60 years, an ongoing discussion has been held about what to call individuals in the United States of African heritage. "African American" is a kind of metaphor linking that group with Africa, "Black" stresses the centrality of skin color, and so forth. If politicians today speak about "family values" but, in fact, mean the values of the Christian right, then "family values" becomes a kind of metaphor disguising the Christian content of those beliefs.

How does one detect metaphors? That is to say, how does one know that, by a particular phrasing or use of words or images, a text intends to signal something else? How do we remove the disguise? The essays in this book will, of course, explain methods to reveal disguises in more detail, but some general ideas can be given here. One method is to look for what is *surprising* in discourse. Metaphors are fundamentally detected by noting unusual or unexpected speech, images, and other components of texts and messages. We notice such oddities and begin to ask what kinds of links and equations might be implied by such ways of speaking. What kinds of patterns and characteristics are shared between the way of speak-ing we have observed and some social issue that might be in disguise here? We can "audition" candidates for likely social issues until we find one that appears to fit.

Another way to look for metaphor is by searching for what we might call *compression*. Even language or images that are not surprising may, upon reflec-tion, have many complex and even contradictory meanings packed within them, so many that some are bound to be in disguise when we use such terms and images in everyday life. Take the terms "terrorism," "war on terror," or even "9/11," for example. Many social issues are signaled by using those terms or by displaying images (e.g., the World Trade Center burning) that evoke them. One might track the use of the phrase "war on terror" to find that it extends to pre-venting Mexican nationals from crossing the U.S. border in the south, to tap-ping the telephones of American citizens, or to developing enough flu vaccine. Invoking "9/11" can signal the need for military preparedness, fear of foreign nationals, a distaste for certain religions, or a call for support of the current administration. So to speak in any of these terms is to allude to a number of social issues that may be disguised until they are unpacked.

For instance, go to an Internet search engine and type in "real Americans." You will get a vast and fascinating array of sites. If you think about it, the term is a little puzzling. It implies that there might be such a thing as "false Americans." It invites examination of the people living around you, if you are in America. A number of questions are then raised as to what a real American is, whether one can go in and out of realness, who might be a false American, and so forth. The possible use of such an expression in many different contexts "hides" a number of social issues in that phrase. One could imagine that being a "real American" might be invoked in certain religious contexts to imply that people who follow another, different religion are *not* real Americans, are sinister and suspect. This expression is thus one of those that might invite metaphorical examination, since it is just a bit odd. You might start examining some of the sites that come up from your Internet search to identify the social issues in disguise when people talk about "real Americans."

Two other principles, *consistency* and *systematicity*, seem to be important in probing metaphorical discourse. The principle of consistency keeps us from overanalyzing, from interpreting a chance remark as if it were structuring whole sets of social issues in disguise. If President Bush describes Iran, Iraq, and North Korea in ways (axis of evil) that may equate them with America's enemies in World War II, we would look to see whether his language in other messages consistently does so. That particular figure of speech may not be used each time, but if he always or generally describes those three countries in the same way, then we are justified in seeing a consistent metaphor (rather than a one-time remark) at work here. Consistency tells us whether we have a real work of disguise under way or just an isolated turn of phrase.

Systematicity is the idea that when we put two things together in a metaphor the implications and connections that occur on one side should, to the extent the metaphor is fruitful and powerful, match implications and connections on the other side. Given that the president speaks of three nations as if they were our World War II enemies, then what characteristics did our World War II enemies have that are matched by characteristics of Iran, Iraq, and North Korea? As we unpack one side, we should find the other side unfolding in the same way, if one is really a disguise for the other. Germany, Italy, and Japan in World War II had powerful, sinister, solitary leaders who became the focus of popular imagination. Does the president in other discourse encourage thinking about the leaders of Iran, Iraq, and North Korea in the same way? The three World War II enemies were allied but largely independent—is that claim being made of the "axis" today? The three World War II enemies developed powerful, secret weapons—is the "axis" doing that, in the president's ongoing discourse?

In the same way, we might look at the metaphors being used by both sides in the current Mideast crisis and ask questions such as these: Cancers often have some pernicious cause; does further discourse identify a cause for this illness? Cancers debilitate you; does the rhetoric on each side complain of debilitation? Cancers can be treated in a variety of ways; do these spokespeople lay out options for "treatment?" Systematicity thus tells us whether and how one issue is being disguised as another metaphorically.

Form

You can think of form as, in some ways, an expansion of metaphor. When we think about the form of a discourse (a speech, a movie, a television show), we are thinking about the basic underlying pattern it follows. Patterns are by their very nature not singular or unique. To become a pattern, the form must be embodied in many different discourses. Form is thus a kind of metaphor on steroids, linking together a great many discourses because it underlies all of them.

No doubt there have been thousands of scholars who have thought about form, and of course we cannot cover all of that work here. So let's focus on just a couple of ways of thinking about form, which will end up being closely connected. We will look at what the rhetorical theorist Kenneth Burke has said about form and the way it connects texts and experiences, and then we will examine something called *homology*, a widely used method of formal analysis akin to Burke's work in many ways.

Throughout a number of his works of the twentieth century, Kenneth Burke explored the ways in which discourse connects rhetorically to our everyday lives. How do literature, film, television, speeches, and the other texts we encounter speak to our lives? For some texts, that question is not a mystery. If the president goes on television and defends a tax increase, that speech connects to our everyday lives directly; the president is trying to persuade us that the increase is needed. If you buy a new electronic gadget, the owner's manual is a discourse connecting directly to your life in that it tells you what to do and how to assemble the machine.

But much of the discourse we consume appears not to connect directly to our everyday lives. We see movies about werewolves and television shows about vampires, and we hear hip hop songs about a context of violence and substance abuse most of us will never know. One way to look at such messages is to say that they are not rhetorical, that is to say, they do not connect to our lives or influence us in important ways. But Burke and many other scholars argue that all discourse influences us in one way or another. Although the obvious, literal connection seems unlikely (we are not troubled by vampires in our everyday lives and yet we love vampire stories), Burkean scholars have identified the form of discourse as a level on which texts may powerfully influence us. Since form is very often experienced outside of awareness, form is a prime way in which social issues are disguised in discourse.

The main principle underlying Burke's discussion of form in several of his books is *connection*. Discourse is *connected* to social issues by way of form. Two examples will illustrate this idea. In an earlier work (*Rhetorical Dimensions*), I discussed two kinds of texts that seem to have no direct connection to everyday life: the 1984 film *Gremlins* (109–24) and vampire films (147–71). Both examples offer audiences rhetorically powerful advice on what to do in life, but at the level of form, I argued. *Gremlins* is *formally* about technology that has gotten out of hand, surely something we all experience from time to time, as when our computers develop minds of their own. The story in the film follows a pattern of ignorance and disrespect for technology, with sinister consequences—so often the same pattern we follow in our everyday lives. *Gremlins* connects with us not because we have actual gremlins in our attics but through sharing a form with how we behave when we encounter technology. Thus, the film advises us on what to do with our machines and how to use them. Vampire films, I argued, follow patterns of conformity and loss of identity, and therefore they connect with patterns that all of us experience from time to time—going along to get along, losing our identity at work, and so forth.

A vampire movie is certainly "about" vampires, but at the formal level it is also about some of the patterns we confront in life. The analyst who wants to lift the "disguise" worn by those social issues needs to be careful to draw *many* formal connections between discourse and experience. The more connections identified, the stronger the argument that the discourse does reference a social issue in disguise. This method is similar to the metaphorical principle of consistency that we discussed earlier, wherein we look for many different metaphorical expressions of the same idea to be sure we are looking at an enduring and important way of using discourse.

Clearly, form is an important way that texts address social issues, but in disguise. Once a text has connected to a social issue at the level of form, the content of that text—what happens at a literal level—can address those social issues. The form of *Gremlins* advises us not to engage technology until we fully understand and respect its social consequences, because its story says one should not keep gremlins until one has wisdom—the connection is formal, the advice is explicit.

To turn to another social issue, consider discourse that follows a pattern of mistrust and fear about the invasion of one's own space. Many examples abound: news reports of home invasion, movies about the mysterious and sinister family next door that just might be aliens, television comedies about the obnoxious relatives who won't stay out of a family's house or their personal lives, and so forth. Such texts *might* (one would need to analyze them closely to see whether the patterns really do connect) follow the same pattern that we see in discourse expressing fear and concern about illegal immigration. In that case, the news reports, movies, and television comedies may be about (may connect to) illegal immigration in disguise, and those discourses may then offer differing advice on how to deal with that social issue (fight back, laugh it off, build a wall, and so forth).

A second way of thinking about form is a method known as *homology,* an idea actually very much akin to Burke's approach and in some scholarship is explicitly based on Burke. It may be useful to think of homology as formal thinking with a wider net. A homology is a formal resemblance underlying many texts and experiences. The idea of homology is used widely in the humanities, natural sciences, and social sciences. Biologists might identify similar physical structures in several different species and work to account for the homology, the form, the species share. Marxist social scientists might identify a similar pattern of social behavior in widely different occupations, locations, or times and identify the homology creating the shared pattern as being structured by economic relations. Some recent work has argued that discursive patterns might underlie different texts and experiences, including experiences of media, so that forms of narrative, figures of speech, and other patterns found within discourse organize not only messages but ways of living in the world as well (Brummett, "Homology," *Rhetorical Homologies*; Olson). A homological analysis is typically more wide-ranging than a Burkean analysis of form, although, again, the idea of rhetorical homologies is built upon Burke's work.

Homological analysis and formal analysis really lie on a continuum; you reach homological analysis as you branch out and consider more and more different kinds of texts and experiences as ordered by the same underlying form. To illustrate, in an earlier work I argued that there is a discursive pattern of ritual injury, in which there is a move from the experience of real injury to treating that injury through ritual (*Rhetorical Homologies* 48–72). Ritualizing injury helps people cope with real injury and formulate ways of responding to that problem as it occurs in everyday life. In the study, I showed the same pattern of moving from real to ritual injury in stories of saints' martyrdoms, old Laurel and Hardy films, "playing the dozens," and televised professional wrestling. The form underlying those texts connects to our lives and allows texts to advise us in confronting experiences that follow the same form. Since we receive social injuries all the time in real life, a rather wide net is cast by this homology, showing how quite a disparate group of texts is connected to, and has rhetorical effect on, quite a wide range of actual experiences of injury.

For our purposes here, we need to consider that, if we are not aware of the shared form in a homology, then in a sense all the texts and experiences are disguises for each other. For instance, in the ritual injury study, I noted that turning actual injury into ritual injury was a central move in the civil rights movement of the 1950s and 1960s, as well as in other social movements since then that have followed the same model. In an important sense, then, when we see a film embodying the form of ritual injury, it may well be coaching an audience on to how to confront the real injuries of social injustice experienced today. Those social issues are therefore being managed in disguise in the texts. If seeing the form of ritual injury enacted on a television program of professional wrestling helps a person confront the real homophobic injuries they receive on the job for being poor or working class, for instance, then professional wrestling is helping manage social issues of class and economic discrimination, but in disguise.

Future Chapters

In this introduction, I have briefly indicated how discourse might be a disguise for social issues and suggested some general methods for unveiling those disguises.

The chapters that follow uncover disguises in considerably more detail, revealing some important social issues in very interesting disguises and showing us methods for digging social issues out of discourses for ourselves.

The book is organized into four parts: Race in Disguise, Morality in Disguise, Politics in Disguise, and Gender and Sexuality in Disguise. It should come as no surprise that as difficult and corrosive an issue as race is should be dealt with indirectly in public discourse. Kristen Hoerl argues that the film *Mississippi Burning* is homologous with the rhetoric of Black Power in the post–civil rights movement era. Thus, although the film is certainly about racial issues and civil rights protests at the level of content, formally it expresses the different dynamic of racial resistance offered by the Black Power movement. Race is entirely disguised in the chapter by Lisa Glebatis Perks, Luke Winslow, and Sharon Avital. They observe a plethora of representations of little people across a wide range of media. The depiction of the dwarf is a kind of Othering often applied discursively to people of color, thus little people can stand in for nonwhites as these discourses reinscribe patterns that contribute to racism. My chapter argues that the film *The Horse Whisperer* reinscribes a white liberal myth of racial history in the United States. The film reinforces a racist discursive pattern, even though few or none of the characters are not white. The analysis thus illustrates the method of homological criticism. Lisa Glebatis Perks's chapter on albinos notes their recurring presence across a range of discourses. The albino is represented in ways that, once again, reinforce discursive practices of Othering, and although they are hyper-white, they are presented in ways homologous with the Othering of nonwhites.

The second section explores morality in disguise. Morality-weighted attitudes toward strangers are explored in a study of three very different discourses by Kathryn M. Olson. She argues that a homology links the discourse depicting sport hunting, hate crimes, and stranger rape. Shared themes of mastery over others are implied by the separate discourses in each subcategory. Luke Winslow studies the rhetoric of pastor and evangelist Joel Osteen. It may be surprising that Pastor Osteen largely avoids explicit discussion of religion and morality in his published works, but Winslow argues that moral issues are disguised as economic issues in Osteen's discourse. His conflation of the two ultimately makes one's financial standing a matter of morality and God's favor.

A wide range of political issues in disguise is featured in the third section. Angela J. Aguayo turns to a surprising text, wildlife documentaries, featuring *March of the Penguins*. This film, seemingly about flightless Arctic birds, also articulates a number of themes commonly found in the rhetoric of the political and religious right. The formal link is enabled by attributing human qualities to the penguins. E. Johanna Hartelius argues that much of the great success of the *Pirates of the Caribbean* films has to do with their homologous relationship to the tension between state and corporation. Americans feel a particular anxiety over that tension, she argues, as state power gives way to the global corporation.

Roger Gatchet examines the discourses that frame witch-hunt tourism in contemporary Salem, Massachusetts. Across the various witch museums, memorials, and tours in the city, Gatchet identifies discursive patterns that disguise both the complex nature of the 1692 hunts as well as the way they connect to contemporary forms of persecution.

The final section explores the linked issues of gender and sexuality in disguise. Teresita Garza examines *Brokeback Mountain,* clearly a film addressing issues of sexuality and sexual identity. Those themes also express, formally, issues of masculinity, class, and culture. In William Earnest's study of the *X-Men* films, it is sexual identity itself that is in disguise. The issues faced by the "mutants" are formally those faced by gays and lesbians in a homophobic society, Earnest argues. The films are about "coming out," difference, and stigmatization.

In sum, this book invites you to be suspicious. All around you are texts that are clearly about one thing, but suppose they are also about another thing? Suppose you are being encouraged to think in certain ways about some important social issues without being aware of it? This book tries to attune you to that possibility and to show you some ways to think critically about the effects of social issues in disguise.

1

Remembering and Forgetting Black Power in Mississippi Burning

Kristen Hoerl

The 1988 film *Mississippi Burning* brought hate crimes from the civil rights era to the big screen. In the film's opening scene, local police stop three men, two white and one black, in a car on an otherwise deserted country road late at night. After the car pulls to the side of the road, a police officer approaches the car, calls the driver a "nigger loving Jew," draws his pistol to the driver's temple, and fires. As the screen goes black, sounds of additional shots ring out, and another man's voice declares, "At least I shot me a nigger." The rest of the film depicts the FBI's struggle to solve the case of these murders. This fictional movie was loosely based on the FBI's 1964 investigation of the disappearance and subsequent murders of civil rights activists James Chaney, Michael Schwerner, and Andrew Goodman. Following the film's opening scene, FBI agents struggle to find the bodies of the missing activists and apprehend their killers in the face of daunting obstacles posed by local Mississippi police. Through their perseverance and commitment to civil rights, the FBI overcome these challenges and arrest the activists' murderers in the film's final scene.

In real life, Chaney, Schwerner, and Goodman came to Neshoba County, Mississippi, in June 1964 as part of the Mississippi Freedom Summer Project. This project was a joint effort of leading civil rights organizations, the National Association for the Advancement of Colored People (NAACP), the Congress on Racial Equality (CORE), the Southern Christian Leadership Conference (SCLC), and the Student Nonviolent Coordinating Committee (SNCC), to bring more than 1,000 black and white activists from the North to register blacks to vote in Mississippi. By depicting events surrounding the activists' disappear-ance, this film brought renewed attention to the violence activists faced during the civil rights era. During interviews with the press, the film's director, Alan Parker, told reporters that he made *Mississippi Burning* because he wanted to bring people "largely ignorant of the events from two decades ago" to "some level of understanding [about events] that radically changed the South and the nation" (Hall C01). Parker suggested that his film would educate audiences about racial violence in U.S. history.

Mississippi Burning created a media stir when it first appeared. The film initially received rave reviews and commercial box office success. It generated $34 million at the box office after it was released to theaters in December 1988 ("Business Data"). The movie was nominated for six Academy Awards for that year, including one for best picture. Gene Hackman and Frances McDormand received Academy Award nominations for best actor and best supporting actress (respectively) for their performances, and the film won the Oscar for best cinematography (Curry D1).

Months after *Mississippi Burning*'s release, however, film critics and scholars passionately condemned the film. Several film critics faulted it for misrepresent-ing the FBI's actual role in the search for the missing men and for downplaying the role of black activists in the civil rights movement (Marquand; Milloy; Ringel). The film never mentioned the names Chaney, Schwerner, or Goodman, nor did it depict events surrounding the Mississippi Freedom Summer Project. The movie also provided a misleading depiction of the FBI's role in the civil rights struggle; in reality, FBI agents frequently ignored cases of police repression of activists. Critics concluded that *Mississippi Burning* symbolically supported white supremacy even though the film's main characters embraced civil rights (Brinson; Madison). Media scholar Kelly Madison argued that the film's emphasis on white men's heroism positioned blacks as nothing more than victims. Critics of *Mississippi Burning* presumed that movies about the past should have a direct correspondence with historical narratives to promote greater understanding of social and political power in the United States. In their analysis of *Amistad,* another film depicting racism in U.S. history, rhetoric scholars Marouf Hasian and Cheree Carlson expressed concern that entertainment films that claim to educate audiences actually obscure "detailed understanding of the actual experi-ences of those who have lived in the past" (43). These scholars suggested that depictions of the past that do not reflect the historic record inhibit awareness about social injustice.

Although critics are correct to point out that *Mississippi Burning* did not faithfully depict historical events surrounding the real-life disappearances of Chaney, Schwerner, and Goodman, I argue that these criticisms overlook some of the ways in which the film advances the cause of racial justice. On a formal level, *Mississippi Burning* evokes the struggles experienced by members of the Black Power movement, a social movement that emerged on the heels of civil rights. Looking at the film in the context of this movement, I argue that *Mississippi Burning* is a homology for the Black Power movement. Barry Brummett describes a homology as a situation in which "two or more kinds of experience appear or can be shown to be structured according to the same pattern in some important particulars of their material manifestations" (39–40). In this chapter, I explain how the film's plot revolves around the types of conflicts and solutions to racial injustice that propelled the Black Power movement.

To set the context for understanding how this film parallels Black Power, I describe the events that propelled the Black Power movement and the rhetoric of Black Power articulated by Stokely Carmichael, a prominent Black Power spokesperson. Then I analyze *Mississippi Burning*'s plot in the context of Carmichael's speeches. By interpreting the film's narrative in the context of Carmichael's rhetoric, I demonstrate how the film's storyline formally embodies the conflicts that Carmichael experienced and described during Black Power's heyday. I also demonstrate how the solutions arrived at by the film's protagonists mirror Black Power's response to racial injustices toward the end of the 1960s. By formally enacting the reasoning processes engaged in by Black Power proponents, the film challenges the justice of the then existing political system. The Black Power movement was an important response to ongoing racial injustices at the end of the civil rights era. By looking at the ways in which the film formally depicts similar responses to injustice, this analysis offers unique insights about the rhetorical role of this "civil rights" film. It also challenges the assumption that historically situated films must represent events with fidelity to the past in order to make a statement about social injustice and political power.

The Historical Development of the Black Power Movement

Emerging on the heels of the civil rights movement, the Black Power movement responded to the political and economic repression of blacks and civil rights activists during the mid-1960s. Jeffrey Ogbar defines Black Power as "a rigorous affirmation of blackness and racial pride and an insistence on the economic and political liberation of black people, independent of whites" (37). This movement signaled a new political consciousness among African Americans. In contrast to the civil rights goals of achieving formal inclusion within the American political system, Black Power sought political empowerment separate from white-governed institutions. Black Power activists also repudiated the civil rights principle of nonviolence in favor of armed self-defense against violent white suppression of blacks. Events in the history of the black freedom struggle as well as the living conditions within African American communities help to account for Black Power's emergence.

Black Power's political philosophy was a response to ongoing civil rights injustices and the dismal living conditions of African Americans throughout the United States. By the 1960s, blacks were still excluded from U.S. educational and political institutions. A series of beatings and murders of civil rights activists pointed to the lengths many whites were willing to go to prevent integration in prevailing institutions in the South. A federal grand jury acquitted Mississippi State Representative E. H. Hurst for the murder of black farmer Herbert Lee on the basis of false charges that Hurst acted in self-defense (Bacciocco 46). Likewise, Medgar Evers's murderer, Byron de la Beckwith, was not convicted for Evers's death until 1994 despite the strong physical evidence against him (Nossiter preface). In addition to the courts' failure to convict men for the deaths of civil rights activists, federal agents passively stood by as state authorities intimidated SNCC volunteers and blacks attempting to register in Selma, Alabama, in September and October of 1963. Public officials who turned a blind eye to attacks against civil rights activists suggested that violence against protesters was condoned by government officials.

In 1964, President Johnson signed the Civil Rights Act into law, making it illegal for states to compel racial segregation or prevent African Americans from voting. Because little enforcement power reinforced the Civil Rights Act, white supremacists throughout the South continued to harass and beat civil rights activists and blacks who attempted to register to vote. Two civil rights organizations, CORE and the SNCC, had been profoundly influenced by violence against blacks and activists in the preceding years. The summer of 1964 witnessed not only the deaths of Chaney, Schwerner, and Goodman but arrests of thousands of peaceful protesters, the bombings of 30 black-owned buildings, and the destruction of three-dozen black churches by fire (Marable 91). That year, white and black civil rights activists from Mississippi organized the Mississippi Freedom Democratic Party (MFDP) to challenge the exclusion of blacks from Mississippi politics. At their national convention in Atlanta that year, the Democratic Party's white leaders refused to recognize the MFDP as a legitimate arm of the party. The outcome of the 1964 Democratic Convention confirmed many activists' position that the nation's injustices would not be eradicated via reform within the system.

Many CORE and SNCC activists concluded that neither formal civil rights legislation nor strategies of nonviolent protest would convince white racists to support biracial democracy and justice. Johnson's dismissal of activists also prompted many of them to believe that the federal government had abandoned them. Edward Bacciocco writes that the generation of black activists who came of age during the 1960s concluded that social change would not be won by working within political institutions (31). Consequently, CORE and SNCC began to part from the more established Southern Christian Leadership Council (SCLC), an organization that held fast to reformist goals and to the principle of nonviolent dissent.

Black activists expressed their growing disdain for electoral politics and formal civil rights in 1966 when SNCC elected Stokely Carmichael and CORE elected Floyd McKissick to lead them. In contrast to earlier, more mainstream leaders such as John Lewis and James Farmer, these younger leaders suggested that black activists must wrest away political power for themselves. The slogan "Black Power" first emerged on the political scene in 1966 during the March Against Fear. On June 5, James Meredith began his one-man march across the state of Mississippi to encourage black citizens to assert their right to vote. Two days into the march, Meredith was shot by a sniper. Civil rights organizations including SNCC and the SCLC mobilized to continue the march. During this march, Stokely Carmichael articulated SNCC's departure from the mainstream movement by supporting the growing militancy of self-defense organizations. Rejecting King's slogan, "Freedom Now," SNCC member Willie Ricks led marchers in calls for "Black Power." On June 16, Carmichael reinforced SNCC's position in his reaction to police harassment against demonstrators: "The only way we gonna stop them white men from whuppin' us is to take over. What we gonna start saying now is Black Power" (Peniel 2).

Carmichael and other Black Power advocates found inspiration in black leaders from the North, where dismal poverty in black communities indicated that integration was not enough to improve living conditions for African Americans. Many black communities in the North and the West also faced ongoing police harassment. Police treatment of African Americans, growing economic disparities between white and black communities, and political struggles sparked race riots in urban ghettos throughout the country, including Detroit, Harlem, and Chicago. One of the deadliest riots took place August 11–14, 1965, in the Watts area of Los Angeles, California, leaving 34 people dead, 1,000 injured, and 4,000 in jail (T. Anderson 132). The growing militancy, anger, and spirit of radicalism in the urban ghettos of the North and the West fueled the Black Power movement (Ogbar 146). As a spokesperson for many people living in these ghettos, Malcolm X laid the groundwork for Black Power by arguing that the entire political system was responsible for black citizens' ongoing economic exploitation and political repression. In his famous April 3, 1964, speech, aptly titled "The Ballot or the Bullet," Malcolm X stated that the federal government had failed black citizens. In a veiled warning to government officials, Malcolm X suggested that, if blacks didn't receive the political representation they deserved, they would take up arms to defend their rights.

Stokely Carmichael's Black Power Rhetoric

The principles of black self-determination, self-defense, and solidarity were taken up by Stokely Carmichael during his years as the president of the SNCC. From the summer of 1966 to the spring of 1967, Carmichael toured the

United States, speaking frequently to both black and white audiences. Carmichael, who took the name Kwame Ture in 1968, organized his speeches around his definition of Black Power.[1] For him, this term meant the ability of blacks to redefine the meanings of blackness and to assert the value of black culture, blacks' responsibility to other blacks, and the importance of organizing the black community to attain political and economic strength (Scott and Brockriede 116). Carmichael's definition responded, at least in part, to his growing disdain for mainstream political institutions. His April 19, 1967, speech at Garfield High School in Seattle, Washington, and his October 29, 1966, speech on the campus of the University of California at Berkeley are typical of the speeches he delivered elsewhere. In his speeches, Carmichael described the problems facing blacks in the United States, the roots of the problems, and the solutions he thought necessary for ending racial injustice. As we shall see in the following section of this chapter, these same kinds of problems, causes, and solutions drive *Mississippi Burning*'s plot.

Carmichael believed that the central institutions governing the United States did not support black people's interests. During his speech at Berkeley, he stated, "It is impossible for white and black people to talk about building a relationship based on humanity when the country is the way it is, when the institutions are clearly against us" ("Black Power"). For Carmichael, the problems for black people were economic as well as political. He argued that poverty was "well calculated" in the United States and that poverty programs wouldn't work because "the calculators of poverty" were administering it. Carmichael believed that the American political, legal, and economic system was corrupted because the individuals assigned to protect the community were also those most likely to maintain white privilege. The Black Power advocate concluded that reforms within the existing political system would not guarantee the fundamental rights of people of color. Working from black philosopher Frantz Fanon's assertion that "man cannot condemn himself," Carmichael argued that the American political system was incapable of recognizing how its political and legal system perpetuated social injustice.

Carmichael believed that fundamental changes to the political system were necessary for blacks to win political and economic power. In part, Carmichael suggested that these changes could be met by reframing the political identity of the black community. Carmichael frequently reaffirmed black people's own entitlement and authority over their lives. In both speeches mentioned previously he insisted, "Nobody gives anybody their freedom." The problem, he argued, was that America had denied blacks their freedom. Instead of recognizing the political authority of the federal government, Carmichael appealed to a higher law of individual autonomy to guide black people's actions. Carmichael entreated audiences at Berkeley to consider how blacks might begin to realize their own political power.

> How can we build institutions where . . . people can begin to function on a day-to-day basis, where they can get decent jobs, where they can get decent houses, and where they can begin to participate in the policy and major decisions that affect their lives?

The Black Power leader suggested that, once black people recognized their own authority, they would be ready to demand recognition from the larger political system. Referencing the U.S. war in Vietnam, Carmichael told Berkeley students,

> We have to say to ourselves that there is a higher law than the law of a racist named McNamara. There is a higher law than the law of a fool named Rusk. And there's a higher law than the law of a buffoon named Johnson. It's the law of each of us.

For Carmichael, the principle of self-determination rendered the authority of the U.S. government illegitimate. "This country is a nation of thieves. It stands on the brink of becoming a nation of murderers. We must stop it." Carmichael appealed to the solidarity among black people rather than the goodwill of existing authorities:

> We are concerned with getting the things we want, the things that we have to be able to function. . . . The question is, will white people overcome their racism and allow for that to happen in this country? If that does not happen, brothers and sisters, we will have no choice but to say very clearly, "Move over, or we're going to move on over you."

As the above passage suggests, Carmichael believed that a cohesive organization of black people would be a strong force for social change.

The principle of self-determination also warranted the activist's support for armed self-defense. Carmichael argued that the appeal to nonviolence was a double standard in American politics; it was senseless to advocate for nonviolent forms of protest when white supremacists had maintained their position of power through violent suppression. Further, he argued, U.S. intervention in Vietnam relied on violence. Carmichael insisted that the only time that mainstream political figures condemned violence was when black people posed a threat to the white establishment.

Carmichael stated that blacks' self-defense from white violence was both legitimate and ethical given that the political system offered black people little protection. At Berkeley, he compared U.S. law enforcement to the German Gestapo under Hitler, asserting, "This is not 1942, and if you play like Nazis, we're playing back with you this time around." Carmichael made stronger assertions of self-defense in his Seattle speech. The SNCC leader drew from Malcolm X by defining Black Power as the "coming together of black people to fight for their liberation by any means necessary." He clarified his position on the role of violence in the struggle for black empowerment. "Yeah I'm violent," he declared. "Somebody touch me, I'll break their arm." Carmichael suggested he would disable anyone who threatened his political autonomy. Further, he maintained that Black Power advocates were not making idle threats: "We're just making it crystal clear to the honky today that if he try to shoot us, we gonna kill him 'fore God gets the news. Period!" Carmichael then explained that the threat of violence was nothing new to the black community: "We have been the recipients of violence for over 400 years. We've just learned well how to use it today." For Carmichael, the legacy of violence against blacks demonstrated that whites' political power in the United States was won at the expense of black people's lives. "Our guts and blood have been spilled for this country. It's time we spill them for our people." With this incendiary conclusion, Carmichael issued a warning to the white community that, if black demands were not met, blacks would rise up to retaliate.

Carmichael's speeches typically followed a pattern of argument that addressed the problems of, causes of, and solutions for racial injustice. In each of his speeches, Carmichael asserted that racial injustices continued to undermine blacks' efforts toward self-determination. He further argued that the central governing institutions in the United States were a primary source of political injustice because they did not recognize the fundamental rights of black people. Thus, injustices against blacks from within the political system warranted blacks' disregard for legal authority and their use of retaliatory justice.

Mississippi Burning as Black Power in Disguise

Although *Mississippi Burning* never mentions Carmichael or the Black Power movement, the film's storyline formally embodies the types of problems, sources, and solutions to racial injustice that drove Carmichael and other black activists. *Mississippi Burning* revolves around the struggles of two fictional FBI agents to solve the mysterious disappearance of three unnamed civil rights activists in fictional Jessup County, Mississippi. Rupert Anderson, played by Gene Hackman, and Alan Ward, played by Wilem DeFoe, endeavor to find the missing men and bring their murderers to justice in the face of obstacles posed by local police. Jessup County Sheriff Stuckey and Deputy Clinton Pell, the film's central antagonists, present daunting challenges to the FBI's efforts to solve the case. The agents' conflicts, their analysis of the problem, and their methods for resolving the case in face of local police obstruction parallel the central themes that drove the Black Power movement. As the following analysis of the film explains, parallels between the film and the movement illuminate how *Mississippi Burning* functions as a homology for Black Power.

ACTIVISTS DISGUISED AS FBI AGENTS

The film's depiction of trenchant racism and disregard for outsiders (non-whites, non-Southerners) by local officials in Mississippi parallels black activists' experiences throughout the United States. This parallel provides an important link connecting the film to Black Power. *Mississippi Burning* depicts Mississippi law enforcement—ostensibly a force for justice—as an agency dedicated to racial segregation. In one of the film's first scenes, Agent Ward describes the station as a "big building in a small town." When the two agents meet Sheriff Stuckey to discuss the activists' disappearance, the sheriff wryly asks, "You down here to help us solve our nigger problems?" Stuckey then states that the activists' disappearance "was a publicity stunt cooked up by that Martin Luther King feller." The FBI's initial meeting with the sheriff establishes the local police force as an overarching and racist presence. A later scene reaffirms the political power of the local police. In this scene, Ward and Anderson struggle to persuade members of the black community to speak with them. One boy, the only person willing to address the FBI, tells the agents, "The reason they don't want to talk to you is they're afraid it will get back to the law." After Ward responds, "We are the law," the boy's father asserts, "Not around here you ain't." The boy tells the agents that they ought to talk to the sheriff's office if they want to learn why the activists disappeared. Overshadowing the FBI's legal authority, local police thus completely control Jessup County.

The film's depiction of local officials as racist and oppressive would be expected in a film about civil rights or Black Power. Indeed, local police often stood in the way of civil rights. In real life, Neshoba County Sheriff Rainey and his Deputy Clinton Pell arrested Chaney, Schwerner, and Goodman and released them into the hands of local Klansmen the night they disappeared (Cagin and Dray). Even when local public officials did not physically harm civil rights supporters, they obstructed black citizens' rights. In an effort to prevent blacks from voting, registrars often gave blacks next to impossible exams when they registered to vote. Whites were never required to take such exams. Outside the South, police brutality was also frequent (Ogbar 84–85).

Despite the film's resonance with civil rights efforts in the past, the film's depiction of the FBI agents is an unexpected reversal in content. *Mississippi Burning* depicts the FBI as the only individuals actively seeking justice for African Americans. The film establishes the agents' commitment to civil rights early in the script. In the first scene with Ward and Anderson, we learn that one of Ward's previous assignments was to protect James Meredith from white violence when Meredith became the first black man to attend the University of Mississippi in 1962. We also learn that Anderson decided to leave his position as a Mississippi sheriff to work with the FBI because he could not stomach the South's racism.

On the level of content, it is paradoxical that the film's primary agents for black empowerment are FBI agents, representatives of one of the foremost political institutions that Black Power proponents challenged. The film's focus on the FBI downplays how black activists played a predominant role in the civil rights struggle and misrepresents the FBI's actual relationship with local officials during the civil rights struggle. In their history of the murders of Chaney, Goodman, and Schwerner, Cagin and Dray reveal that the FBI had an amicable relationship with the Neshoba County police (324). Rather than recall the FBI's friendly relations with local police, these FBI agents' struggles with local police formally recall the experiences of black activists.

Just as officials in Mississippi denied blacks their civil rights in history, fictional local officials deny Ward and Anderson's legal authority. An early scene amplifies the FBI's position in the film. During their first night in Jessup County, the men find a burning cross blazing in front of their hotel room. This marker was a common emblem of racial hatred and warned blacks that they would likely face greater physical dangers for pursuing civil rights. By facing similar obstacles that black activists faced during the civil rights era, *Mississippi Burning* thus positions Ward and Anderson as symbolic stand-ins for black activists. The agents' experiences through the course of the film illustrate why many civil rights activists called for "Black Power" toward the end of the 1960s.

Throughout the film, local police under Sheriff Stuckey collaborate with local Klu Klux Klan members to undermine the FBI investigation. Klan members respond to every development in the FBI's case by terrorizing the black community. The film frequently provides startling images of KKK members beating African Americans in response to the FBI's continued investigation into the activists' disappearance. Likewise, the film conveys spectacular images of black churches burned to the ground and homes firebombed in broad daylight as the FBI agents get closer to solving the case. Depictions of Southern brutality against blacks is not only a reflection in content of civil rights history itself but is part of the film's formal homology for Black Power. Within the context of the film's formal resonance to Black Power activism, these scenes stand symbolically for events extending beyond Mississippi racism in 1964.

A central distinction between Black Power and earlier civil rights was Black Power's insistence that the Southern states were not alone in supporting racial injustice. Reading the film's content alone, a Black Power proponent might critique the film for focusing on Southern racism to the exclusion of other forms of racial injustice that existed throughout the United States. The FBI's relationship with Stuckey and his officers, however, positions the local police as symbols for broader political structures that stood in the way of black empowerment. Just as the FBI stands for the position of black activists during the civil rights era, Mississippi law enforcement serves as a metonymy for the central institutions governing the United States. Metonymies are present whenever a part of something stands in for the whole issue, object, or event.

Perhaps not coincidentally, Black Power advocates frequently used the figure of the police officer to symbolize U.S. political and economic control of non-Western nations. Describing U.S. ties to underdeveloped nations during his speech at Berkeley, Carmichael referred to the United States as a "policeman of the world" willing to wage war against less powerful countries if it suited its interests. The police officer as a metonymy for the broader U.S. political system is a point of intersection connecting Black Power to the movie. From the perspective of Black Power, the intransigence of the police in the film formally recalls the federal government's resistance to black struggles for broader political and economic empowerment.

IRREDEEMABLE MISSISSIPPI

The local officials' failure to find justice for blacks, as well as their commitment to racial inequity, also formally connects the film to Black Power by indicating that injustices are perpetuated by the legal system. Early in the film, Anderson mocks the lyrics to a hate-filled song, "The Klu Klux Klan is here to stay." This line, in addition to several scenes that follow this one, attests to the Klan's prevalence in Jessup County. Klansmen connected to the local police obstruct the FBI's case by threatening local blacks at every turn. In one especially dramatic scene, three white men punish the family of the one boy who dared to speak with FBI agents. The men sneak into the family's barn and set it on fire, killing the family's livestock. The movie projects sounds of cows groaning in desperation as the fire engulfs the barn. As the boy leads his mother and little brother to safety, the Klansmen strike the boy's father and hang him from a rope tied to a tree in front of his house. (The boy unties his father after the Klan members drive off.) Violent images of Klansmen beating black people in response to the FBI's investigation suggest that racism is entrenched in the fabric of Mississippi society.

Other scenes demonstrate that the white power structure in the South supported the Klan's ruthless victimization of blacks. After four Klan members are put on trial for firebombing a black family's house, the county judge concludes that the men's crimes were provoked by outside influences and suspends their sentences. The judge's conclusion indicates that the FBI cannot prevent or hinder the Klan's unmitigated torture of blacks and civil rights activists. By highlighting how local officials treated white supremacists as above the law, this scene illustrates Carmichael's assertion that those governing the political and legal institutions in the United States could not be counted on to support racial justice. This scene also indicates that moral culpability is not treated as a matter of justice in the American legal system. As Carmichael stated in Berkeley, morality is a matter of "who has power to make his or her acts legitimate."

Both the film and Black Power activists indicate that justice cannot be won by working within central governing institutions. A short piece of dialogue from the film closely mirrors Carmichael's rhetoric on this point. Clues about the unknown assailants' identities point to the local sheriff's office. As Ward and Anderson get close to solving the case, Anderson determines that Deputy Pell was with the Klan the night the activists disappeared. After Ward asks, "Do you think he'll crack?" Anderson responds, "Down here they say rattlesnakes don't commit suicide." Anderson's response is a colorful adage for Carmichael's assertion that "America cannot condemn herself." Indeed, Carmichael told his Seattle audience that Sheriff Rainey (the film's character Sheriff Stuckey was loosely based on Rainey) was elected to maintain segregation. Carmichael reasoned that Neshoba County would not indict Rainey for his role in the activists' deaths because doing so would also implicate the county's residents in the activists' deaths. Using the figure of the police officer, Carmichael suggested that reforms within the prevailing system would not achieve justice for blacks as long as white proponents of racist policies remained in positions of authority.

The next scene in *Mississippi Burning* amplifies this point. After Anderson concludes that Pell was involved in the activists' disappearance, the FBI questions Pell about his affiliation with the Klan. Pell denies involvement with the KKK and refuses to answer further questions. Leaving the FBI office, he sneers, "Good luck. If you all get enough to indict me, you'll know where to find me." Outside the FBI office, Sheriff Stuckey mutters, "Don't you worry about a goddam thing." Pell and Stuckey indicate that local officials would not hold themselves accountable for the activists' deaths. Their intransigence vividly illustrates Carmichael's assertion that public officials responsible for blacks' victimization would not promote the cause of racial justice.

The failure of institutions to serve the cause of justice is a key theme throughout the film. Although the agents locate the bodies of the missing activists midway through the film, they can't find physical evidence linking the local police force or local Klan members to the activists' deaths. Indeed, when Anderson questions Frank Bailey, the police officer who shot the white activist in the head in the film's first scene, Bailey tells Hackman, "Still suits in Washington D.C. ain't gonna change us ... unless it's over my dead body [pause] or a lot of dead niggers." Through Bailey, Anderson learns that Klansmen believe that the local police force and the state's judicial system will protect them from punishment for injuring or killing blacks. Bailey admits that he wouldn't give more thought to killing an African American than "wringing a cat's neck" and declares, "There ain't a court in Mississippi that'd convict me." For Anderson, Bailey's confidence in the racism of Mississippi's legal system proves that formal procedures for FBI conduct will never substantially challenge state authorities who sanction violence against blacks. Positioned against the FBI agents, local police are symbolic of a larger political system that will not concede its power to a higher authority. The film's depiction of local police embodies Carmichael's assertion that racial injustices are not the result of isolated actions of individuals but endemic to the political system at large.

RACIAL JUSTICE "BY ANY MEANS NECESSARY"

Based on the conclusion that the roots of racial injustice were embedded in foremost legal institutions, Black Power advocates, as well as *Mississippi Burning's* FBI agents, concluded that justice must be won by going outside the law. In the movie, depictions of local police intransigence to the FBI's case provide the rationale for Ward and Anderson's unorthodox approach to solving the case during the second half of the film. Since they believe that the system is unable to reform itself, the FBI decide to act on a higher authority. Doing "whatever it takes" for the cause of justice is a third theme that runs throughout *Mississippi Burning,* providing another formal link to the Black Power movement.

Early in the film, Ward demonstrates an unassailable commitment to civil rights. After a fellow agent informs him that the manager of the motel where they are staying wants the FBI off his property, Ward instructs the agent to buy the building and do "whatever it takes" for the FBI to continue its investigation. Ward's response evokes the urgency of Black Power advocates' call for racial justice "by any means necessary." Ward aggressively pursues the investigation, calling for 100 naval reservists to search the nearby river bottoms for the bodies of the missing men. Anderson warns him to tone down his efforts and to avoid starting a war between blacks and white supremacists in the area, but Ward hears none of it. As he tells Anderson, "It was a war long before we got here." The conflict between Ward and Anderson echoes the struggle between more moderate civil rights activists and Black Power activists. Sharing Anderson's cautious approach, civil rights activists believed that racial justice would best be achieved by pushing for gradual changes within the white-operated system; by contrast, Black Power activists were more aggressive, demanding fundamental social change as the condition for blacks' freedom.

Despite his reservations about Ward's methods, Anderson is the film's foremost Black Power advocate. Anderson concludes that the legal and political system in Mississippi is inept and unwilling to find justice for the slain activists. Given the injustices embedded within the arms of the law and justice systems, Anderson decides that the federal agents will have to act outside the law to achieve justice for those who have been wronged. Anderson frequently resorts to threats and physical force when local police officers refuse to cooperate with the FBI's investigation. When his efforts to question Officer Bailey prove fruitless, Anderson reaches below his table, presumably grabbing Bailey's testicles. While Bailey groans in agony, Anderson tells him, "We're gonna' be here until this thing's finished." In the next scene, Ward confronts Anderson for intimidating the officers and for failing to follow FBI procedure. "We're not thugs Mr. Anderson. . . . If that was bureau busi-ness, I want to know about it." Although Ward indicates that he is willing to do "whatever it takes" to solve the case, he is committed to following FBI procedure during the first half of the film. Tension between Anderson and Ward thus grows as Anderson becomes increasingly frustrated by the FBI's powerlessness.

Conflicts between Ward and Anderson (both of whom are civil rights sup-porters) parallel the tensions that occurred between mainstream civil rights orga-nizations and younger Black Power proponents. Ward's commitment to rooting out the killers of the slain activists through formal procedures of investigation complement the more mainstream efforts of the past to achieve civil rights from within the prevailing political institutions. Although both civil rights and Black Power organizations sought political empowerment for blacks, the mainstream civil rights leaders strongly opposed principles and strategies within the Black Power movement. Ward's description of Anderson's behavior as thuggery mirrors the mainstream civil rights leaders' initial responses to Black Power. Organizations including the NAACP and the Urban League repudiated Carmichael's appeals to Black Power as "militant" and "threatening." Although Martin Luther King would not sign the statement for fear of strengthening divisions within the movement, he asserted that Black Power "connotes black supremacy and an anti-white feel-ing that does not or should not prevail" (Ogbar 63). Concomitantly, Anderson's charge that the activists' killers can only be apprehended if the FBI uses aggressive force is striking for its resonance with the solutions arrived at by supporters of the Black Power movement.

Despite early vocal disagreement with Black Power principles, civil rights leaders' stances on Black Power softened toward the end of the 1960s. As Black Power support grew, civil rights leaders expressed more openness to Black Power principles. Indeed, in 1967, King averred that white reprisals against Black Power activists only strengthened the Black Power position and "split the Negro from the larger society" (Ogbar 149). As King suggested, Black Power's position strengthened as their analysis of the political situation was reaffirmed by white supremacists' violence.

Just as Black Power activists believed that working within the political sys-tem would not win justice for blacks, Ward and Anderson come to agree that they will not be able to solve the case following FBI protocol. Unremitting Klan violence against the black community through the course of their investigation similarly tempers Ward's stance on proper FBI conduct. After Ward finds Mrs. Pell brutally beaten by her husband for helping the FBI, Ward reconsiders which steps will be necessary to bring the activists' killers to justice. The dialogue between Ward and Anderson toward the film's climax highlights Ward's evolv-ing approach to combating white supremacy. In an effort to stop Anderson from retaliating against Deputy Pell for beating his wife, Ward implores Anderson,

"We're not killers. That's the difference between them and us." Anderson retorts, "That's the difference between them and *you*." Anderson demarcates himself from Ward, suggesting he is not beyond using retaliatory violence himself. After the two men tussle, Ward aims his gun at Anderson's temple and demands that Anderson listen to him.

Ward:	We'll go after them together.
Anderson:	You wouldn't know how.
Ward:	You're gonna teach me how.
Anderson:	You wouldn't have the guts.
Ward:	Not only do I have the guts; I have the authority. No rules. We nail them any way we can, even your way.
Anderson (incredulously):	We do it my way?! With my people?!
Ward:	Whatever it takes.

By endorsing Anderson's methods for solving the case, Ward bridges the divide between him and Anderson. Ward's "no rules" approach to bringing the activists' killers to justice echoes Black Power's approach to finding justice for black people. Likewise, the FBI agents' struggles to assert their authority parallel the efforts made by the Black Power movement to reassert black people's authority over their own lives. Carmichael's appeal to the black community to hold itself accountable only to "the law of each of us" resonates with the FBI agents' final decision to take the law into their own hands.

The scenes that follow portray the FBI agents tricking and terrorizing Klan members to confess their involvement in the activists' deaths. Anderson threatens Deputy Pell in a barbershop with a razor blade positioned at Pell's throat and tricks one Klan member into believing that he needs FBI protection to survive impending attacks from fellow Klansmen. In another scene, Anderson flies an unnamed African American agent to Mississippi to interrogate the town's mayor and threaten him into providing the names of the Klansmen responsible for the deaths of the activists. Through a series of coercive actions, the FBI agents attain the evidence they need to arrest suspects in the activists' deaths.

The threats of violence against Klan members, which were presumably warranted by the Klan's own disregard for the law, enable Ward and Anderson to find some justice for the community. The film's final scenes depict the men involved in the activists' murders, including Sheriff Stuckey and Deputy Pell, being arrested by federal agents. By demonstrating that the activists' killers could only be brought to justice through the FBI's use of "dirty tricks," this film's conclusion suggests that people must sometimes go outside of the law to achieve justice and social equality. Presumably, the FBI's coercive and illegal measures to apprehend the activists' killers are inevitable outcomes of institutionally embedded injustice.

Mississippi Burning is a homology for Black Power, disguised as a false portrayal of the civil rights era. The themes that propel the film's narrative—local whites' disregard for the rights of others, the role of institutions in perpetuating injustice, and the disregard for legal procedure as a response to ongoing injustices—parallel the experiences and rhetoric of the Black Power movement. Both the film and Black Power proponents underscored how powerful, white interests controlled the agencies for social justice; therefore, achieving social justice for blacks could not be won by working within them. Both narratives also suggested that institutionally embedded injustice provided the motivating force for protagonists to eschew the political and legal system. While the parallel structures in these two narratives point to the homological role of *Mississippi Burning*, the image of the police officer and depictions of racial injustice cut through both narratives, linking them together in both form and content.

Conclusion

Mississippi Burning illustrates how films can correspond to political events in form, even though their content contradicts the historical record. Echoing Black Power's analysis of the contemporary political system, this film challenges mainstream perceptions of social justice. At the time of the film's release, few resources in popular culture represented the Black Power movement in content. By making the film's protagonists FBI agents, figures who typically embody law and order, the film masks its resonance to the radical activist movement. This reversal might have helped popularize this film among mainstream film-going audiences. This reversal might also have extended attention to other marginalized groups experiencing political injustices in the United States, including those subordinated by class and gender. The potential for other groups not aligned with the Black Power movement to identify with the film's main characters suggests that homologies are products of the political and economic circumstances in which humans create and reflect upon discourse.

Mississippi Burning is a homology for Black Power not necessarily due to any intentional or conscious efforts of the filmmakers but because both the film and Black Power proponents underscore the experiences of African Americans and groups who have struggled to change oppressive laws, customs, and other structural barriers to political inclusion, economic equality, and social justice. These structural barriers continue to shape many people's lives in the United States and elsewhere. As the Urban League concluded in 2007, significant disparities between blacks and whites remain in areas of income, achievement, health, and legal reform. For example, 25% of blacks live in poverty compared to 8% of whites, black male earnings are 75% that of white males, and 9.5% of African American men are unemployed compared to 4% unemployment for white men ("The State of Black America"). Both *Mississippi Burning* and Black Power rhetoric highlight the contradictions between many people's realities in the United States and the American Dream myth, which tells us that hard work and effort will lead to individual achievement and financial success. The film's counter-myth presents a homology for the ways that structural factors like race, gender, and class pose daunting barriers to the American Dream. Malcolm X, a leading proponent of black empowerment, called this counter-myth the "American nightmare." Fredric Jameson explains that films tap anxieties and aspirations in the historical world that rarely have presence in nonfiction media. As an iteration of the counter-myth of the American nightmare, *Mississippi Burning* figuratively expresses the broader social conflicts and anxieties under which the film was produced. The relationship between Ward and Anderson metaphorically represents contradictions between the American ideals of social justice and equality and the practical realities of life, not only for black people in the southern United States during the 1960s but for all people who struggle against structural barriers to individual success. Black Power activists underscored these contradictions twenty years earlier, but it was the film that projected them into a venue accessible to wider—and whiter—audiences.

The patterns across *Mississippi Burning* and the Black Power movement suggest that films can give meaning to the past even if they aren't explicitly based on historical events. As rhetorical critics, we might look for ways in which struggles experienced by characters—even those in fictional texts—formally embody the experiences of real-life individuals living in times and places removed from the text at hand. Texts that pattern themselves after historic struggles can alert us to ongoing social problems, such as the concentration of power in the hands of a few or ongoing systemic injustices against subordinated groups. Solutions embedded in these texts might also provide insight into the present by suggesting ways in which similar responses can be made even now, but at a formal level.

There are some potential dangers in this approach. Breaks within a film's homology from the outside world could lead us astray. Despite its resonances to Black Power, the film's conclusion contrasted sharply with the history of Black Power during the movement's later years. Although the FBI's strategies successfully lead to the arrests of the corrupt police officers, Black Power's strategies of working outside the political system were largely unsuccessful. The movement declined in the early 1970s, partly due to FBI suppression of Black Power activism. FBI involvement in the shooting deaths of Black Panther Party activists Mark Clark and Fred Hampton attested to the lengths law enforcement authorities would go to curtail movements that fundamentally challenged the American political system (Blackstock; Wilkins and Clark). Rather than attend to the devastating outcomes of radical activism, the film's emphasis on coercion as central

2

Limited Representation

A Homology of Discriminatory Media Portrayals of Little People and African Americans

Lisa Glebatis Perks

Luke Winslow

Sharon Avital

> *Over the last year, I'd come to understand that deep down in the heart of the fear we normals have for dwarfs is a subliminal intuition that they are the ultimate moral tar baby, sticky with our deepest feelings of fear and justice and truth and beauty, and if you touch them even lightly you might never get loose.*
>
> —Richardson (253)

P opular culture has been inundated with little people in recent decades.[1] From major movies like *Willow* and *Simon Birch* to television comedies such as *Seinfeld* and *Dharma and Greg* and even to a reality program dedicated to their lifestyle—The Learning Channel's *Little People, Big World* (LPBW)—little people have become a prominent part of popular media. Indeed, Betty Adelson claims that there are hundreds of films featuring little people (235) and estimates that 9% of Little People of America (LPA) members are involved in the entertainment field (358). As a response to this media trend, we propose to consider the messages that are disseminated in the portrayal of little people.

In this chapter, we argue that mediated portrayals of little people are based on discursive structures of Othering that have been historically applied to media representations of African Americans. Discursive structures, which may be thought of as underlying patterns of language that influence word choice, order, and meaning, inevitably develop out of our use of language to communicate with one another. While these language patterns offer us a shared means of communication, they also organize relationships between people in ways that may empower some groups and disempower others. *Othering*, a term that became widely used after the publication of Edward Said's groundbreaking book *Orientalism*, refers to the ways in which cultural texts–books, films, and various forms of mediated communication–discursively construct groups of people as backward, primitive, savage, degenerate, or otherwise inferior to Western whites. Our observation that similar discursive mechanisms of Othering are at work in the mediated portrayals of both African Americans and little people indicates that these discursive patterns of Othering may be widespread, functioning to marginalize numerous groups of people.

Most of this chapter is spent discussing little people and African Americans, but we want to stress that the discussion is not about little people or African Americans. We use the homology in the media portrayals of the two groups to illustrate that a discursive structure of Othering, which has historically been applied racially, is now being applied to body configuration. But as you read, don't get stuck on race or height: Get stuck on the way language patterns can reinforce a social structure that not only supports racism and heightism but endorses larger categorizes of marginalization and oppression. Being able to identify discursive patterns like these can assist you in discerning mechanisms of marginalization hidden in unexpected places.

Barry Brummett, for example, uncovers a formal pattern of racist Othering in the next chapter of this book. He examines the interactions between rich white New Yorkers and salt-of-the-earth ranchers in *The Horse Whisperer*, observing that the New Yorkers are cast as strangers in the Montana ranch land, marked by the lingering wounds of their violent past, unfamiliarity with the norms of the culture, and an inability to help themselves. While the film does not seem to be about race on the surface, Brummett uses *The Horse Whisperer* to explain that discursive patterns of discrimination can circulate throughout seemingly benign texts, positioning one culture as "normal" and the other as strange or backward.

As you can see, Othering can be accomplished rhetorically through a variety of discursive mechanisms. To determine if little people are Othered and, if so, how they are Othered, we collected and examined a wide variety of films and television programs from the past two decades that include little people. Several formal patterns in the discursive construction of little people emerged from those texts that have homological partners in the mediated portrayal of African Americans. We will focus on three discursive patterns that collectively Other: fantasy magic, anger and violence, and comic relief. By uncovering the formal structure of Othering that undergirds representations of African Americans and little people, this discussion helps expose mediated patterns of Othering that can be used to marginalize many groups. To set the stage for articulating the homologies of Othering, we will first provide an overview of our critical methodology.

Methodology: Homologies of Othering

The method of homological rhetorical criticism involves uncovering formal patterns among disparate texts or experiences. Because everyone is socialized in a particular society, stable categories are created in our consciousness that help us process and organize information. Although texts or experiences may not appear to be related on the *surface*, there may be *formal* discursive patterns common to them that offer important insight into how persuasion works. Indeed, the three of us had seen many of these films and television shows before conducting this research, but not until we viewed them again as a collection of little person texts did we start to see the formal patterns. And interestingly, the formal patterns we observed echoed stereotypes of African Americans in film and television that other scholars had already uncovered, indicating that these stereotypes are built on a widespread discursive structure.

The three themes we discuss, of magic, violence, and comedy, can be loosely labeled mechanisms of Othering because they mark little people as different from the "normal" or "regular" population by presenting them in particular character stereotypes or categories rather than in a diversity of roles that reflect their actual lifestyles and experiences. As people are socialized in a given society and taught how to organize information or create categories in their consciousness, they will likely be exposed to examples of Othering such as these. Said describes how Western nations have historically Othered people from Asian and Middle Eastern nations (for example, the cover of the most recent edition of *Orientalism* depicts a snake charmer, an example of such stereotyping) but also notes that women, the poor, and the insane have been and continue to be Othered. Instead of seeking to understand people who may be different from us, it is perhaps easier to communicate oversimplified and often inaccurate representations of them.

Many social and cultural stereotypes contribute to the process of Othering, and examples may be seen in numerous everyday encounters. In an incident one of us recalls, for example, students were asked to reveal an interesting fact about themselves on the first day of a group communication class. A student who was male, African American, and tall stated that he was attending college on an academic scholarship. Although the student explicitly stated that it was an academic scholarship, the instructor asked him what sports team he played for. One of the stable categories in the instructor's mind seems to have been African American male + tall + scholarship = athlete. This ready association likely would not have happened for a white student, perhaps because the instructor has a greater diversity of categories in his mind for white people. The incident is a primary example of the insidious ways that rhetorical homologies of Othering influence the way people organize information and, in turn, perceive people.

Little people, or the physically disabled in general, may also be considered a group that is marginalized through the ways that they are discursively positioned in society. Their needs and ways of life are often not considered primary, and, as such, they are constructed as deviant from the norm. For example, while there may be particular building codes and regulations that require wheelchair access to public spaces, public places are often not physically accessible to everyone, including little people, unless laws require it. Consider that the height of grocery store shelves and ATM buttons may essentially make little people *disabled,* but little people are expected to adapt to the situation, not vice versa.

Rosemarie Thomson explains that bodies marked by visual difference become cultural deviants as they are "defined through representation, and excluded from social power and status" (8). Othering can come with many surface features, but the underlying formal structure organizes various groups of people into inferior positions based on their differences from a normative center (whether that center is discursively positioned as white, masculine, or of average height, or involves another attribute that has become socially powerful). Thomson's work supports our mission to provide a detailed account of the homologies between mediated portrayals of little people and mediated portrayals of African Americans that will help unmask the discursive structures at work in the Othering of both groups. We now take a closer look at the mediated stereotypes.

Analysis

FANTASY MAGIC

The first type of Othering we explore in popular culture marks marginalized groups as different because of superhuman powers. Although magical abilities may not seem like a negative attribute, consistently portraying African Americans and little people as magical in television programs and films serves to reinforce whiteness and average height as the invisible centers of normalcy. We will first discuss the magical trend in African American popular culture characters and will then describe formal resemblances in the portrayals of little people.

Heather Hicks in her article titled "Hoodoo Economics: White Men's Work and Black Men's Magic in Contemporary American Film" analyzes the spate of recent U.S. films in which African Americans possess magical powers. Hicks explains that what marks the black magical characters in films such as *Ghost, Grand Canyon, The Green Mile, Unbreakable,* and *The Family Man* is that they are not simply magical but that their magic is geared toward saving the white characters playing the leading roles in the films. Similar themes of magical or spiritual powers can be seen in African American characters from *Bruce Almighty, Bedazzled, The Hudsucker Proxy, Pirates of the Caribbean: Dead Man's Chest,* and the television program *Touched by an Angel.* In all of these examples, the magical African Americans also work to help white characters.

Krin Gabbard observes that African Americans are part of a well-established culture of spirituality but argues that many of these popular culture portrayals pull African Americans out of their own culture, situating them in fantasy prejudice-free worlds and offering redemption to white viewers who can easily feel compassion for the Uncle Tom figure (pars. 17–20; see also Appiah). In another essay, Anthony Appiah further suggests that black characters must have saint-like goodness to counteract the racism white audience members feels toward black characters.

The phenomenon of magical African American characters has been prevalent enough to be criticized in the popular press and parodied in *The Simpsons* (see Gabbard pars. 1–3). In a *Time* editorial titled "That Old Black Magic," John Farley comments that, "instead of getting life histories or love interests," African American characters get magical powers because Hollywood scriptwriters do not know anything about their unique life experiences. He cites films such as *The Legend of Bagger Vance* and *What Dreams May Come* as primary examples. In sum, it seems that the magical African American archetype arises from scriptwriters' unwillingness to portray blacks' unique life experiences as well as serves as a method of making African American characters more palatable to a prejudiced audience.

Similar to the exoticism of African Americans in popular culture, little people have often been depicted as magical beings. Adelson describes the ways in which little people have commonly been perceived:

> After the initial shock of reverberating emotionally to physical deformity, the normate may impute to this unknown person the mythological wiliness of trolls, the moral blemish of the evil-spirited dwarf, or the childlike asexual cheeriness of Walt Disney's seven dwarfs—depending on which reference is most familiar. (88)

In spite of the abundance of films with little people, it is rare to find simple love stories or dramatic tales with little people playing a leading role. Rather, little people have been traditionally depicted as belonging to a different realm, a world beyond commonplace reality. Beyond the mythological figures in fairy tales and folk stories, little people up to this day often take part in fantasy or science fiction films in which they usually add to the mysterious atmosphere.

The films *The Lord of the Rings*, *Willow*, *Snow White*, and *Baron Munchausen* and the HBO series *Carnival* are fantasy texts that depict little people in ways heavily influenced by traditional legends and folk stories. The plots often take place in a fantasy world filled with bloody struggles between the forces of good and evil. Little people in these films are rarely the main characters and are almost exclusively a part of a larger group of fantastic characters such as witches and wizards, kings and knights, giants and hobbits, trolls and elves. Just like many magical African American characters, the importance of the little people lies not in their special powers but in their ability to help the normal-height character. In the familiar *Snow White*, for example, the dwarfs' significance derives from the shelter and protection they provide Snow White when escaping from the malicious witch. Similarly, the plot of *Willow* revolves around little person Willow's efforts to save the average-height baby Elora Danan from an evil sorceress.

The visible difference between magical little people and people of normative height is intensified in these traditional depictions through special costumes. In *Snow White* and *The Lord of the Rings*, for example, the dwarfs have long beards, hoods, and axes and are generally unkempt. Unusual costumes proliferate in other films, such as in the *Leprechaun* series with the traditional green suit and hat, along with *Bad Santa*, both of which show a little person dressed as an elf. These unusual costumes act as a visual highlight enhancing the perceived difference between little people and those of normative height.

Little people are depicted as otherworldly even in films situated in a "normal" environment. The film *Simon Birch*, for example, is not of the fantasy genre, yet magic creeps in the back door here as well. Short-statured Simon believes that his life has special meaning and insists that God will make him a hero. In spite of many difficulties, Simon indeed rises to greatness by miraculously saving several children. Simon dies by the end of the film, but not before he is made a hero. His spirit and faith, viewers are told, remain after his death.

Another example is the TV series *Twin Peaks* and the subsequent film made by David Lynch. Both are characterized by a scary and perplexing atmosphere—a woman is murdered in a small town, and an FBI agent is called to solve the mystery. A gratuitous little person was added to the ensemble of beautiful women and crazy men. He had no personality and existence of his own but appeared in people's dreams and told riddles. Since the actor playing the little person spoke backward and was edited to play from the back to the beginning, the impression of his words is frightening. As such he symbolizes the movement from the real world to that of dream and fantasy.

The mere presence of little people in many films appears to signify the plot's movement to another dimension. As Thomson claims, visual disability is usually stripped from any normalizing contexts such that visual difference itself signifies meaning (11). Tito, a little person character in the 1995 film *Living in Oblivion*, comments on the fantastic use of little people in films:

> Have you ever had a dream with a dwarf in it? Do you know any one who has had a dream with a dwarf in it? NOOOO! I don't even have dreams with dwarves in them. The only place I've seen dwarves in dreams is in stupid movies like this. "Oh make it weird. Put a dwarf in it."

The cynical remark beautifully reveals the absurd in the extent to which little people function as a signal of oddity in popular culture. The old association of little people with treasures and magic as well as their connection to mythical creatures such as dragons, kings, and wizards enable directors to plant them in new settings, relying on the fact that they bring the exotic and otherworldly atmosphere with them wherever they go. They consequently spice up the odd atmosphere by functioning as a sign of Otherness.

The association of African Americans and little people with magical realms of existence has become so commonplace that we may rarely acknowledge the negativity of the stereotype. Nonwhites and people of below-average height have been Othered by being associated with magic and sometimes also with service to whites and people of normative height. While it might be entertaining and easy for directors to have a fixed type of character symbolizing different realms of being, it is also disturbing. The discursive structure underlying the fantastical imagery of many African American and little people characters in popular culture can be seen as a mechanism of control by dominant groups. By casting African Americans and little people as different and unusual, a normative center is thereby created as the point from which everyone else deviates. Those who occupy that normative center (i.e., whites and/or people of normative height) benefit by being perceived as average, or ordinary, and can wield much power as the "universal" representatives of a given culture (see, for example, Nakayama and Krizek 102).

ANGER AND VIOLENCE

Perhaps the most egregious stereotype is the one connected to racial Darwinism. George Frederickson reports that arguments from pro-slavery and pro-lynching forces of the 19th and early 20th centuries operated on the stereotype that African Americans had an inherently violent nature (275). African American characters in popular culture today are commonly depicted as violent or angry, thus directly reinforcing the savage stereotype that historically functioned as a rhetorical justification for white patriarchy. Donald Bogle claims that the violent African American film character originated with *The Birth of a Nation*, although the controversy provoked by D. W. Griffith's film temporarily discouraged similar mediated portrayals (13–16). It was not until the blaxploitation films of the 1970s that a version of the savage African American form rose again (Bogle 13–16). Robin Means Coleman observes that African Americans continue to be limited to playing the roles of "pimps, drug dealers, gun-toting gang members, rapists, or murderers" (9). On the contrary, she notes, white characters are often seen as "without dysfunction" (Coleman 196).

Brummett describes the formal foundations of the angry and violent stereotype when he uncovers the "white liberal myth of racial history" in *The Horse Whisperer*. Brummett explains part of the myth as follows: "[P]eople of color bear scars of a lost innocence, an original Edenic happiness that was destroyed in horrible injury and violence. People of color are thus understood to be sullen, resentful, and hurting" (79). The portrayal of African Americans as angry and resentful is similar to contemporary mediated portrayals of little people. Little people in the media are frequently cast as ill-mannered and rude with angry dispositions. They are not social and outgoing but instead are demanding and overbearing to close friends and strangers alike. Little people have quick tempers and are set to combust at the slightest affront. In spite of their small stature, their caustic personalities often result in violent confrontations with larger than average-sized people.

The similar casting of African Americans and little people as angry and violent is fundamental to discursively constructing a savage Other, thus creating distance between what is normal and dominant and what is different and, therefore, inferior. Uncontrolled anger and unprovoked violence are socially deviant behaviors that reflect a primitive and savage personality, thereby subjugating African Americans and little people to the bottom of a hierarchy that rewards rationality and temperance. Overt violence allows for clear boundaries and distinctions to be drawn between exoticized little people and people of normative height. To support this claim, this section analyzes several prominent mediated portrayals of little people, beginning with *Seinfeld*'s Mickey Abbott.

Mickey exemplifies several of the stereotypes in mediated portrayals of little people. First, he is sullen and resentful. He treats most individuals with contempt, even Kramer and his friends, George, Jerry, and Elaine. George is the first object of Mickey's anger and violence after George offers some politically incorrect advice in Mickey's first appearance on the show ("The Stand In"). Mickey complains of the difficulties he is having as a stand-in for a rapidly growing child actor, to which George suggests, "Can't you just switch with another midget?" Mickey is clearly angered by George's use of the term "midget," a word akin to a racial slur in the little person community (Noel par. 5). He slowly approaches George with his index finger extended and gets in George's face, saying emphatically, "It's 'little people'! Got that?" Kramer, who knows Mickey's knack for losing his temper, restrains him.

Later in the same episode, Mickey displays his violent nature by verbally and physically assaulting Kramer on two separate occasions. The first incident takes place in Jerry's apartment, where gangly Kramer and short-statured Mickey get locked in a World Wrestling Entertainment–style stalemate. Jerry finally has to break it up and remind the two to behave themselves. The episode ends in the same way, with Mickey letting out a primal scream and again tackling Kramer as he is seated on a stool. The two fall to the floor as the credits roll.

In another episode ("The Burning"), Mickey and Kramer are hired to act out the symptoms of various diseases to help medical students practice diagnosing illnesses. Mickey's angry and violent personality is displayed again in this episode after Kramer acts out Mickey's coveted cirrhosis of the liver before Mickey gets the chance. Mickey yells, "Hey, that's my cirrhosis! He's stealing my cirrhosis!" Mickey rushes Kramer, throws him from the examination table to the floor and says, "You wanna be sick? I'll make you sick!" The scene ends with Kramer in a headlock while Mickey chokes him. From these scenes, the audience can see how Mickey handles conflict. He is easily offended, quick to anger, and prone to aggressive behavior. Furthermore, the extreme height differential between Kramer and Mickey exaggerates the irrationality of his violent nature.

The Lord of the Rings trilogy also features a little person portrayal that is consistent with Mickey's angry and violent personality. In these films, humans, elves, hobbits, orcs, dwarves, and all sorts of creatures come together in a battle over a powerful yet cursed ring. Even among this host of odd characters, Gimli the dwarf is the one who comes across as ill-mannered, rude, and overly aggressive (in both the Tolkien books and the Peter Jackson films), further reinforcing the fundamental nature of discursive Othering. Gimli is physically short, stumpy, and hairy. He is gruff and blunt and shows a penchant for verbal and physical confrontations. Not only is Gimli's weapon of choice—the battle axe—the most barbaric of all the character's weapons, he is the most eager to use it. Gimli has a combative relationship with most others, even those in his own fellowship. When the fellowship is first brought together and their quest is explained in *The Fellowship of the Ring*, Gimli is the catalyst for an explosive argument when he says, "I'll be dead before I see the ring in the hands of an elf!"

Despite the overall violence in *The Lord of the Rings*, Gimli still comes across as the most violent and bloodthirsty of all the fellowship. In his introductory scene, the cursed ring is displayed, and Gimli quickly draws his battle axe and ineffectively attempts to smash it. He has a simple solution to the problem. Later in the first film, Gimli and the rest of the fellowship come upon the massacred remains of Gimli's cousin and fellow dwarfs. When it is clear that the enemy orcs are coming to attack the fellowship, Gimli looks forward to exacting violent revenge. His excitement for killing orcs overflows as he stands upon a grave and shouts, "Let them come! There is still one dwarf in Mordor who draws blood!"

Mini-Me of the *Austin Powers* films also clearly reflects a homological connection with angry African American portrayals and the deeper form of Othering.

Verne Troyer gained considerable recognition as a little person actor playing Mini-Me, a clone one-eighth the size of Austin Powers's archenemy, Dr. Evil. Mini-Me's violent nature situates him fittingly within Dr. Evil's cadre of deadly assassins. Not only is Mini-Me angry and violent like Mickey and Gimli, but he is savage and animalistic. These related traits of violence and animalism illustrate that he has been marked with an inner penchant for violence, a form of biological determinism. Mini-Me's violent nature is displayed in two prominent physical confrontations with Austin Powers in *The Spy Who Shagged Me* and *Goldmember*. The audience is able to see Mini-Me compensate for his size through his zest for violence. In both of these fights, the much smaller Mini-Me is able to pummel Austin Powers before Austin is ultimately able to gain control.

Even among Dr. Evil's odd team of assassins, Mini-Me's animalistic nature makes him stand out. Mini-Me is indeed violent, but with it comes an unrestrained, animalistic savagery that makes his penchant for violence seem instinctual or interconnected with his small size. In his first scene of *The Spy Who Shagged Me*, he is reprimanded by Dr. Evil for trying to gnaw on a pet cat. Later in the same scene, Mini-Me lunges to attack Dr. Evil's son but is thwarted by Dr. Evil's assistant, who sprays him in the face with a water bottle—just like a pet owner would do to a misbehaving cat. The cat connection is seen again after Mini-Me gets caught in the rafters of the secret hideout; Dr. Evil suggests putting a bell on him. Mini-Me also displays dog-like habits: He is known as a "biter" by Dr. Evil's other henchmen and has to be kept on a leash at times. Austin Powers and Dr. Evil's son make the animal connection clearer: Austin says, "He's so small. He's like a dog or something," while Scott says, "He's like a vicious little Chihuahua thing" (*The Spy*).

Mini-Me's portrayal goes beyond the absurd in the *Austin Powers* films to reflect a deeper homological connection to traditional African American portrayals. Mini-Me's angry and violent nature seems animalistic and instinctual, illustrating that he has been marked with the biological determinism that has also plagued African American media portrayals. Easy laughs come from Mini-Me's absurdly violent outbursts, but beneath the amusement lies a form of Othering.

This violent pattern is prevalent in large roles like those in *The Lord of the Rings* and *Austin Powers* as well as in the smaller portrayals of mostly nonviolent films. *Elf,* a film starring Will Ferrell as Buddy the Elf, is a Christmas comedy much different from *Austin Powers* and *The Lord of the Rings,* but it does feature a little person who is consistent with these personality traits. The little person Miles Finch appears to assist Buddy's father, a book publisher, with an idea for a new book. Miles abruptly enters the meeting room and says in a harsh tone, "All right, let's do this." There are no greetings or pleasantries exchanged as Miles takes a seat at the head of the table and demands his money up front. Once his money is secured, Miles begins to explain a potential storyline, but Buddy interrupts him. In an innocent tone, Buddy asks Miles if Santa knows that he is not in his workshop. Miles says, "You better wipe that smile off your face before I come over there and smack it off." Miles then climbs on the table and delivers a two-footed dropkick to Buddy's chest. He then twists Buddy's arm and flips him back onto the table before Buddy is put in a headlock and spun to the floor. Like Kramer of *Seinfeld* and the orcs in *The Lord of the Rings,* Buddy is extremely tall. The absurdity of a little person physically dominating larger opponents shows their zeal for violence. Not only do they have quick tempers and angry dispositions but their enjoyment of violence is emphasized.

The consistency across genres is illuminating. It does not seem to matter whether the portrayal is in a sitcom, a science fiction film, or comedy, the angry and violent little person stereotype is widespread. Little people are seen as the exoticized Other, to be feared not only because they are rude but also because they are especially skilled in physical confrontations.

COMIC ENTERTAINMENT

Another African American stereotype that has circulated throughout the media for decades is that of the minstrel. A content analysis of 2003 primetime television revealed that African American characters are unusually concentrated in sitcoms as opposed to dramatic programs: 56% of African American characters were in comedic roles contrasted with 34% of whites and 26% of Hispanics (Signorielli, Horry, and Carlton). Toni Morrison opines that the Africanist presence in the United States has inspired literary themes that attempt to deal with "the collective needs to allay internal fears and to rationalize external exploitation" (38). Coleman opines that comedic roles often utilize "negative, stereotypical characterizations of Blackness to promote humor" (8). By occupying a position as object of white amusement (Gray 75), comedically framed African Americans may function to alleviate white angst about racial tensions and power dynamics (Watts and Orbe 18).

African American minstrel stereotypes can be seen as homologous to the little person jester. Adelson reports that the Tang dynasty of China used little people as jugglers and actors for its palace entertainment, a trend that continued through the Middle Ages (144). While the stereotypical, brightly costumed jester image of little people has become rather rare, the exploitation of little people as an entertainment form has continued, varying in severity from relegating little people to comic roles to the physically dangerous practice of little person tossing. The relegation of little people to comedic roles and entertainment spectacles functions as a strategy of containment of difference. Comedic roles trivialize their personhood and help reinforce the unmarked power of normative height bodies.[2]

Many little people in the texts we examined occupy comedic roles, with their bodies used to create humorous scenes. For example, Simon Birch is often the object of laughter. His birth was easy—his mother only had to sneeze and baby Simon unexpectedly popped out. Simon is ogled while in the hospital nursery, laughed at by the townspeople who mockingly call him a mouse, is picked up and passed around by his giggling Sunday school class, and is forced to play the baby Jesus in the Christmas play since he is "the only one who fits in the manger." Seinfeld character Mickey Abbott also finds himself limited to entertainment jobs, which provide comic fodder for the show: He works as the stand-in for a child actor on a soap opera and plays a department store elf at Christmas. The studio audience laughs when Mickey tells of the jobs he has taken. They respond raucously after Mickey's boast, "I stood in for Punky Brewster when all of you was [sic] nothing."

Little people characters often make jokes about their stature. Cracking jokes can be seen as a way for little people to gain acceptance by providing entertainment. Simon Birch amuses his friend Joe with various one-liners throughout the film. As the two dive into a cold lake, Joe remarks, "My balls just turned into marbles," to which Simon replies, "My balls just turned into BBs." Little people also appear in a few episodes of *Dharma and Greg,* providing one-liners for the comedy show. When Greg expresses surprise that Kim (a little person) is an oral surgeon, she quips, "You give your patients enough nitrous, they let you stand on their chest!" This line draws audible laughter from the actors and audience. Perhaps one of the most famous examples of a little person comedian is the now deceased Howard Stern sidekick and member of the "Wack Pack," Hank the Angry Drunken Dwarf. His official Web page explains that Hank quickly became a common figure on Stern's morning show because "Howard was amazed by how drunk Hank was as he told him a bunch of jokes and got more and more loaded."

Pigeonholing little people in comedic roles may have psychological effects on little people and the public's perception of them, but other forms of little person entertainment present more immediate and harmful physical effects. "Dwarf" tossing and "midget" wrestling have sparked much controversy and evoked strong responses from the LPA. Adelson recounts that little person tossing began in an Australian nightclub in the mid-1980s (363). The practice faced strong resistance in Europe but did catch on in a few American cities. The LPA took legal measures against little person tossing due to the physical risks it posed to participants and to the fear that the practice would increase the acceptance of physical aggression toward little people (Adelson 319, 364). Little person tossing is currently banned in New York, Florida, and France (Adelson 364).

The practice unfortunately continues in movies, most recently in the first two installments of *The Lord of the Rings* trilogy, although it is not included in the original Tolkien books upon which the movies are based. Gimli takes a stand against dwarf tossing in *The Fellowship of the Ring,* though it means risking his life by jumping over a large chasm. In the second installment, *The Two Towers,* Gimli asks Aragorn to throw him into battle so that he may help defend a vital bridge. Being thrown or "tossed" is clearly shameful to Gimli and he makes Aragorn promise not to tell his elf friend about the incident. In the LPA newsletter from September 2005, Vice President of Public Relations Dan Okenfuss reports educating a "Lord of the Rings Club" about the dangers of dwarf tossing after they incorporated a "toss the dwarf" game (using a Gimli *doll*, thankfully) into their Middle Earth festival.

Little people wrestling (commonly labeled with the offensive phrase "midget" wrestling) is still legal and seems to have gained in popularity recently. A team of little people wrestlers had prominent roles in the 2006 movie *Nacho Libre*. Also in 2006, a little person wrestler named Little Bastard made his World Wrestling Entertainment (WWE) debut. The WWE has taken even stronger steps to capitalize on the perceived popularity of little person wrestling, beginning a "Juniors Division" in the Friday Night Smackdown. WWE network executive Palmer Canon explains on the WWE Web site, "The Juniors Division will be comprised of world-class athletes at or below 5 feet tall. Midgets, dwarves, the little people; they're all welcome." Aside from the offensive use of the word "midget," which many people liken to a racial slur, the wrestling spectacle has been criticized by the LPA because it is "thoroughly degrading and puts little people out there as a sideshow and entertainment" (Dan Okenfuss quoted in Noel par. 10).

Just as African Americans are often relegated to comic roles in film and television, little people are often stereotyped into entertainment roles—from comic fodder to wrestlers. Positioning little people as a form of comic entertainment rhetorically constructs them as objects, not subjects, thereby potentially diminishing their personhood and discouraging others from treating them respectfully. Comic mockery has been a method of emasculating various groups throughout history, and this discriminatory mechanism also seems to be at work in the portrayal of little people.

Conclusions

So where do we go from here? It is important to ask what types of portrayals of little people are positive, encouraging people to understand the unique features of their lives but still not marking them as exotic Others. Gray warns of the dangers of assimilationist portrayals of African Americans that marginalize "social and cultural difference in the interest of shared and universal similarity" (85). Clearly, universal similarity only strengthens the positioning of already dominant groups as the norm, the center from which everyone else deviates (see, for example, Dyer; Nakayama and Krizek). Such portrayals make already marginalized groups feel not just different but inferior, and we do not wish for little people to be portrayed as such.

Adelson remarks that more positive television roles (not just fantasy or bizarre characters) began to be available to little people beginning in the 1980s but that little people are still very limited with regard to the range of roles they are offered. She suggests that media portrayals of little people would be improved if there were more roles that "illuminate the inner experiences of a dwarf" (235). We believe that The Learning Channel's reality-based program *Little People, Big World* (*LPBW*) represents a step in that direction. *LPBW*, which premiered in the spring of 2006, documents the lives of the Roloff family. Parents Matt and Amy are little people, and they have four children, one of whom (Zach) is also a little person. The opening of the program includes a voice-over by Matt and Amy that provides insight into their lives:

Matt: When you're only 4-foot tall you're feeling like you're living in a world that wasn't made for you.
Amy: We have to face obstacles and challenges just to live an ordinary life.
Matt: So we're making our own life on our 34-acre farm here in Oregon.
Matt: One thing I wish people would understand about little people is . . .
Amy: We can pretty much do what everyone else does, but just in a different way.

Throughout *LPBW* many unique experiences are discussed. The family attends LPA conferences, and Matt and son Zach take a trip to visit little people who are successful in a variety of careers. But in addition to the emphasis on the uniqueness of being little people, *LPBW* also shows Zach and his siblings going through the motions of any regular childhood. Zach and brother Jeremy get their driving permits, go to dances, and play on soccer teams.

Some critics have found fault with *LPBW*, arguing that viewers may treat the Roloffs as spectacle (see, for example, Kennedy). Indeed, we acknowledge that there can be no one perfect portrayal of little people. Media representation of little people, like that of African Americans, should portray a diversity of experiences and a diversity of character types. Unfortunately, that is not the current state of affairs, and both groups continue to be Othered through a multitude of stereotypical media portrayals that cast them as magical, prone to anger, and comic entertainment.

The homology in the portrayal of African Americans and little people demonstrates that discursive mechanisms of Othering may work to marginalize various groups of people, not just on the basis of race but on body shape, gender, or other attributes. Popular culture is a significant vehicle for propagating discrimination by exploiting our human, symbol-using tendency to build patterns and categories in our consciousness. These discursive patterns of Othering perpetuate hierarchal distinctions, functioning as a significant stratifying force in the United States.

The intent of this discussion is not to encourage readers to boycott the deluge of *Seinfeld* reruns shown each evening or to change the channel when *The Lord of the Rings* is shown. There are larger and more important implications that can be drawn from these findings. One goal of this chapter is to encourage readers to recognize how popular media can be a site of struggle, because it often creates hierarchies that marginalize and oppress while masquerading as harmless entertainment. Another goal is to empower readers to recognize the ways that formal patterns may contribute to the Othering of many groups, beyond little people and African Americans. Given just the three mechanisms of Othering discussed here—fantasy magic, violence, and comedy—is it not also possible that the elderly, athletes, and overweight people are Othered through similar patterns? Perhaps it may be helpful to consider the plethora of graying wizards in popular culture, all of the teen movies that depict the school sports star as a big bully, or the many television shows in which the main character has an overweight, comic sidekick. Uncovering a homology between the representation of little people and African Americans makes it possible to discern a rather stable formal image of Otherness, indicating that discrimination is fundamentally based on discursive structures rather than on the color of one's skin or other physical attributes. Understanding these discursive structures and the ways that differences are communicated helps us recognize a new form of marginalization that stretches beyond race and size and calls attention to new ways to understand and respond to our rhetorical world.

Notes

1. We have chosen to use the term "little people" instead of dwarfs because it seems to be the most preferred phrase in their own community.

2. There has been much disagreement in the little person community as to the effect entertainment roles have on the way in which the rest of society perceives little people. It is important to note that we do not aim to condemn little person actors who choose such employment but intend only to explore trends in their representation.

3

Whispers of a Racial Past

Forms of White Liberal History in *The Horse Whisperer*

Barry Brummett

Synopsis

The 1998 film *The Horse Whisperer* is a long, splendidly visual tour de force by Director and star Robert Redford. The film opens on a snowy, beautiful rural scene outside New York City. Thirteen-year-old Grace MacLean rises early in her country estate, saddles up her horse Pilgrim, and goes riding with her friend Judith. The two teenagers ride through beautiful Currier and Ives scenes wearing proper, classical riding attire and gossiping about boys—until they attempt to climb a snow-slick hill. The horses lose their footing and slip down the hill and onto a country road, with Jennifer falling from her mount yet still connected to it by a foot caught in a stirrup. As the girls attempt to control the horses and to free Jennifer, a massive truck rounds the corner of the road and cannot stop in time. Judith is killed, Pilgrim horribly injured, and Grace herself loses a leg.

Summoned to the hospital, Grace's parents—her father, attorney Robert MacLean, and mother, magazine editor Annie MacLean—learn the terrible truth of Grace's injuries. They are consumed by Grace's recovery and their own busy careers over the coming days and weeks. Yet a decision they are asked to face quickly is put off, with terrible cost: The veterinarian asks to destroy the

SOURCE: Chapter originally published in: Brummet, Barry. *Rhetorical Homologies: Form, Culture, Experience*. Tuscaloosa: University of Alabama Press, 2004. Reprinted by permission.

injured Pilgrim. Grace and Annie struggle over the decision, and Annie, unable to devote her attention to the matter fully in the press of her daughter's crisis and her editorial duties, refuses to allow the horse to be put down. The veterinarian does what she can to heal Pilgrim, but he is badly scarred, wild, and unmanageable.

The same may be said for Grace, who sinks into sullenness and depression. Her unwillingness or inability to recover is linked to that of Pilgrim. "We're losing her," Annie says to Robert, and so she seeks a cure. She discovers that Tom Booker, a "cowboy vet" in Montana, is a successful "horse whisperer," able to heal broken animals through empathic methods. She calls him and offers to fly him to New York, but he is unwilling to leave his work and dismisses the offer. Undaunted, Annie loads up the horse, the unwilling Grace, and herself in a car and trailer and drives to Montana.

This is not a decision gladly accepted by Grace or Robert, and it increases some evident strains that already exist in the MacLeans' marriage. The friction between Annie and Robert is an ongoing subtext of the film. It is evident in strained looks and conversations between the two and in Grace's manifest anxiety over that tension between her parents.

Toiling across the vast distances, Annie and her cargo finally reach Montana. With some difficulty she finds Tom Booker on his family ranch which he works with his brother Frank and Frank's wife (Diane) and their sons. An astonished Tom realizes that Annie is the woman he spoke to some days earlier, and reluctantly agrees to work with Pilgrim.

There follows a long period of time in which Grace and Annie move into a guest house on the property and begin to share in the ranch work, while Tom begins the slow process of healing for Pilgrim, which is ultimately successful. Grace's hostility slowly gives way to acceptance and finally she is able to ride Pilgrim again. In the meantime, Tom and Annie begin to fall in love. She is faced with the choice of whether to give up her New York world of sophistication for the utterly alien life of a rancher's wife in Montana—a decision that is brought to a head by her firing as editor due to her long absence.

Robert MacLean arrives unexpectedly for a visit in the midst of this drama. Annie's attraction to Tom becomes clear to him. He expresses his love for her and urges her to make a decision as to where she will live. Robert returns to New York with Grace. Sadly, Annie decides that although she loves Tom she could not live the life of a rancher, and so she follows her family to New York with Pilgrim in tow.

White Folks

The real star of *The Horse Whisperer* is Montana. Beautiful, lush scenes of vast prairies and grand mountains captivate the viewer. The people of Montana are also depicted as quite attractive. They are strong, virtuous, polite, sociable—and White. In scene after scene of cowboys and their families at work, at barn dances, relaxing on the front porch at the end of the day, we see no people of color whatsoever. Tom has an affecting story about an Indian he knew years ago as a youngster, and Grace and Annie stop at the Little Big Horn battlefield memorial on their way to Montana, but no actual Indians ever appear on screen, much less Hispanics, African Americans, or Asians.

And yet, if one looks not for the literal presence of color but for the form or pattern of color as a narrative element in American cultural myth then black, brown, and yellow faces begin to emerge from beneath the white skin tones. For the people of color in this film are the MacLeans, exotic sufferers moving west to seek healing and redemption—but in whose story? In this essay I argue that there is a liberal, White, mainstream American myth (hereafter, The Myth) of the racial history of this country, a discursive form—a recurring pattern—that generates many explanations that this empowered demographic tells itself in films, television, around the dinner table, and in school curricula. The Myth is a form creating a homology underlying many texts of popular culture and of White, liberal constructions of history. By homology, I mean a formal resemblance occurring across many different texts and experiences. As new texts (such as *The Horse Whisperer*) emerge, they embody the form once again and recreate the homology each time, perpetuating a powerful ideology that props up the well mannered dominance of White liberalism in mainstream American thought, politics, and culture. The Myth thus also orders the behaviors and the perceptions of those who share it. History itself, as lived experience, as story, as perceptions of others, becomes part of the homology grounded in The Myth.

In this essay I will show the homological bones of the film as I read it according to that mythic discursive form. In this way, I hope that a reading of the film can reveal some characteristics and nuances of The Myth at the same time that The Myth can be used to open up interpretive possibilities in the film—thus modeling the same possibilities in other critical efforts. This essay should help the reader to see ways in which racism is expressed *formally*, in ways that may not look like racism but nevertheless are. Let me begin by considering the overall structure of the mythic homology, and then returning to this unhappy family, the MacLeans, stripping off the content of the masks that they wear and revealing the roles they enact as people of color within this great White liberal American myth of racial history.

What's the Story?

Although it is alive and well in pockets here and there, outright racial bigotry has gone out of fashion in the United States. In the way of all successful tools of empowerment, racism dropped the tiring strong-arm practices of Jim Crow and standing in the schoolhouse door in favor of the more genteel masks of *hegemony*. If an empowered group perpetuates the idea that their empowerment is natural, acceptable, and preferable—especially if such ideas are accepted by the disempowered—we would say that such a group has hegemony. Hegemony is created and perpetuated by a rhetoric of common sense, a rhetoric of the natural. Of course, hegemony is often refused, struggled over, and subverted by those unwilling to accept it. The idea may be traced in the twentieth century to Louis Althusser and to a later, more sophisticated treatment by Antonio Gramsci.

Systems of empowerment based on constructions of race have employed a myth, a discursive structure, that underlies many texts and practices in Western culture. This myth has enough narrative cohesion and plausibility (I do *not* say that it is *true*) to find adherents and collaborators among all races (although we must acknowledge that many people also struggle to fight against The Myth). The homology it creates links seemingly many different texts and practices in creating a powerful understanding of how the West, and specifically the United States, came to be the way it is in terms of racial politics.

Expressed at a general level of abstraction, The Myth is told from the standpoint of White, Western culture in the United States, and it sounds like this:

> There is a race of people (them) who have had a horrible, violent, and injurious past. They have been overcome in the past through superior Western technology and social organization. These injuries may well have been inflicted by people *like us*, but it was not *us*. At any rate, the victims in the past (and/or their compatriots) were complicitous with their injuries and are thus partially responsible. Pain, anger, and a capacity for violence are the legacies of these injuries. As a result of injury and as a possible ground for healing, *they* have come to *us*, making cultural, psychological, and physical journeys. We offer healing and wholeness (we can do it, we have the "technology"), but through *integration* with us on our terms, in our space, literally on our grounds. Of course, we mean a guarded integration: They will always be exotic and different, but we'll take them in—they can sleep *over there*. This is a totally free choice we offer; there are no constraints on either side. But sadly, so many of *them* refuse the bargain. They return—sometimes physically, sometimes culturally, sometimes psychologically—to the less than idyllic historical/cultural/psychological/geographical places from which they came. They leave *us* sad but blameless, for we had extended our hand.

This is "history" told about Africans who came west in slavery, Indians who were pushed west to clear the land, Hispanics who came north to pick the crops, Asians who came east to build the railroads—and the descendants of these people. That every American of European descent made the same journey (west) is usually forgotten as White, homogenized, mainstream culture becomes the discursive center, the default, the culture always already in place. *We* have *always* lived in the castle.

The Myth provides a homology ordering and generating many discourses as well as behaviors. It is essentially the form beneath the film *The Green Mile,* for instance. In that film the viewer is given to understand that the tormented but angelic, exotic African-American character is the way he is because of a racist society—and we see the cautious, arms-length efforts of the White power structure in the prison to help him—but ultimately such efforts fail and the prisoner goes gently, even eagerly, into that good night. It is the form beneath news stories of families of color that succumb in successive generations to crime or to poverty despite the best efforts of White-dominated power structures to help them.

As we saw in the first chapter, every retelling of the discursive structure underlying a homology is a new version that introduces new elements, with rhetorical effect. *The Horse Whisperer* embodies The Myth, and in doing so helps us to see some dimensions of The Myth—but also carries its own freight of rhetorical impact. To understand how such a long (160 minutes), rich film embodies The Myth, I will first turn the discussion to the main characters and their experiences, up to the point at which they encounter the West.

Dark Folks

Of course it is outrageous to claim that the MacLeans are reindividuations of The Myth's construction of people of color. But perhaps it is no more outrageous than were the frequent humorous comments that Bill Clinton was the "first Black president." Both attributions depend upon a discounting of information and an attention to patterns of experience, style, and conduct. I trust that my analysis here will show that the MacLeans embody The Myth in that way consistently. To offer up one example by way of appetizer before the complete analysis: The central character in the family, Annie MacLean, although White is in fact an exotic foreigner, being British by nationality but having lived all over the world. She has come West as a stranger, to a Western culture already in place (in New York), and we are constantly reminded of her strangeness in the text of the film and in her British accent every time she speaks. She is not the British-regal *Anne* that her heritage and high-powered job would seem to demand, she is the folksier, working class, more American *Annie.*

The rest of the family, in their own ways, rings to the frequency of this strong central character who is enacting the strangeness and movement toward the west attributed by The Myth to people of color. The fact that the actual racial identities of the characters, on the level of content or information, is White suggests an interesting reversal—and the rhetorical effects of that reversal will be discussed later as well.

The Myth depends upon constructing people of color in certain ways. The MacLeans and their horse, Pilgrim, represent not only reindividuations of particular types of people in The Myth, but also dimensions attributed to the characters of people of color. The Myth constructs an image of Otherness in people of color, based on certain recurring attributed dimensions of those people. As The Myth is reindividuated in particular texts, stock characters may be created to embody those stereotypical dimensions. Later in the film Tom Booker will affirm the status of each character as but a dimension of a complex mythic character when he claims that the horse's recovery is integral with Grace's healing, and by extension with Annie's and Robert's as well. The relationships among these characters/dimensions is complex, and the ways in which a network of relationship in *The Horse Whisperer* emerges to express Third-World character will take some unpacking.

However, to preview that structure: One recurring dimension of The Myth is the emasculation of people of color. Strong males and, more importantly, male principles of control, law, and dominance are understood by The Myth to be recessive if not downright absent. These absent male principles are metaphors for the homeland fathers long ago who lost control, who let their people go, but who in some sense remain to keep open the door for a return. So it is with Robert MacLean, who is clearly less "high powered" than is Annie and who is in fact absent for much of the film as he remains in New York while his family travels to Montana. He is an echo in the collective memory of his family. In the absence of the male principle, The Myth posits the rise of a strong, controlling female presence—in this film, clearly the mother, Annie MacLean. Yet in The Myth this female principle is ultimately ineffective and weak, emerging elsewhere in tales of single parent households and welfare mothers unable to control their unruly children. The Myth thus imagines a waspish but ultimately ineffectual Sapphire, an imposing but fundamentally impotent mammy.

In The Myth, people of color bear the scars of a lost innocence, an original Edenic happiness that was destroyed in horrible injury and violence. People of color are thus understood to be sullen, resentful, and hurting—as is Grace MacLean, the once innocent thirteen year old who is torn in mind, body, and spirit. She is unreasonable and unreachable in her pain, as is the enduring sense of injury in The Myth. Finally, The Myth maintains the image of a lurking potential for violence among people of color. The more liberal The Myth, the more it is understood that this violence, this power waiting to erupt, has good reason to be so because of injuries and oppression suffered in history. But violence is nevertheless deplored, and the inability of people of color themselves to do anything about that lurking violent proclivity is likewise deplored—and here we see, obviously, the powerful, wounded horse, Pilgrim.

These mythic forms used again and again to construct people of color emerge clearly in the discursive construction of these exotics, the MacLeans, from the start of the film. Let us turn now in detail to the personae of the MacLean family to see how they express these attributions of The Myth in the first part of the film, in their "homeland" of New York and during the "middle passage" to Montana. We begin with the father, Robert MacLean.

As the film opens, Grace awakens in her room in the MacLeans' country estate outside the city. She peeks in at her sleeping father on her way to her fateful ride. Her mother is at the family's apartment in Manhattan, finishing the week's work. Robert MacLean is thus pictured as master of the homeland, the original ground on which Grace lives out her life of Edenic innocence. Yet he is a sleeping lord of all he surveys, not awake to warn Grace of the slippery conditions that might exist in the snowy world outside as she slips off to go riding.

After the accident, it is Robert who is positioned as the centering influence at home. He is first at the hospital to be with Grace, and breaks the news of the disaster to his breathless wife. As Annie rushes around managing affairs, bossing nurses and fussing over IV bags, Robert is the one nursing the stricken Grace, stroking her head and apologizing to the hospital staff for his wife. The same solicitous care for humanity continues at home. Grace slips and nearly falls rising from the dinner table, yet spurns Robert's quick rush to her side to help her. Later, Annie scolds him for this caring sensibility: "You've got to stop doing that. . . . helping her all the time, running to her every time she trips, anticipating her." It is Robert who promotes familial togetherness by suggesting a vacation: "Why don't we go someplace warm, the three of us . . . Bermuda, or the Bahamas"—a trip to Third-World warmth that Annie rejects on the practical grounds that Grace could not wear a swimsuit or sun dress in such tropical places. It is Robert who maintains the social unit even outside of the family, as he goes by himself to a dinner with people because, after all, "we're still friends" with them, as he explains to Annie.

All this social nurturing is one of several reversals in the film, in which Robert the father figure is emasculated and cast into more traditional (under patriarchy) female roles. He is the nurse, the homebody, the keeper of the flame in the family hearth. Although he is allegedly a high powered lawyer in Manhattan, we never see him at work (as we do Annie). Although he tries to assert his voice in family decisions, it is Annie who decides to take horse and daughter into the great West to see the mysterious horse whisperer, and Robert's initial objections turn to capitulation. As his family heads off to the strange West (Grace and Pilgrim most unwillingly and in virtual captivity), Robert remains behind to keep the home places going on a skeleton crew. In this way he enacts The Myth's construction of the spirit of the original homeland for people of color (whether that be Africa, China, the forest primeval of Pocahontas, or some other scene): a present but emasculated masculinity, a fatherland that in some sense is intact and waiting but no longer where the action is in terms of the "family" unit. In The Myth, the "spirit" of the original scene is barely active as its people journey to the strange and distant West.

Annie MacLean is clearly positioned as the center of control in this family, although that will evaporate as the family moves into the distant West. We first see her running (not "jogging," as she will later correct Tom Booker) near the family's Manhattan apartment. She goes to her work as editor in chief of a large, glitzy magazine, with assistants and functionaries running here and there at her bidding. From that seat of power she calls Robert at their country home and is clearly "in charge" of the situation, telling him when she expects to arrive and refusing his offer of a ride, saying she will take a taxi from the train station.

Annie's scene of power is another of the film's interesting reversals, for although it is culturally of the West it is functionally of The Myth: the production of a magazine, like Annie's running, requires furious energy that results in ultimately ephemeral, even futile, real outcome—an attribution frequently made about Third World economic prowess. Positioned in a seat of power, but in the world of entertainment, Annie is placed in as de-Westernized a place of control as can be. But in that site she is queen, and tough as nails. Scolding her boss on the telephone for his timid reaction to a lawsuit, she says, "You're not going soft on me, are you?" Later she will order her staff around to bring her information on horse healers that she needs for her personal life, and will do so imperiously: "I want it *now*." With her staff around her she ticks off the merits of the latest cover's photography, layout, cropping, and so forth, but then says: " . . . and I am so bloody bored," and orders them to do it over again.

Arriving breathless at the hospital, Annie is task oriented and domineering. Told that "Judith is dead" by Robert, she pauses, considering, then gets to the point: "What about Grace?" When informed that a leg has been removed, she objectively assesses the situation while keeping emotions in check: "Which leg?" she asks, as if it mattered. She orders the hospital staff around while her husband comforts their child. "I'm gonna get to know all the nurses' names; it's good to know that," she declares. Annie orders her husband around, directing him to remain with Grace while she runs errands. She is just as no-nonsense with the veterinarian, who asks that the horse be "put down"—"You mean *shoot* him," Annie replies. When Grace refuses to return to school because she is gawked at her first day back on crutches, Annie reads her the riot act: "Well you're not going to stay home all day feeling sorry for yourself, you're going to get up and figure this thing out." Rebuffed by her initial attempt to fly Tom Booker to New York, she imposes her desire to drive Annie and Pilgrim to Montana on the rest of the unwilling family.

Yet this Iron Lady shows signs of weakness and ineffectuality, which grow as she moves toward the West. Asked to give permission for Pilgrim to be destroyed, she cannot make the decision: "I cannot deal with this now, Liz, if you need a yes or a no then don't do it, OK?" Visiting Pilgrim for the first time with Grace, Annie stares at the broken, wild horse with an expression of despair on her face. The task of going West is daunting, and she knows it. Once the thrashing, flailing horse is put into the trailer the veterinarian asks Annie, "You got a gun just in case?" "Of course not," she replies. To which the vet returns a prophetic warning: "You may want to shoot *yourself* halfway through Ohio."

Huge trucks on a rainy highway on the journey frighten her. Battling a sullen Grace the whole way, Annie's imperious office manner gives way to weak, mocking impersonations of her daughter behind her back. During one of their many fights, Grace accuses Annie of having imposed her will on others: "It's all about you, about you being right." To which a confused Annie replies, "I don't have all the answers." She runs off into the night to collapse weeping by a park monument. What power there is in this community is thus shown to be more bark than bite, and much of it evaporates as these strangers approach the golden West. In this pattern we see The Myth's construction of non-White society as matriarchies governed by dragon ladies, big mommas, and other paper goddesses who prove to be unequal to the task of maintaining true power.

Grace herself is the site of injury, pain, and loss; she is damage personified. Pain constructed as a child, she thus raises questions of *guilt*: what more could we have done, who is responsible, who was watching out? Her loss is nicely (from the perspective of how The Myth works) balanced between complicity and fate: she could have done things differently, but on the other hand this just simply happened (in the past). The Myth thus neutralizes the pain and loss suffered by people of color in the past, and blunts connections to ongoing structures and processes that sustain that pain.

On the morning of the accident Grace awakens in a scene of Edenic innocence, a quilt covered bed in a child's room filled with statues and images of horses. She meets her friend Judith as snow slowly coats the countryside with purity, and they gossip about boys as they ride along. In this state of [g]race, she controls the power and violence represented by the horse easily. In the first of what will be a recurring image, once she has taken Pilgrim from the stall she shuts its door with a decisive clang of a black iron clasp. That mark of physical control over the powerful horse, the clasp, is matched by the gentleness of her mastery through love, as she sweet-talks the horse in echoes of the boy-gossip she shares with Judith. Grace will maintain this control until the injury; it is Judith, not Grace, whose horse loses its footing and who tangles her own foot in the stirrups. Grace is injured as she comes to Judith's aid.

The accident scene is horrifying but also surreal. It is shot in quickly alternating scenes that show the panic and fear of the girls and their animals as the White man behind the wheel of an enormous truck slides his overwhelming technology inexorably towards them. The moment of loss, the accident, the source of pain is thus remembered as in a mirror darkly; it is a confused image from the past. The Myth preserves the horror of the original loss at the same time that it refuses to remember historically specific events that might raise uncomfortable questions of responsibility (How fast was the truck going? Who owned the slave ships? Was the driver sober? Who profited from the cheap labor? Who eats all that fruit? and so forth).

The loss is terrible. The living envy the dead. The pain shared by Grace and by the embodiment of power, Pilgrim, is explicitly equated. After seeing Pilgrim for the first time after the accident, wildly in pain, Grace says, "I've decided about Pilgrim. I think we should put him down. It's not fair for him to suffer." As Annie begins to applaud Grace's calm maturity in such a decision, Grace drops the other shoe: "Maybe we should put me down, too. I'm not much use any more," a statement that stuns Annie in its pain and grief and prompts the trip to the West. The lost innocence of Grace represents the theme in The Myth of people of color as damaged, torn beyond repair, with parts removed. The loss suffered by those who come to the West, in The Myth, is so great that accommodation and prostheses are all that can be hoped for; there will never be wholeness.

The broken, fallen, former innocents who arrive in the West are also problematic, for their loss has emerged in an uncontrollable rage and violence. The bad things that happened to them have created terrible resentments, perhaps understandable under the circumstances but now wholly out of control. These resentments, this enraged power, must be managed in some way if social accommodation is ever to be achieved. This dimension of The Myth is clearly enacted in Grace's loss of control over Pilgrim. It is foreshadowed by her inability to control Pilgrim entirely, as she and Judith slide into the road. Recuperating in bed, Grace watches videotapes of herself riding Pilgrim in steeplechase competition, gracefully mastering his power. But that control is gone. She wants to see Pilgrim, and so goes to the veterinarian's barn. "Hey, hello beautiful boy," she coos to him in tones of old, and is shocked by the eruption of violence and power that is Pilgrim's reply. She is horrified by the sight of his still raw flesh, red and oozing on muzzle and flank. Backing away in a panic, she understands that the ability to control power has vanished with her innocence.

Grace's ability to control anything at all has vanished. She becomes a social outcast. One wonders where her friends are in all of this; at any rate, nobody is seen visiting her, nobody is kind to her at school, she cannot manage to keep up her social connections. "I don't want to come back, that's all" she tells her mother. Taken unwillingly on the trip to the West, she fights Annie all the way. When an exasperated Annie asks if she wants to return, Grace expresses her powerlessness: "What are you asking me for? You didn't ask if I wanted to come in the first place. Now *I* get to decide?"

As for Pilgrim: Twilight scenes of horses running open the movie, bringing the animals' power to the foreground. The original unity between this power and innocence is established in camera shots that alternate back and forth between Grace and Pilgrim as she saddles him up and as they ride toward their shared doom. Embodied power is "alright" as long as innocence is unharmed. With pain and loss comes an unappeasable drive to violence. Uncontrolled, angry power bursts forth from the wound left in the body of innocence.

The anger and violence represented by the horse is an important part of The Myth, which sees that violence as inherent in the complex of character that it attributes to people of color, and sees it as always in danger of eruption. Pilgrim is full of fire and spirit even before the accident, but he is mastered by Grace. Faced with the oncoming truck, he rises up to strike at it with his hooves, futilely opposing physical force to unopposable technology (as spears and arrows were once opposed to musket and cannon). When Pilgrim's body is broken, so is the hold that Grace has over his power. That hold was fragile to begin with. Reading about horses after the accident, Annie learns this: "A million years before man they grazed the vast and empty plains. They first came to know man as the hunter, not the hunted . . . the alliance with man would forever be fragile, for the fear he struck in their hearts would never be dislodged"—and the first pictures shown to accompany this narrative are of American Indians and what would appear to be Assyrians. This "fragile" balance is destroyed by the historical disaster that befell Africans, Asians, Indians, and so forth, and the potential for violence is thus on the loose. As the wild, eruptive stallion is locked into the trailer for the ride into the West, we see another closeup of an iron latch being clanged shut, emphasizing the strength that must be contained within the aluminum walls.

It is important in The Myth that violence is made to emerge from this afflicted people because of the pain they have suffered. The connection to injury provides a justification, although the violence is nevertheless regrettable. This connection to pain is what makes this a liberal myth rather than one of simpler racist attributions of violence; The Myth is a more complicated racist attribution of violence. In the film, the hideous injuries suffered by the horse are clearly marked as the cause of its newly emerged violent behavior. We see the horse first after the accident taking refuge under a bridge. The condition of his injuries, in which flesh hangs from him in strips, takes the veterinarian's (and the audience's) breath away. "Oh, Jesus!" exclaims the veterinarian. The horse overpowers her efforts to control it, overwhelmingly violent even in its injured state. It is eventually subdued, but even under tranquilizers in the hospital it is violent, kicking out with its legs against the stall. The change wrought by injury is made clear by the veterinarian: "Well Grace, you see, Pilgrim just isn't the same horse he used to be." She is more blunt with Annie: "This animal's beyond help."

The stage is thus set for these dimensions attributed to people of color, these complex interlocking parts of The Myth's racial theory, to reenact the historic journey to the West. With an unwilling Grace and a drugged Pilgrim, an uncertain Annie weighs anchor on her SUV and makes way for a distant land. We have had early indications that they will be strangers in that strange land. When Annie first called Tom Booker to solicit his help, she confidently announced, "This is Annie MacLean, from *Cover*. . . . you know, the magazine." Tom stares impatiently into the middle distance, completely unimpressed by this meaningless declaration of her tribal affiliation. "Is there something I can do for you, ma'am?" he queries. The strangeness that the MacLeans will represent as they move into the West becomes clearer the farther they go. Hip-hop and oldies radio begins to give way to the sounds of farm reports, country-western, and evangelists even as the land flattens while mountains rise in the distance. The strangeness that people must have felt arriving from Africa, Asia, and other parts of the Americas is echoed as these New Yorkers enter the West, and their own strangeness will be made plain to them once they get there. A significant break in the narrative of the film occurs as Annie, Grace, and Pilgrim arrive in Montana and declare themselves to the man of the West, Tom Booker.

The Man of the West

Tom Booker is a stereotypical cowboy, that mythical personification of White, patriarchal America. His rugged, weatherbeaten face exudes strength and confidence. As noted, we first see him in a telephone conversation with Annie as she tries to impress him with her magazine credentials and woo him to visit darkest New York. He stares into the far horizon, mastering impatience to be on the trail, refusing to leave his grounded place in Montana. He is who The Myth would like to imagine the benign patriarchs of the West to be, there to suffer the entreaties of the matriarchal societies that fate has brought to his shores.

Tom Booker will also enact The Myth's conviction that people of color, represented often in female form, are attracted (physically and spiritually) to the men of the West. The sexual attraction Annie will come to feel stands in for the social attraction imagined by The Myth. "They" want "us," says The Myth, even as the men of the West make the fulfillment of that desire a perfectly "free" choice for "them." Tom Booker does very little to woo Annie, other than to be himself; she falls head over heels giggling in love. This attraction is also expressed in other ways. Reading about horse whisperers in general, Annie learns that "Since that Neolithic moment when a horse was first haltered, there were those among men . . . who could see into the creature's soul and soothe the wounds they found there." All of the whisperers pictured in the film at that moment are White. The men of the West are thus pictured as sources of healing and love, waiting for wounded people of color to come to them.

Moving ahead of the approaching MacLeans, the camera first shows us Tom in Montana tending an animal as his brother, Frank, and Frank's adolescent son look on. Tom's nephew is relating a story he heard in school about how geese can "imprint" on an airplane and follow it around, and he recommends that the family try to get a foal, newly born on the ranch, to imprint on them. Tom smiles and says, "Might be alright for geese to grow up thinking they're an airplane. A horse, far as I can tell, can't fly." This is precisely the kind of parable that an older generation of racists might have used to explain why birds of different feathers ought not flock together—a version of racism that The Myth updates and replaces—and at that precise moment, the car and trailer from New York pull into their yard with its freight of strange, exotic birds from distant lands.

Assuming her best managerial style, Annie extends her hand to Tom: "Annie MacLean, from New York. We talked on the phone. I had a little trouble finding the place, there are *nooooo* signs." Annie natters on in her British/New York urban sophisticated way while Tom regards her as if she were a Martian newly dropped from the skies. "Oh, there are plenty of signs, just not many that are printed," he replies, thus laying claim to a knowledge of how to negotiate *this* place that is denied to this exotic. She implores him again to examine Pilgrim, and when he begins to demur she snaps at him, "Look, please don't do the 'shucks, ma'am' thing again," a rather grating thing to say under the circumstances. She practically summons him to the motel, then returns to his car. Tom never answers, staring at her all the while. His is a communicative strategy that Annie and Grace will both encounter and engage in often during their stay in Montana: questions go unanswered, remarks go unremarked. The film thus enacts The Myth's assertion of a lack of connection and communication among people of diverse backgrounds, and suggests that the snippy social manner of the matriarchal Others may be largely to blame for the disjunction.

Annie and Grace appear as Other to Tom when he goes to their refugee camp, disguised as a motel, to examine Pilgrim. There he sees for the first time Grace's artificial leg. Annie is in another room doing her magazine business by phone. Grace is watching the television show *Friends,* about as un-Montana as you can get. "This your first time in Montana?" Tom asks, and Grace makes no reply. "Is she gonna be long?" he asks of Annie, still on the phone. "Probably, she's on the phone twenty-three hours a day," says Grace. Then she offers up this gracious observation: "Just in case she hasn't told you, which she probably hasn't, I don't want to be a part of this, OK?" Difference, separation, lack of connection mark the interaction from the start.

I have mentioned before the extent to which locks and clasps appear regularly in the film. Entering Pilgrim's stall, Tom undoes a heavy metal chain. He uses a coiled rope, an instrument of constraint and control, to wave at Pilgrim in an attempt to subdue the horse, as if the rope were a talisman. Pilgrim has not been led around in months, much less ridden, but he still wears a bridle. The film features close-ups of these instruments of mastery. In the context of the racial history of America, they are also reminders of the physical bondage of people in slavery, incarceration, and other situations of oppression, and they emphasize the position of Tom as the White man of the West, and of the MacLeans and their horse as the exotic Third World.

However, the film embodies The Myth by granting the man of the West his instruments of physical (if need be, brutal) control but locating the real source of his power in his spiritual purity, social dominance, and strength of character. In the corral we see the first of many episodes in which Tom will look deeply and intently at the horse, as if divining the secrets of his soul. Annie remarks at the immediate effect: "Well, you're the closest anyone's come" to Pilgrim. Tom's plan for healing emphasizes the connection between Grace and Pilgrim, between damaged innocence and unruly violence in the Third World: "I need to know something right now. It's a question for Grace. You see, when I work with a horse, it's no good just me doing it, the owner's got to be involved, too." When she objects that she cannot be involved since she cannot physically ride, he dismisses the argument: "Either you want to or you don't." In doing so he shifts the problem with Grace (and with these people) from a physical one to a moral one: her disability is restated as one of will, not of historical fact. It is a way in which The Myth urges "moving on" beyond the fact of historical injury, to overcome that history by an act of will and moral transcendence. Of course, the man of the West is thus placed in a position of moral superiority and judgment. When Annie also objects, Tom overrules her: "This is her decision, not yours," thus speaking for and directing this social group that has come to his place, and empowering the man of the West over these exotic strangers.

Back home with his brother Frank and family, Frank's wife Diane has all kinds of objections to Tom's working with the MacLeans. "Well, I just think she's got a lot of nerve showing up here and that, you know, poor animal and that child." She all but wonders why they don't go back where they came from. The strangeness of the MacLeans is emphasized gastronomically. Frank hypothesizes that Annie eats "Big salad. . . . I believe women from New York eat big salads," which prompts another assertion of difference and strangeness from Diane: "Well that's just what we need, a vegetarian from New York on our cattle ranch." In this episode the characters reenact The Myth's attribution of legitimate grievance for Whites, at the same time it notes their patient acceptance and assistance of people of color.

Themes in The Myth that have been established so far are continued and elaborated upon as the film progresses. In his first sessions with Pilgrim on Tom's own ranch, we see more close-ups of coiled rope, which Tom has in his hands often and waves at the horse so as to control his movements. Ropes are used to lead Pilgrim through water. Annie's attempts to exercise her own poor power in this context are shown to be useless, especially as she questions these attempts to control the horse's power. "What's he doing? Is this some kind of physical therapy?" she asks, and is ignored. Many of the scenes in which the MacLeans' questions are ignored are situations in which force is being used to subdue the violent horse. In this way The Myth shows people of color the futility of questioning the "legitimate" use of state power in controlling expressions of rage. During this episode Annie's cell phone goes off, sending the horse into a flailing panic. Officiously, she chides Tom: "Mr. Booker, I'm really not comfortable with you taking these kinds of risks." She clearly has no idea of what she is talking about, nor any standing to make such a comment. The Myth uses the film to position the West as exercising a necessary control over the unruly power of people of color, a control which is questioned by the ignorant, ineffectual sites of matriarchal power. The Myth thus legitimizes means of coercive control as serving a higher, even spiritual purpose that will not be understood by those being controlled.

The spiritual grounding of ropes and chains in The Myth is made clear by what follows this scene. Pilgrim is allowed to run off, with Tom following. The horse stops in a meadow, and Tom simply stops as well, some yards from him, and sits, staring intently at the horse. Annie, not understanding the higher purposes that are being served, querulously asks "Are we in the way? Should we leave?" And when she is completely ignored, as she is so often, she says, "I guess we'll go then." Tom waits in the meadow the entire day, until toward dusk the horse gives up the spiritual struggle and comes to him, bowing his head. Capitulation of angry power and a move toward the ground of, the site of, the man of the West is regarded as a great spiritual victory. Tom's only comment is to chide Annie for her major link to the homeland: "From now on, leave your phone somewhere else."

Once anger has bowed its head, even if only for the moment, the exotic MacLeans are deemed civilized enough to be invited in for dinner, which Diane does. Their utter difference from this centered Montanan family is clear: they scarcely know what to do as the family prays before dinner, and their conversation is about restaurants in New York as the family attempts to discuss different breeds of cattle. Frank, in a moment of generosity, offers Annie and Grace the use of a spare house on the ranch while they are there. From the amazed expression of Tom and the appalled expression of Diane, it is clear that he has committed a *faux pas* in actually inviting these people into the neighborhood, but the deed has been done. Diane's subtle objections are hardly noticed, and Annie seems not to pick up on the cues that she might not be welcome. Grace pipes up that the house would be a good place to receive Robert when he comes to visit, prompting Diane to ask, "Where *is* your dad, sweetie?" "He's at home, working," she replies, but her embarrassment at her disunified family is clear.

This episode expresses the discomfort inherent in The Myth with meaningful integration—a conviction that integration must be done on the ground of the West (*they* must come to *us*)—and a sense that the brokenness asserted for people of color is an embarrassment to them, a looming scandal of which they are always aware. That embarrassment continues *en famille* as later that evening Robert asks Annie, on the telephone, "So when are you coming home?" Annie replies evasively, "You know, I asked him that tonight he doesn't know"—a reply that places decision making for this family with the man of the West, Tom Booker. Once she hangs up Grace asks her, "Did you ask him to come visit?" to which Annie replies, again evasively, "You already did." The dysfunction of the family is clear, as it is in The Myth.

The next day, Tom is again in the corral with Pilgrim. He throws a rope over the neck of the horse and wraps the other end around himself, using his own body as a lever with which to control the horse's wild running and rearing. Questioning *this* use of force by the man of the West to control violence, Annie asks "How is it going?" of a ranch hand—and is again ignored. Pulling the loop (the noose?) around the horse's neck tighter and tighter, in what can surely be read as an echo of lynching, Tom finally brings the horse to a standstill. Pilgrim walks calmly to Tom, as he did the day before, and *again bows his head* before the man of the West, allowing the rope to be removed. At this point Tom and the ranch hand exchange knowing looks and brief nods, a confirmation of Tom's success in controlling violence and restoring order—but also an exchange that completely excludes Annie, making success as an achievement of these two White men as they exercise their secret and powerful knowledge.

If the point about control over violence were not yet clear, there follows a long passage of scenes showing the branding of cattle. Rambunctious calves are shown on the ground, irons becoming white hot in the fire, the scorching of flesh as the brands are pressed to hide. A major component of The Myth is the complicity of people of color with their own misfortunes, the idea that Africans sold Africans to the West, Asians and South Americans willing came here to work, and so forth. Into these scenes of branding, of violent control, come Annie and Grace to observe. Tom asks each of them to "make yourself useful," and they are quickly put to work helping willingly with this work of mastery and marking. Annie is laughed at good-naturedly as she falls in the corral, landing in Tom's arms at one point to her embarrassment. Grace likewise learns to brand, and presses a hot iron onto live flesh with a smile on her face. Annie wears her difference like a signboard, asking an incredulous Tom, "Is it cocktail hour yet?" Tom recruits Grace even further into the project of control and mastery, saying "You handled that pretty well. I think it's time you started earning your keep around here," and suggests that she groom and feed the horses. "Think you can handle it?" he asks. "That's not a question, is it?" Grace replies, to which he says, "No." She does not object, and thus damaged innocence is willingly recruited in the project of mastery and control.

The Myth understands that strangers came here with history, but that history is usually understood as one of pain and suffering. The West is positioned as the site of a rich, positive history that is the center to which other, less privileged cultures come. In *The Horse Whisperer*, the Booker family is pictured as such a center, having lived for generations on their ranch laying down a sedimented history and family tradition. This point is made in the evening of the branding day, when a picnic supper shows real cowboys who could well be straight out of Western movies, playing guitars and singing around campfires. In this site of venerable grounded (if imaginary) history, Tom and Frank's aged mother tells stories of the family. She asks Annie, "Where do you call home?" Answering for her from a position of dominance, Tom replies, "She's from New York, Mom." But Annie explains that her strangeness is even stranger: "I'm from all over, really, my father was a diplomat, we moved all over." And although Mrs. Booker praises Annie for such an exotic life, Annie mournfully replies, "It's not like *knowing* a place like this." She remarks as she views pictures in the old-fashioned parlor, "This family has quite a history." Diane says, "Yup, it's a story alright." Diane relates stories of Tom and Frank's Western boyhoods as Annie sees a picture of a close family life unfold.

Annie's lack of centeredness continues to be made clear as she wanders onto the front porch and finds Tom demonstrating a string game to the children. He offers her his jacket as she sits and fidgets. "Don't you ever sit still?" he asks. "Well, you sit still too long in New York and you get renovated," she replies, marking herself as Other. She also marks herself as disempowered:

> "Why is it, Mr. Booker, that sometimes I get the feeling that you're laughing at me?"
> "I don't know, why?"
> "No; you're supposed to say you're not laughing at me."
> "Oh I see, you take care of both sides of the conversation."
> "It's a man's world, Mr. Booker, most women have to."

She is the wanderer, a visitor from a foreign place but also the disempowered woman, come to a patriarchal society that seems always to have been here, that seems naturally grounded in the land. "It's beautiful country, and I can see having some kind of vacation place or retreat, but don't you miss the rest of the world?" Annie asks. "What's to miss?" Tom replies. Annie lists museums and opera and so forth, to which Tom replies that he enjoyed those things when he lived in Chicago, a revelation that surprises Annie. The man of the West thus lacks nothing; his groundedness does not come at the expense of sophistication. He knows which fork to use as much as the next gent. But he also belongs somewhere, a groundedness denied this vagabond, exotic female.

Annie's Otherness is also apparent the next morning, when she confronts Tom out early; he is riding, she is running. "Oh, a jogger, eh?" he asks her. "I don't jog, Mr. Booker, I run," she replies. "Oh, that's lucky for you, the grizzlies around here mostly go for joggers," he returns. It is clear that her seeking exercise for its own sake is a mark of difference on this hard-working ranch, but she is also marked with naivete in her ignorance of the danger from bears in that country.

This man of the West introduces his exotic visitors to his customs. It is revealed that Annie used to ride in her youth, although "I've never ridden Western before," she demurs, emphasizing her sojourner's status. Tom shows up with a horse for her to ride and gradually teaches her the ways of riding on his own grounds. Likewise, he later shows up at the guest house with a pickup truck (a novel technology for a Manhattanite, surely) and insists that Grace drive it, even with her artificial leg. She is reluctant, claiming her disability, but he insists and she eventually proves capable of mastering this new machine. Tom thus enacts The Myth's claims that the exotic visitors to this land need training and exposure to new practices and technology that will improve their lives.

The learning is not reciprocal; The Myth makes little room for the visitors to bring anything with them worth sharing. Annie's urban, even global sophistication has little or no value in the West. She envies old Mrs. Booker because "It must be great to be her age and to be at that point in life where you have no more guesswork, no more impossible decisions to make." Tom replies by asserting the currency of that certitude among the men of the West generally: "I don't think you have to wait to be her age to find that kind of peace." He gets it by "waking up on the ranch, knowing what I'm supposed to do that day, knowing I'm home." Annie replies that she wakes up full of doubt, and she surely wakes up in a strange place, whether Montana or back home in one of her two dwellings. "The more I try to fix things the more they fall apart," she says, displaying her ineffectuality. Tom invites her to let them do so, thus encouraging her weakness, although it is pretty clear that he does not do so himself in mastering the land and cattle of his home. Her place in the West is uncertain even to her: "do you think I was right to come?" Although The Myth is happy to raise that issue, it puts the man of the West in the position of granting at least the appearance of perfect freedom to make a decision about whether to stay or not, for Tom replies, "I can't answer that, Annie." His own wife, from whom he is divorced, made the wrong decision in coming, however—"Too much space, she said"—and thus returned to where she came. Tom makes clear his groundedness where he is and his unwillingness to be on anyone else's turf.

The pain and ineffectuality of these exotics continue to be displayed. Cooking a meal for the Bookers, Annie clumsily drops pans and curses audibly from the kitchen. She wails despairingly to Tom, "It's been so long since I've done this." When he buttons her undone dress in the back, she simpers and frisks like a schoolgirl; gone is the strong leader of the New York magazine. As the Bookers take their leave, a fight erupts between Annie and Grace; Tom takes it upon himself to tell her how to manage her family: "Don't let her turn you away." In the ensuing conversation, these exotic women expose their own pain and ineffectuality. Annie complains, "Whatever I do, it's wrong, whatever I say, it's wrong." When Grace accuses her of *pushing*, she replies "I don't push for me, I push for you so you don't spend half your life not knowing where you belong"—as, clearly, Annie has done. Grace reveals her own pain by breaking down in grief and crying, "Who's ever going to want me like this?"

The ability of the man of the West to manage power is compared to the inability of these strange visitors to do so. One short scene shows Tom sitting in a corral with his back to Pilgrim, working on a complicated harness that may well be used on Pilgrim. Pilgrim observes and walks around the corral but does not trouble Tom, a serenely confident center of power. However, the next scene shows Grace summoning the courage to enter Pilgrim's stall. But it is clear that he is unwilling to be approached and mastered by her; scenes of the accident flash by and he displays the old signs of violence and unmanageability, leaving Grace in tears. Hope for taming the angry violence brought by people of color to these shores is thus invested in the man of the West, according to The Myth.

Tom will be a source of healing for Grace as well, as The Myth puts very little stock in the ability of those who are injured to help themselves. Grace tells Tom that she is ready to talk about the accident, which she does in tears, showing her pain. Tom absolves Grace by saying, "You didn't do anything wrong." He then tells the story of (pointedly, from the perspective of The Myth) an *Indian* boy who used to work on the Booker ranch (of course). "He and I were really good friends," Tom says, but this person of color suffered a violent injury (of course) and became a (helpless) quadriplegic. Tom went to visit him a few times after the accident, but "his mind, his spirit, whatever you want to call it, just disappeared. The only thing left was his anger." Grace reinscribes her equivalence to people of color generally by saying, "I know where he goes." Tom says, "I know you do. Don't *you* disappear." She begins to respond to this call from the man of the West in ways that she never did among her own people.

Tom and Annie become increasingly close, spending time together, laughing and talking. A cattle drive takes the whole party out camping for a few days, where the relationship strengthens. The growing closeness is observed with concern by Grace and by Diane, Frank's wife. Differences in communication styles between Annie and Diane enact The Myth's stereotypical attributions, for Annie is indirect and stylized in her expressions (the signifying African, the inscrutable Asian) while Diane is plain spoken and gets to the point. Annie beats around the bush but eventually admits, after an initial denial, that "fired" is exactly the right word to describe what has happened to her in terms of her magazine job. Diane replies, "I guess you don't have to figure it out until you get home," which of course raises anxiety for Annie since she does not know whether "home" is where she wants to be. "Did you always know this was the life you wanted?" she asks Diane, who responds with a certainty equal to Tom's, "Well, I was a rancher's daughter, it wasn't too far to go to be a rancher's wife." Annie hems and haws in asking about Tom's wife, at which point Diane goes to the point directly and comments on their different styles: "Hey look, Annie, I'm no good at this sort of talk, goes round and round something and never gets to it so let's just say what it is. . . . Don't you go looking here for whatever it is you're looking for," she warns. Sisterhood clearly only goes so far, and the woman of the West is not willing for this exotic stranger to get too close to the family.

Later that evening, Tom and Annie, on walks away from the others (Tom walks out first, Annie comes to *him*), share a first kiss. Love seems to be in the air, but lo! upon their return to the ranch they find that Robert has arrived, having arranged a last minute surprise visit. They enact the happy family for the Bookers, but it is clear that they are strange and exotic. Tom looks at Annie with appraising eyes as Grace and Robert repeat family stories of how the parents met: Annie was a journalist for an English magazine who stumbled upon Robert, a Peace Corps worker on a hiking holiday, in farthest India. The longer the story goes the stranger (and more Third World) do the MacLeans appear in the context of centered Montana.

Later that night, Annie's face is a picture of confusion as she and Robert prepare for bed. It is clear that she does not welcome physical closeness. She says, "You have every right to be here" but her arm is shaking and it is clear she feels ambivalence in her utterance. Thus The Myth expresses its ambivalence as to whether the spirit of the fatherland really belongs in the West, really has a place with its separated and disempowered relics that it has sent here and whether the displaced people who are *in* the West really feel a connection to their home.

Tom maintains a careful neutrality since Robert's arrival, enacting The Myth's depiction of the Third World wanting and needing the West more than the West wants and needs the Third World. Annie confronts Tom over his sudden distance. He is putting the decision entirely in her hands: "You've got to figure out what you want." Annie replies, "Do you know what *you* want?" He says, "I do know what I want. . . . Annie this is where I belong, this is who I am. Is *this* what you want?" He thus expresses his chief priority as groundedness in the West rather than in terms of social bonding with the Other. When she says yes to his question, Tom replies, "Can you tell that to your family? To Robert, to Grace? If you had a chance to go home and change things, would you?" Annie replies, "You can't ask me that, it's not that simple." Tom responds: It *is*." Annie's inability to act prompts Tom to take things in hand. In the very next scene we see him in Pilgrim's stall saying "there's something you've got to do tomorrow, boy." Tom is going to "change things" for the family by finally healing Grace and Pilgrim.

This exchange between Annie and Tom is a key expression of The Myth in this film. It positions the West as desiring integration with people of color, but it removes the West entirely from any position of *need* for such a thing; it's Annie's decision, after all, and she had come to the man of the West seeking healing in the first place. The Myth in this film expresses the belief that one alternative for the Third World is that things can be "changed" and the alleged brokenness of people of color can be healed, but not by remaining as whole, authentic people in the West. On the one hand, people can change and become Western. On the other hand, the promise of a return, whether physical or spiritual, to the place of origins is offered as an alternative to the preferred option of forsaking that origin and one's roots, giving up one's wandering and becoming one with the West, on the West's own terms and on its ground. In the end, the West is to take pity and do what must be done to heal people of color, since they cannot do it themselves.

In the corral the next day Pilgrim is bridled and saddled; we see lots of close-ups of metal buckles, ropes, and other instruments of mastery. Grace tries to mount the horse conventionally, but he refuses her. Frank assures her,

"Tom'll get him alright." Tom and a ranch hand prepare a complicated rig of roping and hook it around Pilgrim's leg. As in the past, the impending use of forceful control over power is questioned; Grace says, "It's not gonna hurt him, right?" For once she is answered, but obliquely, for Tom says: "Nothing we've done has hurt him. Grace, this is Pilgrim's chance, and it's yours, too." The atmosphere is sinister; we know that something akin to punishment, surely some act of control and restraint, is about to occur.

Sure enough, Tom uses the rope system to hobble the horse, raising one leg off the ground. Pilgrim fights it, but in the end Tom drops him to the ground as the family watches in fear. Considered in terms of The Myth, parallels to lynching seem unavoidable. Grace cries out, "That's enough, stop!" Tom and the horse eye one another in a contest of wills, but in the end, rope, control, technique, and the man of the West win out. It is then that Tom, sitting on Pilgrim's side, strokes him lovingly (once he's down!). He invites Grace to do the same: "Grace, this is where you come in. . . . He's OK, and you never did anything to let him down. Grace you've got to do this. Trust me one more time." Grace is also invited to stroke the horse, and she does so, weeping. Pilgrim relaxes, and makes sounds that the film presents in ways that resemble weeping as well. Tom says, "Now we're gonna show Pilgrim here how to help you get on him. Because you see there's a point where neither one of you's gonna need me any more. And we're there. . . . I'm *not* asking." Tom wraps caring inside a position of mastery and control: the man of the West is going to heal these folks whether they like it or not. Grace sits on the saddle; Pilgrim rolls to his feet and stands upright with Grace astride him. It is an epiphany for all. They begin to ride while everyone looks on, transfixed. Robert and Annie hold hands. The family seems reunited. Tom helps Grace to dismount, they hug, and then Grace runs to her parents to embrace them.

The family prepares to return, Robert and Grace by airplane, Annie to follow with Pilgrim in the trailer. Robert confronts Annie and tells her to "take your time" in returning: "I sat there looking at that horse and I swear I felt the same thing was happening to me. . . . I can either fight the way things are or accept them." He says he knows what is going on and depicts himself as always having loved Annie more than she loves him. He articulates Annie's indecisiveness: "You don't know how you feel about me. You don't know if you want a life with me any more." He gives her a free and open choice to "come home" or not, but not until she knows how she feels. He and Grace drive away.

Annie is left by herself to finish packing. She wanders Tom's house seeing all the Western decorations and seems to come to a decision as to where she belongs. We see a final closeup of the latch on the trailer being lifted as Annie walks in to see Pilgrim, who is now perfectly tame. Tom arrives on the scene. Annie says, "I don't want to leave you." Tom replies, "I don't want you to." But she knows she must go. Indirect to the end, she asks him to prepare horses for one last ride. As he does so, she drives off, thus avoiding the last goodbye.

Conclusion

I have observed before that *The Horse Whisperer* has a number of interesting reversals. A myth about people of color is manifested in a movie about White people. The father figure, or male principle, for Third World people is represented as having more traditionally female characteristics of nurturing than is his domineering wife. In enacting a form that also underlies many other texts, the film thus introduces content or information that is the reverse of what one might expect. As we noted in the first chapter, such information often piggybacks on form, and is thus one of the sites of rhetorical appeal in texts.

The underlying claim that the film is homologous with The Myth is supported if one considers a trajectory of homology among related texts. The "original" idea of horse whispering was introduced to a mass audience in Monty Roberts's book about his own experience with horses, *The Man Who Listens to Horses*. This book is less well known, less widely distributed, than are the film and the book upon which the film is based, Nicholas Evans's *The Horse Whisperer*. Horse whispering as described by Roberts has little or nothing to do with domination and control. The link between horse and whisperer is spiritual and equal, one of respect and cooperation. Domination and empowerment of the whisperer over the horse is emphasized in the more popular Evans book. That antagonistic position between human and horse ends differently in that book than it does in the film, for in the book Tom Booker is killed by a herd of still "angry" and defiant horses in the end. The film, as we have seen, is an unambiguous celebration of domination and control, and its triumph over the horse—and the film is the most popular of these texts. As a text increases in popularity and distribution in American culture, then, it aligns more closely with themes of power over "lesser beings" that is central to The Myth.

Given the nature of the reversals in this film, an important rhetorical effect is that The Myth is affirmed, perpetuated, and reindividuated in disguise. Since it is about White people on the level of content, it seems not to be saying anything about people of color. Since everyone displays the same pigmentation on the level of information, the film seems not to be about the history of race in America. It can therefore deliver its message without the accuracy of the message being questioned. The Myth comes in under the critical radar. The film reinscribes a way of thinking that has often been used to think about race, but it does so without being about race on a content level. Nevertheless, it exercises a formal muscle, a formal potential, in the minds of specifically American (especially White) audiences, a formal faculty that has been used to perpetuate what is obviously an instrument of racist hegemony and domination.

The film thus calls our attention to the importance of form over content. Especially for critics who want to intervene in social conflict by advising readers and students about the ways in which inequities are perpetuated rhetorically, attention to form rather than to the literal level of content or information is a vital strategy and an important task of vigilance. We must likewise teach our students and readers to see political work at a formal level in addition to the more easily detectable work of claims, assertions, propositions, and accusations at the level of information.

If it is possible for a film that shows no literal people of color to be about color, *The Horse Whisperer* also suggests that race in America is not *only* based upon physical features. In other words, race itself is not really about color, nor are the rhetorics that maintain race and racism. Race as a concept and racially based domination is based upon certain symbolic strategies that are fundamental, that cut across many times and places and that can transcend the historical specificities of particular constructions of race. Patterns based upon emasculation, assertions of terrible loss and injury, Otherness and exoticism, and so forth are always already *available* in American thinking. If domination over people of one socially constructed racial group some day no longer serves hegemonic interests, the formal pattern is there to extend The Myth homologically into new situations so as to underlie the construction of new historical specificities of race, group, and identity. This study thus illustrates the importance of thinking about rhetorical homologies as highly adaptive engines for ordering social consciousness in the service of power.

4

The Evil Albino

Cinematic Othering and Scapegoating of Extreme Whites

Lisa Glebatis Perks

They are ghosts, or, at least, tips of a historical iceberg jutting into the present. And, as such, they are provocateurs, forcing latent troubles into the light of day.

—Hicks (51)

Albino characters in films and novels are ethereal and ghostlike, clearly marked by absence. Hypopigmentation (having little to no pigment or color) and the ideologies that accompany pale skin, eyes, and hair lend a uniqueness to albinos that make them appealing to authors and film producers.[1] For example, one of the most prominent characters in Dan Brown's 2003 worldwide best-seller *The Da Vinci Code* is Silas, a murderous albino monk. Despite complaints from the National Organization for Albinism and Hypopigmentation (NOAH), Silas is still depicted as an albino in the film version because, as producer Brian Grazer explained to *Time* magazine, Silas's albinism "drives the eeriness of the movie" (quoted in Gordon 106).

Albinos are a small subset of the population—there are around 17,000 people with albinism in the United States (NOAH Web site, 11 Nov. 2005)—but their representation in popular culture seems to be of greater proportion. Albino characters have been included in numerous major Hollywood films including *The Princess Bride, The Firm, The Bodyguard, The Matrix Reloaded, Cold Mountain,* and *The Da Vinci Code.*[2] Dermatologist Vail Reese has observed an increase in albino film characters, cataloging 20 in the 1990s and already 24 between 2000–2004 (NOAH Press Release, 6 Jan. 2005). Aside from their increasing popular culture presence, another unusual feature is revealed when delving deeper into albino portrayals: in all of the previously listed films, the albino characters are assassins, villains, deranged stalkers, or henchmen of sorts.[3] The purpose of this chapter is to better understand the communicative and social implications of the trend in albino vilification.

While there are many novels and films that include evil albinos—NOAH President Mike McGowan notes that there have been 68 films since 1960 that include an evil albino (cited in Elsworth)—I have chosen *The Da Vinci Code* as the primary text for analysis because of the depth of its portrayal. Albinos generally do not serve as main characters but are sideshow villains. Silas's character development is one of the richest of any popular culture albino, and many details are provided about his life history, his thoughts, and his emotions. To situate Silas's portrayal in relation to nominal albino characters, I will also note similarities to other albino roles.

Obviously, the trend of evil signification may cultivate discrimination toward albinos, but the consistent correlation of skin color with morality may have more severe consequences for collective society. After exploring the rhetorical construction of Silas and several other popular culture albinos, I conclude that the evil albino archetype sneaks ideologies of racial hierarchization into the texts, and I offer two related arguments to support that claim. First, the evil albino represents a form of racist Othering. Wicked albino characters are an inverted (or light-skinned) version of the Manichean allegory of darkness as evil. This inversion allows the racist ideology of the savage Other to be disguised and sustained via attachment to visually white characters. Second, the Othering of albinos can be seen as a primary step in Kenneth Burke's scapegoating mechanism. With scapegoating, evil traits are projected onto one group of people (who may be united by a common religion, appearance, nation of origin, or other characteristic), thus effectively enhancing the perceptions of purity and innocence of an already dominant group. I will discuss in the coming pages how Burke used the scapegoating mechanism to analyze Hitler's rhetoric of Aryan superiority and also how albino vilification works to purify normative whiteness, making whiteness the superior center from which other racial groups deviate.

Othering and "Racing" Albinos

Edward Said's 1978 book *Orientalism* inspired critical scholars to explore processes and patterns of Othering. Othering refers to cultural representations that depict groups of people as backward, primitive, degenerate, or otherwise inferior to

Western whites. Said attributes such representations to early 19th-century biological determinism, which divided "races into advanced and backward, or European-Aryan and Oriental-African" (206). The rhetoric of biological determinism has been transmitted through anthropological, historical, and cultural texts, and this rhetoric functions to Other nonwhites, thereby constructing a moral and material hierarchy that benefits Western nations. The Western world has historically "gained in strength and identity by setting itself off against the Orient," thus justifying intervention in Othered people's cultural, political, and economic lives (3).

Albinism is a genetic condition in which melanin is not produced at normal rates, resulting in little to no pigment in one's eyes, skin, and hair. Albinos can be of any race or ethnicity and consequently may have various physical markers of racial distinctiveness. To explain how a group of people with a genetic skin condition can be rhetorically constituted as one race and Othered, Barry Brummett's method of homological criticism is a fruitful tool. This critical method looks past surface features to uncover underlying formal persuasive appeals among disparate texts and experiences. Brummett explains that "race itself may not be so much a matter of specific physical attributes as it is a model of expectations, relationships, perceptions and behaviors modeled on a discursive structure" (*Rhetorical Homologies* 210). In other words, racially indistinct groups of people, such as albinos, may be Othered and raced through the way language is used to communicate with them and about them.

In a previous chapter of this book, Brummett exposed forms of Othering in *The Horse Whisperer*, a text that few viewers would perceive to be related to race in its surface content. To explain how the interactions between rich white New Yorkers and white Western ranchers are laden with issues of race and racism, Brummett begins the essay by articulating an underlying pattern of Othering that he terms the "White liberal American myth of racial history." This myth neatly summarizes a common strain of imperialist rhetoric and will be a useful foundation to see how Silas's character is tainted with principle elements of Othering. Brummett explains the myth as follows:

> There is a race of people (them) who have had a horrible, violent, and injurious past. . . . These injuries may well have been inflicted by people *like us*, but it was not *us*. At any rate, the victims in the past (and/or their compatriots) were complicit with their injuries and are thus partially responsible. Pain, anger, and a capacity for violence are the legacies of these injuries. (*Rhetorical Homologies* 77)

This white liberal American myth of racial history is woven with the ideologies of what Abdul JanMohamed describes as the hegemonic phase of colonialism. During this phase, imperialist discourse is fixated upon "civilizing" the savage (62).

Consumers of popular culture in the United States can be exposed to the formal foundations of Othering (including the white liberal American myth of racial history) by reading classic novels, attending to current events, learning about our nation's history, or engaging in any number of socialization rituals. Discriminatory premises may more easily slip beneath viewers' and readers' critical radars by utilizing *formal* patterns of Othering and not necessarily engaging in surface racism. These patterns continue to circulate in part because they are gratifying for many people: Hierarchies embedded in Othering may help "control the terrors of *mystery,* which is the perception of difference, strangeness, and alienation between people," thereby providing a measure of comfort when faced with cultural differences (Brummett, "Burkean Scapegoating" 255). Socialized individuals have been provided with these ideological tools of order and sense-making; consequently, films and novels that engage in the practice of Othering may be enjoyable because they resonate with a pre-existing mental schema.

You have likely been exposed to many patterns of Othering in daily life and in encounters with media. One widespread example is the informal hierarchy of regional accents in the United States. When I first began attending college in the Southeast, I was told by an acquaintance that I needed to lose my New York accent in order to appear more intelligent. This form of Othering was not subtle, and I took offense to the suggestion. In fairness to my acquaintance, he had worked to get rid of his own Southern accent after facing discrimination himself. Real-life Othering on the basis of regional accents and media stereotypes of people with such accents are likely mutually reinforcing. Consider that television personalities who are supposed to seem smart (such as national news anchors) have "no accent" and that various comedians such as Jeff Foxworthy (who speaks with a Southern accent) and Andrew "Dice" Clay (who affects a stereotypical Brooklyn dialect) have become successful by perpetuating stereotypes of stupidity and ignorance.

Although many people learn about unfamiliar people, places, things, and experiences from media portrayals, relying on media to understand our world is fraught with "ideological risks," according to Bill Nichols (76). These ideological risks stem from the creation of an unnatural hierarchy that subjugates many groups and benefits a select few. Even with his moral reservations toward the hierarchy embedded in mediated narratives, Nichols maintains that ordering is *essential.* We must ask why such a process is essential. One possible answer is that racism and rhetoric both thrive on the ability of language to create difference. The formal foundation of racism and colonialism is not necessarily based on physical features but on the way difference is discursively manipulated. Opposites, negations, and discursive polarizations harness rhetorical power. They motivate individuals by convincing them to identify with a particular group and thus to differentiate themselves from others. In Burke's *A Rhetoric of Motives,* he describes identification as "compensatory to division," arguing that war is the "ultimate *disease* of cooperation" (22, emphasis in original). The naturalization of difference has notable consequences, facilitating public support for racism, imperialism, and wars throughout history. It is important to keep such dire consequences in mind when questioning how and why albinos are discursively distanced from normative whites.

The subject of "brown" villains in media has been explored through analyses of the ideologies represented (Cloud) and the audience's responses to such characters (see, for example, Cooper; Oliver), but the negativity of albino portrayals has been largely ignored by communication scholars. Media criticism of African American and Latino villains has likely flourished because of its logical connection with colonialism and racism; by pointing out a trend in media stereotyping of marginalized groups in society, scholars may be helping to expose and undermine discriminatory ideologies. Michael Osborn explains that light and dark archetypal metaphors subsume moral terms. In the dichotomy he discusses, Osborn connects the standard pairs of darkness/evil and lightness/good. But, perhaps due in part to media criticism of dark-skinned villains, the signifying pairs may have reversed in popular culture. As Claude Lévi-Strauss observed, it is very rare for a mythological system to "exhaust all the possible codings of a single message, even if this is achieved through the apparent inversion of signs" (332). By simply shifting the evil connotation to extreme lightness (whiteness), the polarity Osborn observed still operates formally, just with different surface content.

Although there can be albinos of any race, those portrayed in popular culture generally appear to be European American. The vilification of European American–looking characters may seem to be a positive step in balancing media portrayals, potentially providing gratification for African American and Latino/a consumers of popular culture who may be frustrated by seeing people in their image often cast as villains. Although it may seem positive that "whites" are being cast as villains, there is a crucial division between albinos and normative whites. Albinos are representative of what Richard Dyer terms "extreme whiteness," a historical symbol connected with Nazism that is signified by blond hair, blue eyes, and a pale or literally white complexion.[4] Dyer argues that extreme whiteness reinforces "ordinary" (or what I term "normative") white people's position as the "average" representatives of humanity. This universal identity is very powerful according to Thomas Nakayama and Robert Krizek, who argue that it allows whiteness to be the privileged position against which all others are measured and marked. The Othering of extreme whites further reifies the powerful position of ordinary whiteness by making it more refined, more pure, and distinct.

Othering Albinos: Priming the Fatalistic Scapegoat

Extreme whites can be rhetorically Othered in many ways, but a very simple form of Othering is represented in the naming of popular culture albinos. The albinos in films such as *The Firm* and *The Princess Bride* are not provided with proper names but are only labeled by their visually distinct skin color, a discriminatory discursive device Toni Morrison also observes with African American literary characters. In *The Firm*, for example, a mafia-connected henchman is described as having "long blond hair, almost white, and weird blue eyes." One of the few unnamed major characters of the movie, he is referred to as an albino in the dialogue and credited as "The Nordic Man." Naming characters solely on the basis of appearance exposes the manner in which albinos may be Othered through their appearance and the language used to describe their appearance, for if they embodied "ordinary" whiteness, such labels would not differentiate them from the many other white men in the movies. Furthermore, these pigment-based labels cast albinos as objects and spectacles, maintaining a rhetorical distance between albino characters and the audience.

Although *The Da Vinci Code*'s albino character is given a proper name, the book soon describes his violent life and how he came to be called Silas. In the beginning of *The Da Vinci Code*, Silas's piteous childhood is described in a sympathetic tone. As the book progresses and his evil acts become more extreme, however, Silas is Othered rhetorically for the audience, unweaving any threads of identification and foreshadowing his death.

Throughout his life, Silas's hypopigmentation makes him an outcast. People respond to Silas with awe and fear during his childhood in rural France: "A *ghost*, they would say, their eyes wide with fright as they stared at his white skin" (Brown 55, emphasis in original). The boy's "embarrassing condition" angers Silas's father, who abuses both wife and child (55). As a teenager Silas kills his father, thus beginning his life of violence and carrying on what may seem to be a genetic proclivity for rage in light of his father's abusive nature. He is eventually imprisoned and wishes for death to deliver him from misery, but instead an earthquake answers Silas's prayers. Fate guides him to the doorstep of Bishop Manuel Aringarosa, and Silas dedicates his life to chastity, poverty, celibacy, physical penance, and the service of his faith.

While the backstory revealed in the first half of *The Da Vinci Code* may evoke reader sympathies, the latter half of the book focuses heavily on the violent acts Silas commits in the present part of the narrative. As the book progresses, Silas is portrayed as increasingly unremorseful about his sinful acts and thus crafted as vicious and "Other." Silas is described as "amused" and "smirking" as he kills (4). Toward the very end of the book, he is labeled a "monster" (278). Said observes that the shift from "subservient beings into inferior humanity" is common throughout imperialist rhetoric (*Culture* 168). Silas's newfound religious faith allows readers to contemplate what Christopher Diller describes as the "sociological view of human nature in which internal essences interface with environmental conditions and thereby become at least potentially malleable" (29). The eventual emphasis placed on Silas's immoral adult acts overshadows his chasteness, thereby functioning to crystallize his evil essence. This shift in his characterization from abused youth to evil adult allows readers to perhaps toy with the emotion of sympathy, but then be absolved of guilt regarding Silas's eventual condemnation.

Unabashed cruelty is a common thread throughout many albino portrayals. The dread-locked albino twins of *The Matrix Reloaded* smirk and smile as they mow down innocent pedestrians in pursuit of protagonists Morpheus and Trinity. Bosie, from *Cold Mountain*, gleefully dances on a fence, torturing the woman whose fingers have been placed between the lower railings. *The Princess Bride*'s albino happily tells prisoner Westley of the torture regime that awaits him in "the pit of despair." Silas's malevolent character trajectory and the glaring cruelty of many albino characters highlight evil as an innate trait of the Other.

The evil acts and unrepentant nature of Silas and several albino characters not only Other them but also naturalize their positions as scapegoats. Burke argues that authors may prepare the scapegoat by pointing "the arrows of the plot [so] that the audience comes to think of him as a marked man" (*Philosophy* 40). Silas eventually dies, meeting the fate that also awaits albinos in *The Firm*, *Cold Mountain*, and *Powder*. It is perhaps poetic justice that Silas is involved in a gunfight toward the end of the book and ends up accidentally shooting Aringarosa, the man who facilitated Silas's religious conversion and impelled him to engage in his last killing sprees. Silas's last sacrifice is to carry Aringarosa to a hospital, neglecting and exhausting his own fatally wounded body. In his final conversation with Aringarosa, Silas's "soul thundered with remorse and rage" (Brown 418). Silas appears neither sad nor repentant, humane emotions that would have represented a recognition of his own moral fallibility. The thundering of Silas's soul encourages readers to infer that he is still unable to contain his "lurking violent proclivity," which Brummett argues is an important element in the ideological construction of an Othered group (*Rhetorical Homologies* 80). As audiences are exposed to more and more evil albinos, hypopigmentation becomes a visual shortcut for Othering, entrenching the arrows that point to albino characters as "marked" men or scapegoats.

Burkean Scapegoating: Silas as Vessel of Sin

Othering is an ideological mechanism through which dominant groups keep themselves in power and is usually the means to a sinister end such as the exploitation of a group of people. I argue that the vilification of popular culture albinos has been a consistent trend not because of benefits derived from exploiting or subjugating actual albinos but, instead, because it empowers normative whites through their differentiation from "evil" extreme whites, who then become the vessels of guilt and sin. To more clearly explain this argument, it is necessary to provide a more thorough explanation of the relationship between Othering and scapegoating.

Othering and scapegoating both refer to ideological mechanisms of managing fear and guilt. Othering has a fairly direct relationship with guilt relief. It alleviates imperialist guilt by casting the targeted country or group of people as savage and in need of Western influence, which will allegedly improve life for its inhabitants and thereby save the natives from themselves. In the scapegoating process, the guilt or vices of one group are projected onto a *separate* person or group of people (or object) who are then figuratively or literally sacrificed to purge the ills. Communication scholars have applied the principles of scapegoating to explain rhetorical strategies in a variety of situations: presidential campaigns (Brummett, "Burkean Scapegoating"), the U.S. government's "war on drugs" (Mackey-Kallis and Hahn), and Hitler's rise to power (Burke, *Philosophy*). There are innumerable additional illustrations of scapegoating; one could argue that homosexual men were scapegoated at the start of the AIDS crisis and that immigrants to the United States have been scapegoated throughout history. Because scapegoating involves the projection and transference of guilt for illogical reasons (see Burke, *Permanence* 16), it can be more complicated to critically trace than Othering. To clarify the application of theory here, this essay interprets the albino scapegoating mechanism as a method to alleviate normative white American guilt, thereby promoting normative white solidarity and superiority.

Burke describes two types of scapegoating, one that he calls an "explicit ritual," which involves the formal appointment of a scapegoat, and another more insidious form, the "concealed pseudoscientific variant" (*Philosophy*). This second form of scapegoating more closely resembles the scapegoating mechanism I have observed and may indeed be the most common; it involves an unspoken or implied projection of evil onto the scapegoat that naturalizes evil as a "'scientific fact' about the scapegoat's 'true nature'" (*Philosophy* 45). This naturalization of evil may occur through the practice of Othering, thereby priming the scapegoat for the sacrifice. Examples of the "concealed pseudoscientific variant" of scapegoating can be found in many sports rivalries. The New York Yankees are a very polarizing force in baseball—they are loved or hated with a vengeance and have even been dubbed the "evil empire" by the president of the Red Sox organization. Judging by the postings to baseball message boards, it seems that, even if the Red Sox do not perform well, some fans can be relieved of their disappointment and anger if the Yankees fail, too, and are therefore figuratively sacrificed.

Although the Yankee/Red Sox rivalry may seem simplistic, scapegoating utilizes a complex interplay of multiple parties, not just a two-sided relationship between the exploiters/exploited that operates in Othering. Burke explains that the scapegoat mechanism flatters "a sick psyche by proclaiming the categorical superiority of one's 'kind,' and by organizing modes of injustice that are morbidly considered advantageous to the conspirators as a class" (*Rhetoric of Motives* 285). In other words, the scapegoating mechanism involves the negotiation of positions in a moral hierarchy, positions that are not discrete but are defined only in relation to other groups. To continue with the baseball example, scapegoating the Yankees may broaden the Red Sox's fan base, ultimately helping them when competing against other baseball teams. Occupying and maintaining an advantageous position in a moral hierarchy through scapegoating may empower a particular group to act in their own interests throughout a variety of situations, potentially resulting in dire consequences for third parties (not just the Othered factions). For example, the scapegoating of homosexual men at the beginning of the AIDS crisis strengthened the perceived normalcy and morality of heterosexual marriage, thus not only disempowering homosexual men but also homosexual women, heterosexuals who do not marry, and others with various lifestyles.

In his analysis of "The Rhetoric of Hitler's Battle," Burke dissects Hitler's rhetorical strategy of scapegoating Jews (*Philosophy*). Ironically, in that essay and other explications of scapegoating, Burke positions Nazis and fascists to be scapegoats themselves, lending support for drawing the same conclusions about albinos. For example, Burke provides a list of characteristics that make a scapegoat "worthy" of sacrifice, including, first, that the scapegoat "may be made worthy legalistically (i.e., "by making him an offender against legal or moral justice") and, second, that the scapegoat may have a "personal flaw" such as "*hubris,* punishable pride, the pride that goes before a fall" (40, emphasis in original). Burke more directly labels Nazis scapegoats, explaining in a footnote that it is rational and justified to scapegoat fascists due to their historically situated cruelty: "That is, the fascist was, in the most objective sense of the term, an enemy" (48).

The Nuremberg trials, the U.S. Holocaust Memorial Museum, and the inclusion of Nazi villains in contemporary films such as the *Indiana Jones* series, along with many other examples, illustrate that the evil Nazi archetype still occupies a prominent place in the U.S. cultural imaginary. In the next sections I will describe homologous links between Nazi rhetoric and Silas's racial and religious pride, thus forging a discursive connection between the visually similar figures. The discursive connections revolve around the theme of rebirth, which signifies the beginning of an unhealthy transformation toward fanaticism, and the expressions of inborn superiority that result from the transformation.

SYMBOLIC REBIRTH

After the sacrifice of the scapegoat, the person who has been dialectically purified is reborn, involving *"the obliteration of one's whole past lineage"* (Burke, *Philosophy* 41, emphasis in original). In his analysis of Hitler's rhetoric, Burke explicates the theme of rebirth, citing Hitler's declaration that the Aryan bloodstream was distinct from Hebrew lineage as an indicator of the conversion (*Philosophy* 42). Silas's past was so traumatic that, before being imprisoned, he had erased memories of his family and had forgotten his original name, indicating that the only way to survive would be to start his life over.[5] Silas's rebirth parallels the rise of Aryan pride through its erasure of the past and its religious symbolism. After the earthquake breaks Silas's prison walls, he struggles through a mountainside and is left on Aringarosa's doorstep in a state of exhaustion. Delirious while recovering in the church, Silas sees visions of Jesus who tells him, "*The stone has been rolled aside, and you are born again*" (Brown 57, emphasis in original). He is given new hope and a new purpose to serve God and Aringarosa.

Burke explains that rebirth or reidentification may be symbolized with the adoption of a new name (*Philosophy*). Aringarosa renames his amnesiac convert Silas based on a parable from Acts. Silas responds to his renaming, thinking he "had been given flesh. *My name is Silas*" (Brown 58, emphasis in original). Silas discursively highlights his rebirth, referring to his previous existence as a "past life" and claiming that he had died and was "born again by the hand of Bishop Aringarosa" (393).

The idea of cleanliness, a purging of the soul, is related to rebirth. Silas's physical penance, a practice he undertakes as a dedicated Opus Dei member, is one of the many controversial elements of *The Da Vinci Code*. Silas wears a spiked cilice belt that cuts into his thigh "as a perpetual reminder of Christ's suffering" (14). He engages in self-flagellation, cutting his flesh with a knotted rope to atone for his sins, reminding himself throughout the process that "*pain is good*" (14). While the book vividly describes the wounds of the cilice and knotted rope, the visual power of the movie more strongly conveys the pain Silas endures: He walks continually with a limp, his face is wracked with pain when self-flagellating, and viewers see his thigh ooze blood as he tightens the cilice, leaving his sock drenched with the sickening signs of his ritualistic cleansing.

By professing to enjoy the self-inflicted pain and often appearing naked to self-flagellate, Silas's cleansing rituals enhance his savage imagery and contribute to his Othering. An interesting duality of violence and piety are captured in the image of Silas's sadistic efforts to purify his soul. These contradictions help exemplify that it is only through the dialectic between good and evil that we can conceive of good or evil existing at all (Burke, *Rhetoric of Religion*). Similar dialectical tensions can also be seen in *The Bodyguard*. In this 1992 film, an albino stalker writes threatening letters to an African American celebrity, calling her a "whore queen of darkness" and admonishing that her "purity of soul can only be regained by a painful and violent death." These interrelated dialectical tensions of light/dark, good/evil, and violence/purity can be seen as essential to the scapegoating mechanism as the polar interplay opens up a figurative space for the transference of sin. Burke explains, "ultimately the idea of cleanliness attains its full modicum of personality, in the idea of a fitting personal sacrifice" (*Rhetoric of Religion* 216). Cleanliness or whiteness is a shifting signifier representing purity of the soul (good), as well as the ability to receive the sins of others (evil).

INBORN SUPERIORITY

Inborn superiority and extreme racial pride have been used throughout history to justify imperialist Othering. And, as noted previously, inborn superiority can be construed as a punishable pride worthy of scapegoating. Whites and the Western world may Other or scapegoat groups that advocate strong racial, religious, or national pride in fear that those groups may become too powerful and seek to alter hegemonic structures. Pockets of white pride can also be alarming, evoking strategies of containment such as Othering and scapegoating. As Dyer argues, whiteness has been associated with death because of the World War II Holocaust and the Ku Klux Klan's emphasis on their skin color and literally white robes. Interestingly, *The Da Vinci Code* protagonist Professor Robert Langdon discusses the symbolism of a KKK headpiece, noting that it arouses feelings of hatred and racism in the United States (Brown 35). In the movie version, Langdon features KKK costumes and several swastikas in a slide show presentation in an opening scene. Collectively, these symbols may make the connection between whiteness and death more salient in the minds of readers and viewers. Throughout *The Da Vinci Code*, Silas expresses great pride in his white skin. Because of the connections between racial pride and ethnic cleansing exemplified by the swastikas and Ku Klux Klan costumes referenced early in *The Da Vinci Code*, viewers are primed to fear Silas's expressions of inborn superiority. These characteristics help Other Silas, making him a person who must be contained or killed.

Burke retraced the growth of Hitler's anti-Semitism, observing that poverty was a trigger for Hitler's hatred (*Philosophy*). Shifting the blame to an extraneous source enabled Hitler's feelings of Aryan superiority. Silas is also ostracized and abused as a child, but he develops a sense of superiority after undergoing his symbolic rebirth. He begins to view his albinism, his whiteness, as a marker of divine superiority. Aringarosa serves as the catalyst in this change, encouraging him:

> [Y]ou were born an albino. Do not let others shame you for this. Do you not understand how special this makes you? Were you not aware that Noah himself was albino? . . . Like you, he had skin white like an angel. (Brown 167)

The story continues that "over time, Silas learned to see himself in a new light. *I am pure. White. Beautiful. Like an angel*" (167, emphasis in original). It is only after embracing his whiteness that Silas is able to carry out Aringarosa's sinister orders with a sense of divine purpose.

The following passage appears after Silas commits a murder and performs physical penance; it illustrates Silas's reverence for his appearance: "[Silas's robe] was plain, made of dark wool, accentuating the whiteness of his skin and hair. Tightening the rope-tie around his waist, he raised the hood over his head and allowed his red eyes to admire his reflection in the mirror" (31). The color contrast between skin and robe highlights the inversion of the light/dark metaphor, illustrating the electric interplay of good and evil that courses through Silas's hyper-white body. Silas views his whiteness as a symbol of a clean soul, projecting an indivisibility of racial and religious pride: "*Purge me with hyssop and I shall be clean,* he prayed, quoting Psalms. *Wash me, and I shall be whiter than snow*" (31, emphasis in original). The previous passages are referenced not to suggest that Silas should be ashamed of his albinism but to illustrate the misguided pride he feels as a white, angelic soldier of God. By committing physical penance in the name of God, he retains a superior purity; he is whiter than heavenly snow.

As *The Da Vinci Code*'s mysteries unravel, it becomes clear that each character has different motives for seeking the Holy Grail. Readers exposed to Silas's inner thoughts gain the sense that he sees the world as divided into believers and nonbelievers. Throughout the passages involving his violent acts, Silas often rationalizes based on this religious binary, picturing himself as the participant in a holy war. When proposing that Silas become an assassin in order to retrieve the Holy Grail, Aringarosa explains, "Our battle, like all battles, will take sacrifice," then asks, "Will you be a soldier of God?" (195).

In Burke's analysis of scapegoating in *Mein Kampf,* he quotes this passage as a demonstration of Hitler's demagoguery: "I am acting in the sense of the Almighty Creator: *By warding off Jews I am fighting for the Lord's work*" (*Philosophy* 198). Throughout his killing spree, Silas reiterates a similar religious justification for his brutality. He reminds himself that his actions were "holy in purpose. Acts of war against the enemies of God had been committed for centuries. Forgiveness was assured" (Brown 13). The film version makes Silas's religious fanaticism even stronger as Silas spits at his nemesis Sophie Neveu: "I am the messenger of God. Each breath you take is a sin, for you will be haunted by angels." Given the erasure of his past and profound reverence for his skin color and faith, Silas embodies the shift toward racial and religious superiority composed by Hitler as he orchestrated the rise of German fascism. This homological connection between Silas and the most infamous segment of the Aryan race makes clearer his position as a scapegoat; by echoing Nazi imagery, he, too, is the enemy.

Conclusions

Throughout *The Da Vinci Code,* Silas is described as a ghost, effectively foreshadowing his death. Paraphrasing Heather Hicks's quote from the beginning of this chapter, it is important to question what latent troubles this albino ghost is forcing into the light of day. I have argued here that the evil albino insidiously advances ideologies of racial stratification through two primary means. First, the vilification of Silas and various popular culture albinos exposes repeated formal patterns of racist Othering. Contrasts of light/virtuous versus dark/evil have pervaded racist and colonialist rhetoric. In this mutated example of the Manichean allegory, the contrast of normative whiteness and hyper-white albinism has harnessed the rhetorical power of difference and imbued it with moral significance. Morrison argues that Othering fulfills a collective need, often discursively evading open dialog about racial tensions by encoding the issues in a "substitute language" (9). It is important for communication scholars to be vigilant in uncovering homologies of racism and Othering, no matter what groups of people are directly stereotyped.

Second, Othering represents a step in the scapegoating mechanism, which serves as an outlet for guilt held by a group of people. Burke explains that, through scapegoating, "the 'bad' features can be allocated to the 'devil,' and one can 'respect himself' [*sic*] by distinction" (*Philosophy* 196). The albino as a symbolic Nazi embodies the tainted history of a group whom Americans, particularly normative white Americans, view as having committed acts more indecent than their own oppressive exploits. The Othering of hyper-whites may therefore represent an attempt to symbolically distance normative white Americans from the Aryans of fascist Germany in order to maintain an advantageous moral hierarchy.

Whatever the conscious or unconscious reasons for creating and consuming popular culture texts with evil albino characters, it is important to consider potential rhetorical motives and consequences. Dan Brown has answered criticisms of his evil albino, stating: "Silas' skin color has nothing to do with his violent nature—he is driven to violence by others' cruelty, . . . not by anything inherent in his physiology" (Dan Brown Web site).

Anyone can be driven to violence by cruelty, but it is important to note that Silas was treated cruelly *because* he was an albino. His skin color and appearance are necessarily rhetorically intertwined with his pitiless childhood. Burke offers a potential explanation for an author's amnesia of intent: "[H]aving woven a rhetorical motive so integrally into the very essence of his conception, the writer can seem to have ignored rhetorical considerations" (*Grammar of Motives* 37). Said reiterates this point, arguing that the ideological construction of the evil Other allows the colonialist author to become a disinterested, "invisible scribe" (*Culture* 168).

In light of this analysis, it is important to consider whether other films and popular culture texts contain hidden or seemingly unintentional patterns of Othering and scapegoating. While not guaranteed to reveal any mechanisms of social stratification, you may find it useful to question if there are patterns in the characteristics of villains throughout popular culture. What does the text suggest as their national origin? What do the villains look like? How do they speak and act? How do the other characters treat them? And what is their fate in the film—punished, killed, repentant, free? As noted previously, Nazi villains still have a presence in contemporary popular culture, even decades after World War II, and "Communist" or Russian villains are also common, although the Cold War has ended. FOX network's popular antiterrorist drama *24* has created one of the most recent controversies about villain stereotypes, often casting Muslims as terrorists. In the wake of controversial post-9/11 racial profiling, the importance of scrutinizing such portrayals is particularly salient.

Although I am not satisfied with Dan Brown's defense of his evil albino character, my intention for this chapter is not to blame him and other producers of popular culture texts for Othering and scapegoating albinos and various villains. Indeed, many character stereotypes already exist in our cultural psyche, and the author or producer may be recirculating a pattern of representation that they have not critically thought about. To be sure, before conducting research for this chapter, I never would have guessed that there have been 68 evil albino characters in films since the 1960s. The main focus of this discussion is to expose deeper causes for these patterns of representation—to explain why evil albino characters have proliferated and why they are presumably resonating not only with the creators but also with the consumers of popular culture texts. My conclusions about racial stratification through Othering and scapegoating are surely not the only ones that might be reached when critically examining the portrayal of evil albinos, and I hope this chapter marks the start of a continued conversation.

Notes

1. As *The Da Vinci Code* heroine Sophie Neveu observes, an albino monk is "impossible to miss" (Brown 368).

2. All of these classifications are supported by dermatologist Vail Reese on his list of over 80 movies featuring albinos (<http://www.skinema.com/AlbinismList2005.html>). Interestingly, the book version of *Cold Mountain* does not describe Bosie as an albino, but he becomes so in the film. The White Witch from *The Chronicles of Narnia* was also drawn with dark hair in the original book illustrations, but she adopted blond dreadlocks for the 2005 film version. These film adaptations may indicate that the visual rhetoric of albino hypopigmentation is more powerful than the written form.

3. Not all albino characters in popular culture are evil, but there have been enough of these stereotypical roles to generate a critical response from NOAH. The popular culture industry has responded with albino discrimination jokes on comedy shows such as *The Tonight Show with Jay Leno* and *Saturday Night Live*. There is also a Wikipedia entry dedicated solely to "evil albinos."

4. For the purposes of identifying examples of the evil albino archetype in popular culture, it is important to note that having red or pink eyes is a common misconception about those with the condition—the majority have blue eyes.

5. The film version differs slightly; instead of having a narrator recount the story of Silas's childhood, the transparent figures of young Silas and his parents are superimposed on the screen to depict his life history. The visual imagery makes it appear as if viewers are witnessing Silas's own memories.

the remaining Native Americans" (xix). Drinnon's reminiscences imply a symbolic link, almost interpretive interchangeability, among three types of impersonal violence against sensate beings: sport hunting,[1] stranger rape,[2] and physical violence against people because of their perceived "Other-ness" in racial or ethnic classification, religion, or sexual orientation (e.g., "hate crimes").[3] Although Drinnon's passage suggests that, in early U.S. history, these violent physical activities may have been interchangeable, that is no longer the case. I will contend, however, that in modern America the talk of actual sport hunters, "hate criminals," and stranger rapists about their activities exhibit formal similarities that suggest a larger common interpretive framework funding all three types of impersonal violence and possibly others.[4] By impersonal violence, I mean acts against admittedly sensate targets whom one claims no motive for hurting or retaliating against as an individual, but only as a representative of a particular class (e.g., deer, ducks, women, gays, Jews, Muslims, Native Americans, Asian-Americans, Euro-Americans, African-Americans). Although the common interpretive framework demonstrated from the discourse of those who act consistent with it may not account for all sport hunting, "hate crimes," or stranger rapes, it reveals a powerful, internally consistent symbolic pattern that impersonalizes victims/prey, yet relates the violent actor to them as sensate beings in some shared hierarchy that the actor perceives is significant. A symbolic and nuanced relationship of domination—and the domination of an animate "Other" viewed as worth dominating rather than use of an objectified "thing"—emerges in these texts.

This essay detects a rhetorical homology facilitating all three types of impersonal violence and discoverable in the discourse of many people known to participate in any one of these activities. It does not suggest that a contemporary American individual who already participates in one activity supported by the framework (e.g., sport hunting) will shift to or be more prone to become involved additionally in the others (e.g., stranger rape); that issue, by definition, is an empirical question that rhetorical criticism cannot answer and that the scant existing empirical evidence does not support. In fact, there is some reason to believe that those proficient at one individuation of the interpretive framework's "justified" activities would not switch to others. Rather, my argument here is that there are formal parallels in how sport hunters, "hate criminals," and stranger rapists symbolically construct their victims/prey and their own relationships to those victims/prey and sometimes to other violent participants as a result. I will argue that this homology is less a deviation from contemporary mainstream American rhetoric than a systematic variation on this society's relentless emphases on competition and hierarchical dominance, both by classes and individuals, and so it is a matter of shared responsibility. Finally, I go beyond criticizing "what is" to raise one possible alternative framework that encompasses the competition and hierarchy motives featured in the homology in a systematic, yet more pro-social way: an interpretive frame constructed from Jesus's recommendations for impersonal behavior as recorded in the New Testament gospels.

Rhetorical Homologies and Impersonal Violence

According to dictionary definitions, a "homology" is the quality or condition of exhibiting correspondence or similarity in position, value, function, or structure; for example, a seal's flippers are homologous to a human's arms, says *The American Heritage Dictionary*. A rhetorical homology is a formal parallel that cuts across seemingly dissimilar discourses (Brummett, "Homology" 203). It reveals itself at a level of generality higher than an analogy (i.e., one text to one other text) and differently than a genre. By detecting formal resemblances across bodies of texts that appear disparate and do not share the same general content, homologies operate at a high level of abstraction in order to "relate whole systems of practices together in complex ways" (Brummett, "Homology" 214). As such, they are positioned to facilitate comment on any of the items linked by these formal similarities or on the link itself (Brummett, "Homology" 214). Although a viable genre claim demands that one demonstrate a recognizable constellation of situational, substantive, and stylistic devices (Campbell and Jamieson 18), a homology argument emphasizes formal resemblances across discourses *in spite of* their apparently disparate contents and situations. Such formal parallels might include the symbolic characterization of conflict, roles, and stakes (Brummett, "Homology" 204). Through a homological approach, a critic "may profitably 'break' ... source-defined boundaries to consider how they participate in homologies within wider mosaics, thus understanding discrete texts as symbolic constructions that are continuous with wider constructions of context and subjects" (Brummett, *Rhetorical* 97).

The significance of identifying homologies rests on the assumption, elaborately developed in Kenneth Burke's *Counter-Statement,* that a text's form plays at least as important a role in its persuasiveness as its content. Formal resemblances can "carry and ... reinforce persuasive messages, *independently and in addition to* the content of those messages. ... Homologies, or formal resemblances among texts and experiences, are a pathway of persuasive influence at a formal level" (Brummett and Nam 320). Although content and form can never be disengaged completely from one another, they may operate at compatible or cross purposes. In other words, the form of a text or body of texts may either enhance or undermine the persuasive purposes of its content (e.g., Olson, "Function"). So, although form cannot be studied independently from content, it is possible to separate hypothetically its persuasive influence from that of a particular content and so to trace its parallel vectors in discourses with very different content. A homological approach to rhetoric provides a means to observe formal parallels that might indicate a larger systematic interpretive framework that rhetors discussing very different content nonetheless hold in common.

Although, at first glance, seeking rhetorical homologies may appear to be a structuralist undertaking, it is not. Homologous patterns are "structural but not structuralist" (Brummett, *Rhetorical* 73). The similarities sought include correspondences of function, value, and position, not only structure. The social relevance of identifying symbolic structures, argued Burke, is that such structures serve some function for those who embrace them in achieving a larger purpose (*Philosophy* 74). Although a homology falls short of the coherent constellation of situation, substance, and style that represent a genre, the formal correspondences detected are rhetorical ones and so inevitably imbued with purposeful function and inherent valuation. Furthermore, to observe similarity at the level of a rhetorical homology, one must see a formal pattern that actually recurs many times and across discourses with disparate contents; this requirement does not apply to rhetorical genres (e.g., Black 137; Campbell and Jamieson 24). Most importantly, the notion of rhetorical homologies sets aside structuralist assumptions that the formal parallels observed are products of the human psyche writ large or are otherwise universally derived. Instead, meaning-making patterns apparent at the abstract level of homologies are socially or culturally derived and exercised symbolically by group members making meaningful order of their experiences (Brummett, *Rhetorical* 73–75). As Barry Brummett argued, corresponding forms in discourse should "be read and applied *as* socially held and strategically applied forms, even if that was not the original intent of the scholars who identified them" (*Rhetorical* 96).

In this case, I present the rhetorical homology explicitly as a recurring socially held and strategically applied symbolic pattern within contemporary American culture, rather than one emerging from nature or from humans' psychological structures or even from the human capacity for symbol use itself. Three Burkean assumptions justify this approach. First, texts are strategies for encompassing situations or answering assertions that the rhetor sees as posed by a perceived situation. Texts encompass or answer situations, in strategic and stylized ways, by sizing them up, naming their structures and outstanding features, and naming them in ways that contain attitudes toward them (Burke, *Philosophy* 1, 109). Second, critically examining the strategic and stylized interrelationships in a text reveals a set of motives and a perspective on a perceived situation. Even though rhetors make some conscious choices about how and what to communicate, they "cannot possibly be conscious" of all the motivational and situation interrelationships, regularities, and assumptions revealed by their discourse. However, because discursive interrelationships are publicly available in a text, Burke argued, critics reliably can probe both a rhetor's motive and situation, which "is but another word for motives," by analyzing texts for their strategic and stylistic choices and patterns (*Philosophy* 20). Third, critically examining texts that seek to encompass situations involving physical phenomena (e.g., violent acts, disease) reveal more about the rhetor (or namer) than about the named phenomena. The locus of such assertions, Burke claimed, is the structural powers by which the rhetor encompasses them, not the material aspects of the phenomena themselves. According to this critical perspective, the discursive encompassment of a situation that justifies response provides a "caricature" of the first persona, or textually implied communicator, that is an "oversimplifi-cation" of his or her actions and "hence, most easily observable because it is an oversimplification" (*Philosophy* 18). As such, texts are cues to cogent, recogniz-able, and motivated perspectives for encompassing situations. So, although genre theory assumes that situations perceivable as similar recur and hence so do rhetorical patterns (Black 133), this essay argues that the obverse is also true: rhetorical patterns recur, hence so do humans' perceptions of situations as being of certain recognizable types.

The following homological analysis demonstrates how recent American sport hunters, "hate criminals," and stranger rapists discursively configure the larger society's priorities of competition and hierarchy in a formally similar, systematic way to justify impersonal violence of sorts usually viewed as unac-ceptable by the society's majority.[5] I contend that late twentieth-century American sport hunters, "hate criminals," and stranger rapists create a non-consensual relationship with a party selected not as a unique individual but by virtue of con-venience combined with that party's observable marks of differential group clas-sification and that they justify impersonal violence within this non-consensual relationship through homologous symbol use. The common pattern recurs in initiators' own discourse, whether it precedes or follows their violent actions. As Murray Edelman noted, "Once a group of people have committed violent or aggressive acts[,] they develop shared perceptions of a kind that justify their actions" (107).

Such analysis must turn on discursive evidence from or for those known to participate actively in the kinds of impersonal violence at issue (i.e., sport hunting, "hate crimes," stranger rape). Although some thoughtful works on the connection between speech and impersonal violence against categories of beings exist (e.g., Freedman and Freedman; Whillock and Slayden) and the fol-lowing claim has some notable exceptions (e.g., Kellett), most scholarly litera-ture relies exclusively on other professionals' comments *about* those individuals or groups who engage in impersonal violence (e.g., psychological evaluations, legal representations, or sociological theories on causes of anti-group violence) or on advocates' self-serving characterizations *of* the impersonally violent (e.g., anti-hunting sources, feminist activists on rape and pornography laws, or political groups with a stake in legal definitions of hate crime). Also useful, but partial, in understanding the symbolic dimensions of impersonal violence is scholarship that unravels the grander, whole-cloth hate philosophies officially advanced by hate groups. As Laurence R. Marcus contended, "[I]t would be short-sighted and inaccurate to believe that all hate-based activity comes from [established] extremist groups" (20). Further, America's most physically violent haters are those who do not ally themselves with any major hate group with a well-established, publicly available doctrine (e.g., the Ku Klux Klan), but those who borrow from various hate group philosophies and/or act indepen-dently of any organized hate group or philosophy. California State San Bernadino criminology professor Brian Levin observed that most potentially dangerous force are "freelancers," or independent individuals, such as Timothy McVeigh, who do not belong to a particular group, but draw inspiration from various philosophies. Levin supported his claim, saying, "With the exception of some well-known shootings, the people committing the most violent [hate] crimes are not members of hate groups" (qtd. in Worden). Such evidence underscores the importance of critically seeking predictable patterns in hate criminals' own discourse beyond formal hate philosophies. This analysis relies primarily on discourse actually created and/or actively used by actors known to engage physically in the impersonal violence featured.

Sport hunting magazines, newspaper columns, and television programs make discursive samples from, discussions among and from, and ads for lethal implements for active sport hunters abundant. Sport hunting differs from "pot" or "meat" hunting in that the latter is undertaken from necessity for survival and the former as a leisure activity. Although self-respecting sport hunters always use or give away the animal killed—to do otherwise is "un-sportsmanlike" or "slob-bish" and damages one's status among fellow hunters, while being "flush" enough to donate from one's conquests for others' use elevates one's status (e.g., Marks 20–22, 25, 72, 211, 266–67)—killing from necessity rather than for the sport gen-erally marks one as lower status among both pot and leisure hunters (see Hahn; Marks 20, 72, 266–67). Thus, hunters and non-hunters all agree that it is one thing to kill willingly from necessity and quite another to do so for pleasure, although the valence of these distinct motivations tends to be opposite among hunters and non-hunters (Cartmill; Marks). Given acknowledged differences in both motivation and symbolic characterizations of their activities by hunters themselves, this study focuses on the discourse of and for active sport hunters, for whom hunting is a voluntary leisure activity. The primary texts employed here are hunting and gun specialty periodicals published from 1998 to 2001 (e.g., *American Rifleman, Buckmasters, Deer and Deer Hunting, Field and Stream, Mossy Oak Hunting the Country, North American Whitetail, Outdoor Life, Petersen's Hunting, Shooting Times, Wisconsin Sportsman*) and television programs aired from 1998 to 2000 (e.g., *American Shooter, Bass Pro Shop's Outdoor World, Bill Jordan's Realtree Outdoors, Buckmaster's White Tail Magazine, Cabela's Sportsman's Quest, The Chevy Sportsman, Great Outdoors, Mossy Oak Hunting the Country, Remington Country, Under Wild Skies, World of Ducks Unlimited*), as well as news-paper columns by sport hunters. Such texts are written and consumed specifically by sport hunters, who can afford the clothes, leisure trips, and gadgets advertised, not "pot" hunters seeking survival through hunting.

Given the illegality of their activities, such discursive evidence is far more difficult to locate for those who commit "hate crimes" or rape strangers. A bur-geoning wealth of hate speech is available in cyberspace (Etchingham; "The Year"), and stranger rape scenarios saturate popular culture and pornographic texts in every medium, but the degree and actual uses made of such materials by those who physically engage in hate crimes and stranger rape are unclear. Thus, this study relies on discourse created specifically by those known to engage in such impersonal violence as it seeks to identify how these actors experience and symbolically construct their actions. Further, a homology argument seems more secure if built on actual discourse from documented or admitted physically violent "hate criminals" and stranger rapists either *before* they are influenced by their lawyers (e.g., Aaron McKinney's "gay panic" defense; Colin Ferguson's proposed "black rage" defense [Kelly]) or *after* their convictions/admissions of their acts, when there is little reason to fabricate. Transcribed, usually open-ended interviews with admitted, already-convicted stranger rapists (e.g., Beneke; Stevens; Sussman and Bordwell) and recorded statements of and writings by known hate criminals serve as the remaining two discourse sets.

Four Points of Homological Correspondence

Four key points of homological correspondence form this common interpretive framework: (a) the rhetor symbolically constructs and physically initiates an adversarial relationship with non-consenting victims/prey class members, (b) victims/prey class members are selected opportunistically and constructed impersonally as relatively interchangeable class representatives, (c) rhetors distance and impersonalize victims/prey, without objectifying them or diminishing their presumed potency or the status accompanying conquering them, and (d) rhetors express a desire to physically assert—and take pleasure in exhibiting—dominance and superior hierarchical status.

Rhetor Symbolically Constructs and Physically Initiates an Adversarial Relationship with Non-consenting Victims/Prey Class Members

There is something about the hunt's unique challenge that is portrayed discursively as motivating and intrinsically satisfying by the sport hunter. Hunter Wilmer Leviner explained the notion of "hunting as a sport," by saying: "Well, it's getting to know how to kill things. A lot of thrill in killing a rabbit or something and him moving like that. You show your skill and all. A deer's complicated. . . . They're hard to kill. And then you've got to know what you're shooting at [a buck or a doe], too" (qtd. in Marks 216). Sport hunting involves pleasure in a symbolically different, more adversarial way than skill-shooting at even moving insensate targets where "the beauty and pleasure of shooting sporting clays" is the game's simplicity (*Under Wild Skies*) or hunting animals for physical survival. Asked what part of hunting he liked best, one sport hunter responded, "Well, I would have to say the kill. Just the kill. I did it [hunting] mostly for sport, like I said, and to keep from cleaning the rabbit I give it away" (qtd. in Marks 215). The point of many hunting programs and magazine articles is to coach better skills (and sell improved products) for besting a prey as well as out-hunting one's peers. What sport hunters constantly must defend to non-hunters, then, is not their enjoyment of the fruits of the hunt, but of the kill itself—which could be why need-based hunting finds greater acceptance than sport hunting among non-hunters.

When sport hunters construe the hunt as a head-to-head contest, for one adversarial partner to win, the other must lose. A much-reproduced Realtree camouflage gear ad slogan succinctly sounds this theme: "Blend in or go hungry." That the hunt is a competition, an "us or them" contest of unnecessary, but absolute stakes (at least for the prey), is a constant refrain in hunters' discourse. An ad for Jennings Archery bows reiterates the symbolic construction of the sport hunt as a competition: "This is not a game, but I am keeping score." A December 1999 article title in *Deer and Deer Hunter* underscores the adversarial nature of the symbolically constructed hunter-prey relationship: "Uncommon Senses: Five Reasons Why Deer Defeat You." Compared statistically to American non-hunters and to those who hunt primarily for meat or to commune with nature, their survey responses show that sport hunters

> manifested a rather strong negativistic attitude toward animals. Apparently interest and affection for animals is not typical of those who report sporting enjoyment as their primary reason for hunting. Sport hunters were very dominionistically oriented, suggesting that displays of skill, expressions of prowess, competition, and mastery over the animal were important motivations in this activity. (Kellert, "Perceptions of Animals in American Society" 542)

In fact, the most dominionistically-oriented animal activity groups were trappers and all three types (nature, meat, and sport) of hunters (Kellert, "American" 96).

Hunters congratulate themselves and each other on their craftiness with respect to the prey when camouflage techniques and authentic-sounding animal calls prove successful. When unsuccessful, the result is attributed to the adversary's perceptiveness (e.g., the ducks here now are "well-educated"), battle-readiness ("They [the ducks] all seem to be wearing a full metal jacket"), scheming coordination (e.g., hunters portray ducks as "circulat[ing] information" among themselves), and/or agility (e.g., when one shooter misses a quail, another consoles him by saying "those are tough birds" [to hit]) (*World of Ducks Unlimited*; see also "'Smartest'"). In "From Trust to Domination," Tim Ingold observed that the relationship between predator and prey is essentially antagonistic and zero-sum, "pitting the endurance and cunning of the hunter against the capacities for escape and evasion of his quarry, each continually augmented by the other through the rachet mechanism of natural selection. The encounter, when it comes, is forcible and violent" (3). Although big game trophy hunts take this emphasis on unnecessary competitive achievement to its logical extreme, the challenge of conquest and the prey's death as proof of one's skill animates all sport hunting. The challenge of matching skills with a worthy opponent, factoring in the terrain and elements and according the prey a "fair chance," animates sport hunting (Marks 77, 78, 181).

In sport hunting, the individual prey gets symbolically positioned by the hunter as a relational partner to such an extent and in such a way that its impersonal conquest may be sexualized. For instance, the weekly opening to Kawasaki's outdoor program *Under Wild Skies,* accompanied by appropriate music and visuals, clearly constructs an eternal hunter/hunted adversarial relationship, saturated simultaneously with sexuality and sexual conquest:

> Here in the domain of the untamed beats the unrelenting rhythm of the wild. Beneath moonless dawn and sunlit dusk, through sudden cloudburst and fiery sky, beyond the path of the last hundred years, so far from comfort and so close to conquest. Where instinct and mastery bind animal and man in the sweet sweat of pursuit, passion, and fair chase. Invisible to all but hunter and game—and, now, you. Under wild skies.

Thus, a key associational aspect of "hunter" is its status as relational, and this relationship is initiated by the hunter. The constructed relational partner could exist without a hunter and outside the relationship and be named otherwise (e.g., deer, duck, or rabbit instead of "prey"), but, by definition, a "hunter" cannot exist without symbolically naming a "prey." Once hunted, the one pursued, willingly or not, acquires the relational role of prey.

Likewise, "hate criminals" symbolically construct an adversarial relationship with their victims' group. They discursively portray encounters with particular unwilling relational partners as a zero-sum game in which one must lose for the other to win. White supremacist Chevie Kehoe dreamed of creating, by whatever means necessary, a whites-only nation that he would call the Aryan People's Republic; he was implicated for trying to finance that goal through acts of robbery, murder, and kidnapping targeting Jews (Thomas). Similarly, African-American author Nathan McCall eloquently expressed the adversarial "us or them" relationship that he and his teenage buddies perceived between themselves and Caucasians, a situation that motivated them to commit impersonal violence against numerous white individuals. And, according to Aaron McKinney's girlfriend Kristen Price, McKinney and his buddy Russell Henderson wanted to put the gay Matthew Shephard, whom they did not know personally but happened to encounter in a straight bar, in his place. The two men were charged with kidnapping, aggravated robbery, and first-degree murder (Thernstrom 274). Price recounted what McKinney said to her when he arrived home that night: "[A] guy walked up to [Aaron] and said that he was gay and wanted to get with Aaron and Russ. [Aaron] got aggravated with him and told him that he was straight and didn't want anything to do with him and he walked off. Then later Aaron and Russ said, 'Let's pretend we're gay and we can—we'll rob him and take his money.' They just wanted to beat him up bad enough to teach him a lesson, . . . not to come on to straight people and don't be aggressive about it anymore" (qtd. in Thernstrom 271). McKinney later admitted that Shephard had neither approached nor propositioned them, yet he still characterized the "relationship," even in private to his girlfriend, as adversarial. At trial, Aaron's account of that night highlighted his own violent prowess during the struggle. Asked if the bound Shepard ever requested that McKinney and Henderson stop beating him, McKinney replied, "Well, yeah; he was getting the shit kicked out of him" (qtd. in Thernstrom 274).

Hatred, someone once noted, is not the opposite of love; indifference is. Hate is a relationship that, like hunting, connects the hater *with a group* rather than a recognized individual to whom the hater wishes ill. "Anger has always an individual as its object," observed Aristotle, "whereas hatred applies to classes. . . . One who is angry might feel compassion in many cases, but one who hates, never; for the former wishes that the object of his anger should suffer in his turn, the latter that he should perish" (II.iv.31). The comments of white supremacist Kehoe, while serving life in prison for anti-Semitic acts of impersonal violence, seem to confirm Aristotle's analysis: "In my entire life, my dad always hated this or hated that and never gave me something to love or something to work toward. It was extremely confusing because you get left with this bag of anger, and you have no place to focus, you have nothing" (qtd. in Thomas). The common interpretive framework detailed shows how diffuse animosity can be made coherent and construed as "meaningful" impersonal violence.

Paradoxically, either success or failure may encourage a "hate criminal" to seek more prey. For instance, after luring from a bar, tying to a fence post, and beating senseless gay college freshman Shephard, McKinney and Henderson were distracted from their plan to rob Shephard's home by an encounter with members of a different victim class. McKinney and Henderson verbally harassed and then fought two Hispanic teenagers, but did not best them. After McKinney, who was shouting slurs, cracked one of the teens in the skull with a gun so hard that the wound required twenty-one surgical staples to repair, the other pulled a big stick from under his coat and hit McKinney in the head. McKinney and Henderson fled the scene as the police arrived, leaving behind their truck and its incriminating contents with respect to the Shepard attack (Thernstrom 271, 274).

Conversely, if a "hate criminal" loses some adversarial battle, he or she may be more motivated to win the next round. In this autobiographical passage, McCall described how he and his black friends beat an anonymous white teen, who happened to ride past them on his bike, solely because of his color:

It was automatic. We all took off after him. We caught him on Cavalier Boulevard and knocked him off the bike. He fell to the ground and it was all over. We were on him like white on rice. Ignoring the passing cars, we stomped him and kicked him. My stick partners kicked him in the head and face and watched the blood gush from his mouth. . . . [W]ith each blow delivered, I gritted my teeth as I remembered some recent racial slight: "THIS is for all the times you followed me round in stores. . . . And THIS is for the times you treated me like a nigger. . . . And THIS is for G.P.—General Principle—just 'cause you white." (3–4)

McCall's testimonial goes on to establish irrefutably that the violent beating was retaliation against the group of which this unlucky individual happened to be a member; the victim was a general or representative, not a specific, "you." "When we bum-rushed white boys, it made me feel like we were beating all white people on behalf of all blacks. We called it 'gettin' some get-back,' securing revenge for all the shit they'd heaped on blacks all these years. They were still heaping hell on us, and especially on our parents. The difference was, cats in my generation weren't taking it lying down" (4). Once transportation became available, McCall and his friends stalked vulnerable victim class representatives more widely: "After my older brother Dwight got his driver's license, a group of us would pile into my stepfather's car some evening and cruise through a nearby white neighborhood, searching for people walking the streets. We'd spot some whites, get out, rush over, and, using sticks and fists, try to beat them to within an inch of their lives" (4). To the initiators, this was a contest where an adversary won or lost each battle, even though the war dragged on, unresolved, and where the victim was adjudged and treated as a class representative rather than for his or her own culpability.

Many stranger rapists, though by no means all, claim to want to defeat or overcome an adversarial challenge from their victims and/or law enforcement. For instance, for "Ray" the competition was "not like keeping a scorecard," but "just seeing how many [women] you can rape, you know, before you get caught" (qtd. in Sussman and Bordwell 121).[6] For others it was about besting their victims. As Les Sussman and Sally Bordwell concluded after their extensive series of interviews, "few rapists believe that women want to be raped. They know the truth because, as they state, they would not enjoy rape if the women did" (9). An anonymous rapist, quoted in that book's introduction, says, "It wasn't because I couldn't get sex. . . . In a way it was a thrill for some reason because they were scared. You know—'I gotcha.' They didn't want to do it, and that's what really turned me on. I was making them do something they didn't want to do" (5). This rapist saw rape as a competition, which he could win only at the victim's expense.

The accumulated formal pattern of stranger rapists' discourse symbolically constructs an antagonistic relationship that is dissolved or devalued by the victim's cooperation or, worse, voluntary consent:

I ask Zeke what would have turned him off in terms of raping a woman. He answers quickly. "If they said, 'I want it.'" "Why would that have turned you off?" "Because I wasn't in there for her to want it," he says irritably. "She turned me down. She said no from the beginning. That's why I have to take it." (Sussman and Bordwell 38)

For these participants, the relational partner's consent destroys the zero-sum, win-lose competition. "Chuck" answered the question "what could your victims have done to keep from being raped?" with: "If they'd said, 'Okay, go ahead, do anything you want,' I don't believe I would've raped. If a girl had said, 'Take me, I'm yours,' I know I would've turned and walked away. It just wouldn't have been there for me. I didn't want somebody to be passive for me. I wanted somebody to show me the fear and the hurt that I had to show" [to the powerful women in his personal relationships] (qtd. in Beneke 79). Victim consent removes the adversarial component, making the rape symbolically unsatisfactory to these rapists. "Amos" recalled his dissatisfaction with one "completed" rape's progress:

All my life I've been taking women and then there's a person that's offerin.' . . . But I backed up from it because I feel messed up emotionally. It won't be rape. But in the event I did it. . . . [Qu: Why did it turn you off when she said you should rape her?] . . . If you play a game with yourself and then the game's exposed to you, you back away from it. This is how I felt. Like I would have raped her, like if it was a thing where I was in one of my lustful states, something I looked at and I gotta have it, and she says no, I'm gonna get it. But the vibes I got from her when she says, "You have to rape me," it kicked up a nerve. I hunched my shoulders, and something just went through me. It's a feeling— I can't even explain it. It was just like a cold shiver. Then I got hot. Then I did it anyway, right? But in that one session, knowin' that she wanted to be raped, I really didn't have no gratification out of doin' it. (qtd. in Sussman and Bordwell 72–73)

This interpretative framework's organization of predator-victim relationship as zero-sum competitions among adversaries from different classes relates closely to this homology's second characteristic.

Victims/Prey Class Members Are Selected Opportunistically and Constructed Impersonally as Relatively Interchangeable Class Representatives

Although sport hunters, "hate criminals," and stranger rapists sometimes view their prey as individuals *in addition to* class representatives, they always recognize the particular victim as, or sometimes only as, a class representative. Unlike Ahab, the whale hunter in *Moby Dick,* sport hunters rarely seek only a specific animal that they have encountered in the past. Rather, they tend to hunt for deer or quail generally, as species. Some prey might be favored over others, when there is a choice among class members, but that preference is based on the animal's relative proximity to the size or maturity ideal for its class rather than its intrinsic individuality. For instance, on one episode of *Cabela's Sportsman's Quest,* sport hunters are admiring a large bull moose—a "keeper, definitely a keeper" with "big bones"—who is out of range, when a smaller moose "spooks" the large one. Although the smaller moose is within range, the sportsmen decide it is too small and do not shoot. Likewise, on *Babe Winkelman's Outdoor Secrets,* the hunters pass up a shot at a "nice buck, just not exceptionally big" in hopes that "the king of the hill" eventually will appear. As the context of this discussion shows, "the king of the hill" refers not to a specific deer, but to any one perceived to be extraordinary in relative size based on the species' average. Sometimes an acceptable class representative will be taken, if a more nearly ideal specimen proves too elusive. A speaker on one episode of *Mossy Oak Hunting the Country* comments: "We got a big one in, probably not the biggest one we could have got, but we got it nice. . . . He's got good mass. Pretty good deer." Such substitution of an adequate class specimen when an exceptional one cannot be found or downed is symbolically acceptable because the class members are interpretatively interchangeable.

The emphasis on the size of a class specimen's body or trophy body parts (e.g., antlers) relative to other species' members is underscored in a televised caribou hunt featured on the TNN Outdoor network's program *Buckmaster's White Tail Magazine with Jackie Bushman.* After discussing the excellence of both one bull's large antlers (in "full velvet") and body weight, the hunters down it; their conversation proceeds: "That's a big bull. He's big!" . . . "Golly, look at this caribou here! That's an impressive bull." . . . "[W]e saw four bulls and a cow. And I saw the tines on that, and I said, 'Man, look at that front.' Those other three bulls were nice bulls, too, but he stood out; he really stood out from the other bulls, that's for sure." As this last comment also illustrates, much of the prey choice among species members is opportunistic. For instance, duck hunters will aim for those that break away from the group, and any hunter may choose among only those class representatives that cross his or her path within shooting range.

Whenever an animal is bested by a sport hunter, its attributes are accentuated and aggrandized by the hunter or his or her companions: "Isn't he nice? Man, oh man, what a buck! Isn't that a great buck?" (*Buckmaster's White Tail Magazine with Jackie Bushman*); "What a buck, what a beautiful digger! Fat, healthy. Look at that, I got half a cedar tree in his horns. Ten big long points, one little kicker. Man, what a dream buck!" (*Mossy Oak Hunting the Country*); "Oh, man, look at the size of that deer! Look at the size of that deer! Oh, goodness, folks! That is unbelievable, unbelievable. Oh, folks, you can't believe this. I am so excited. We have been watching him for two hours!" (*Bill Jordan's Realtree Outdoors*); "Pintailed Mallard cross; what a bird! . . . Never shot one of those before. I shot it! . . . I harvested a unique specimen" *World of Ducks Unlimited*); "He's a nice bull. Look at the velvet, full velvet. He hasn't started do shed at all. He's got everything you need. All these tops, . . . two shovels . . . , and he's just a good all-around bull" (*Buckmaster's White Tail Magazine with Jackie Bushman*).

This exchange from *Bill Jordan's Realtree Outdoors* illustrates the specific prey's role as class representative nicely: "Good buck. I didn't think I'd gonna be able to stop him!" "What is it? What is it?" "A ten—perfect. Big body. Look at the body on him!" "He's huge! When I heard you shoot, I thought, 'That is unreal!'" "It's fun when you hear that! What a buck, what a buck! That is awesome; that's an awesome buck!" Even if bigger or otherwise "better" prey escaped the bullet or arrow, the catch is portrayed as a worthy partner in the adversarial relationship: "We got a big one in, probably not the biggest one we could have got, but we got it nice . . . He's got good mass. Pretty good deer. He's got a neck all swelled up. He's got a good body on him" (*Mossy Oak Hunting the Country*).

Because hatred targets whole classes, the "hate criminal," like the hunter, views relational partners from these groups as fundamentally interchangeable, not as distinct individuals. Drinnon's comment that he might have shot Native Americans as easily as he did pheasants foretells the search for any available, minimally acceptable adversary from the target class, not a specific individual. Individual "hate crime" victims rarely are chosen deliberately. Rather, they tend to be those members of the hatred group unlucky enough to cross the hater's path at a vulnerable moment. For instance, the Filipino-American mailman shot by Buford Furrow, Jr., just happened to be the first person of color whom Caucasian Furrow encountered after shooting up a Jewish kindergarten. African-American McCall's recollection of his own "hate crimes" emphasized that white victims were selected based on happenstance, not design. His victims were whichever whites happened to be walking the streets of their own neighborhoods when McCall and his buddies passed through or who turned up, vulnerable, in the wrong place at the wrong time:

> The fellas and I were hanging out on our corner one afternoon when the strangest thing happened. A white boy, who appeared to be about eighteen or nineteen years old, came pedaling a bicycle casually through the neighborhood. I don't know if he was lost or just confused, but he was definitely in the wrong place to be doing the tourist bit. Somebody spotted him and pointed him out to the rest of us. "Look! What's that motherfucka doin' ridin' through here?! Is he *craaaazy?!*" It was automatic. We all took off after him. (3)

Just so, the stranger rapist's readiness to act violently rests on a perceived relationship to the generalized target group, not the unlucky, vulnerable individual member of it who opportunistically crosses the predator's path. To avoid empathy that may abort the attack, the stranger rapist must impersonalize the victim; yet, to "justify" the rape interpretively to himself, he simultaneously must position the victim as sharing the same category as women with whom he does have, has had, or hopes to have a *personal* relationship. It is a symbolic balancing act. "Phil," serving time for five rapes, though he admits to having attempted twenty to thirty, described his behavior during attacks:

> Very little verbal contact. There was some. There was no attempt to kiss the girls or to relate to them as human beings or as individuals. That's not where I was at. I was using them strictly as a sex object in which to act out all these conflicts and blocked relationships with my wife. (qtd. in Sussman and Bordwell 170)

Apparently, perceiving women, whether strangers or intimates, as individuals rather than primarily as class members is recognized by rapists themselves as incompatible with their behavior. "Phil," who claims to be reformed and is working on a book entitled *Ex-Rapist,* points to his new respect for "a woman's uniqueness and her individuality, her right to her own body and own mind" as evidence that he has changed from a man who would "take" women into one who might have a relationship with one as an individual (qtd. in Sussman and Bordwell 173–74). Likewise, "Julio" distinguishes who he was while raping from who he is since his incarceration based on a new stance toward potential victims:

> My attitude has changed completely. . . . My attitude now is that I don't think I'm superior [to women]. I'm not scornful. I understand now that they have their own opinions, their own attitudes about certain things. I appreciate the differences because I think that I grow behind that. But there was a time where I couldn't be comfortable with a woman and just sit down and speak with her, because I always thought I was better than they are. (qtd. in Sussman and Bordwell 54)

To recognize the individuality of and develop a personal relationship with a victim would change the symbolic valence or compromise the violence's meaning.

Stranger rapists also portrayed female strangers as symbolically interchangeable. When asked whether he singled out a particular type of woman to rape, "Ray" responded, "Not really. I'd rape any woman" (qtd. in Sussman and Bordwell 117). Asked how he selected one particular victim, "Sal" answered, "It wasn't that I just picked her, it was just that she was the person around. I don't believe I was looking for any type of—you know, any color hair or anything like that she was built in a special way. She was just the one that was there when I was cruising" (qtd. in Sussman and Bordwell 155). "Kasim," who "blamed all women for being the same as [his ex-girlfriend] . . . and spent most of [his] life trying to get even," was high the night he raped a woman exiting his neighborhood park; though he does not remember, the victim reported that "Kasim" talked about his general hatred for women as he raped and sodomized her (Sussman and Bordwell 79–80). "Julio" argued, "All the women is the same in nature" (qtd. in Sussman and Bordwell 55). "Zeke" admits that, when he raped, he perceived any victim as "every" woman:

> I tied this girl down in a position where she couldn't move. And I just used her.
> I did everything I wanted to do to her, as Shirley [the stepmother he claimed
> had raped him] did to me. . . . I felt at that time it was my rightful payment for
> what had been done to me. This is why I took it out on her. . . . I said, "This is
> what somebody did to me, let me see how you feel, how you like it, being that
> you're a woman and this is what you did to me. . . . You're mine to use the
> way I've been used, and there's nothing else to be said." (qtd. in Sussman
> and Bordwell 32)

When the stranger rapists interviewed expressed a level of discrimination in selecting female victims, their preferences still were cast in terms of "types" of women, rather than individual women. For instance, like sport hunters, some rapists looked for women who approximated certain ideals of size or beauty as representatives of their class. "Qu: 'Was there any special type of woman you were looking for?' Sal: 'Yes. Big tits. The bigger the better'" (qtd. in Sussman and Bordwell 63). "Ray," himself a repeat stranger rapist who also raped his wife, explained the victim selection process, when based on anything more than opportunity, as possibly turning on the specimen's physical characteristics: "After your first victim you want to get another one. Maybe she's better-looking or something like that—the way she walks, the way she smiles and talks or something" (qtd. in Sussman and Bordwell 122).

Other stranger rapists chose among potential victims based on their physical resemblance to particular women with whom they were angry. "Amos" characterized his second victim as "every bit the image of my mother" (qtd. in Sussman and Bordwell 73). Such men characterized their stranger rapes as justified, though impersonal, payback to the class of interchangeables, another or others of whom had hurt them personally. "Chuck's" explanation communicates the overarching perception that women are basically interchangeable and that superficial physical similarities telegraph this interchangeability and validate an unfamiliar woman's violation in retaliation for personal hurts inflicted by other women: "The three girls I attacked represented to me my real mom, my stepmom, and my wife. They all had special features that reminded me of them" (qtd. in Beneke 75–76). After his biological mother abandoned him in infanthood, his stepmother abused him in childhood, and his wife cheated on him in adulthood, "Chuck" claimed that he

> started hating all women. I started seein' all women the same way, as users. . . .
> I'd thought about murder and other ways of getting even with women and
> everyone who'd hurt me. I was just waiting to explode. . . . When I seen that
> [porn] movie [featuring a rape], it was like somebody lit a fuse from my child-
> hood up. When that fuse got to the porn movie, I exploded. I just went for it,
> went out and raped. It was like a little voice saying, "It's all right, it's all right, go
> ahead and rape and get your revenge; you'll never get caught. Go out and rip
> off some girls." . . . So I just went out that night and started lookin'.' . . . As I did

it to her, my head was back one night where my wife just lay there like a bump on a log and didn't show any pleasure. That's one thing that was in my head. She was just layin' there doin' nothin.' It wasn't a victim no more; it was my wife. . . . I felt like I'd gotten even with different girls who'd fucked me over. . . . I . . . went lookin' for my next victim. (qtd. in Beneke 73–75)

Notice that "Chuck" represents the rape he witnessed in the pornographic movie as the fuse that crystallized his interpretive framework and gave shape to a potential response to his perceived experiences, not its cause. Rather, this symbolic representation validated for him a violent act that "made sense" within his larger interpretive framework. When "Chuck's" sisters asked him why he raped, he "told 'em I wanted to hurt you females in my family, just like I'd been hurt. . . . The three girls I attacked represented to me my real mom, my stepmom, and my wife" (qtd. in Beneke 75–76). Both these physical criteria—approximation of some beauty ideal or resemblance of an intimate of the rapist's—still recommend rape victims mainly on their relative appeal as class representatives instead of individuals.

Even more important than a woman's approximation of some physical beauty idea or resemblance to a woman with whom the rapist has had an unsatisfactory personal relationship, though, is the stranger rapist's perception of a potential victim's vulnerability at the time of the attack. Dennis J. Stevens's study of sixty-one serial rapists' descriptions of their attacks showed that sixty-nine percent of them characterized "victim vulnerability" as the means by which they selected a particular prey from among members of the targeted class (i.e., women); in addition to those who were "easy prey" as a result of their personal characteristics (e.g., the young, the elderly, the physically incapacitated), stranger rapists looked for vulnerability created by the woman's situation (e.g., solitary occupation, disorientation by an unfamiliar location, alone in an isolated location, temporary incapacitation by shopping bags or a dependent child's presence). "Harold," for instance, cruised around in his car with a toy pistol; he selected a woman carrying a child, coerced them into her car by threatening to hurt the child, drove the captives to another location, and raped the woman (Sussman and Bordwell 154–55). "Phil" noted that, while he did not blame his victims, he would warn women against putting themselves in vulnerable situations or not paying close attention to self-interest because men like him were out there "looking, looking, looking" for a woman doing "stupid things" to "pick up and rape" (qtd. in Sussman and Bordwell, 175–76).

Such opportunistic victim choices (versus "random" choices or "confusing responses") comprised a whopping eighty-four percent of predatory rapists' own explanations for their victim selections; if one also includes "randomness," an opportunistic explanations account for ninety-five percent of predatory rapes (Stevens 55–67). Personal accounts published in other sources confirm that stranger rapists, like "Zeke" and "Julio," seek women who already are vulnerable (what "Julio" referred to as "the type of woman that's easy . . . fair game") and that they perfect techniques to maneuver them into even more vulnerable situations (see, for example, Sussman and Bordwell 34–35, 50–51). Those who plan stranger rapes might stalk physically vulnerable victims, waiting for maximum situational vulnerability to coincide with that physical vulnerability. For instance, "Ray" admitted to planning one of his many rapes, this one against a juvenile: "What I did, I watched where she lived at, and I followed her where she lived, where she would go certain places—this and that—and where she went at night, what time she got back. And when I figured out where was the best spot to get her, I made my attack" (qtd. in Sussman and Bordwell 115). Stevens concluded that "the primary mission of most serial rapists is to have immediate sexual contact with a female, any female," however they justify it (98). Like sport hunters and "hate criminals," stranger rapists are opportunists who generalize by class when selecting victims.

Rhetors Distance and Impersonalize Victims/Prey, Without Objectifying Them or Diminishing Their Presumed Potency or the Status Accompanying Conquering Them

Under the adversarial relationship staged in sport hunters' discourse, hunters require a worthy opponent to preserve the notion that this is a contest with a respectable challenger. "A hunter never apologizes to his prey. He just thanks it for the contest," reads a 1999 Wizard Works Realistic Hunting and Adventure Games ad. Perhaps because the prey is constructed as a relational partner, hunters rarely characterize their own actions as killing or even shooting (gun or bow), relying instead on an astonishingly broad lexicon of euphemisms including "harvest," "take," (as in, "Take him!"), "fall," "drop," "hit," "stop," or "bring down" (see also Cartmill 285). In fact, the use of such terms as "kill" and "dead" are so rare as to be striking when used by hunters; for instance, in reviewing hours of videotaped hunting programs, I only heard "kill" uttered twice and "dead" once (*Remington Country; World of Ducks Unlimited*). One only can have such a competitive relationship with an adversary who somehow is capable of reciprocating or resisting, of feeling pain at losing. To bother initiating an adversarial relationship at all, the interpreter must perceive some level of comparability, even similarity, between self and prey. A *Mossy Oak Hunting the Country* article subtitle implies that a sport hunter also must identify with a prey to some extent in order to prevail: "Decades of predator hunting yield tricks to harvest tricksters" (Bynum 55). Another indication of the hunters' identification with their prey as more than objects is the fact that sport hunters almost never refer to a large prey animal as "it," but consistently identify the target by gender as "he" or "she." The animal-human distinction gets even fuzzier in discussions taped at the moment of an actual kill: "That's a big bull. He's big! That's a *man* right there!" and "Handsome, handsome devil" (*Buckmaster's White Tail Magazine; World of Ducks Unlimited*).

Judging from hunters' symbol use, part of what makes the hunting relationship worth the effort rests on the ability to establish the prey symbolically as a worthy foe. This task may involve exaggerating a class representative's potency, relative imperviousness, or arrogance. For instance, a menacing pair of green, unmistakably non-human eyes peering out of the darkness appear in an ad for black, green-lensed Predator binoculars with the caption "Nothing escapes these eyes." A 1999 *World of Ducks Unlimited* program depicts hunters discussing potential prey in classic combat terms, such as "they all seem to be wearing a full metal jacket." Perhaps offering the most insight into this feature of hunters' interpretive framework are advertisements in which a voice is projected for the prey animal. For example, the prairie dog in an ad for a Simmons V-Tac gun scope says: "I can handle hawks, a few coyotes, and an occasional rattlesnake, but I sure get the 'willies' when Simmons shows up." The statement is framed as that of a seasoned competitor who understands and is prepared for lethal intergroup contests. Even more telling is a commercial, which appeared during a 1999 *American Shooter* episode. Here the talking prey, a deer, insultingly taunts the hunter's prowess in an unmistakable parody of one highly confrontational Clint Eastwood character: "I know these woods like the back of my hoof. I've locked antlers with the biggest of bucks and dodged five years of bullets and arrows. I can pick up your scent at half a mile and be gone before your next heartbeat. So I gotta ask ya; do you feel lucky, punk?"

Impersonalization without objectification or depersonalizing seems key to the interpretive perspective of "hate criminals" as well. The victim must be perceived as different enough from oneself to short-circuit the attacker's empathy, yet similar enough to oneself that one can accurately anticipate the sensations of and possible enjoy the victim's suffering. McCall's recollection of his group's assault on a white teen reveals that much of their satisfaction and pleasure came from hurting and humiliating a recognizably sensate being that they acknowledged could experience pain in the same ways and places that they might:

> I kicked him in the head and face, where I knew it would hurt. Every time I drove my foot into his balls, I felt better;. . . . [O]ne dude kept stomping, like he'd gone berserk. He seemed crazed and consumed in the pleasure of kicking that white boy's ass. When he finished, he reached down and picked up the white dude's bike, lifted it as high as he could above his head, and slammed it down on him hard. . . . Fucking up white boys like that made us feel *good* inside. (3–4)

The victim's expiration or pain is intrinsic to the predator's satisfaction and motivating sense of superiority. Thus, I disagree with the popular notion that "hate criminals" objectify or depersonalize their victims. "Hate criminals," like sport hunters and stranger rapists, may distance themselves to avoid empathizing with a victim's recognized pain, but they cannot objectify or depersonalize them totally nor deny some level of sensational similarity between themselves and the victim or the interpretive motive sponsoring the pleasure taken in the violence evaporates.

Stranger rapists' discourse likewise communicates a pattern of impersonalizing rather than depersonalizing victims. A predator cannot be gratified by an object's submission; only surmounting an "Other's" resistance, forcing submission, and possibly causing humiliation or physical pain completes the interpretive circuit. Convicted stranger rapist "Ray" recounted his experience of his attacks: "They was in great pain. I just laughed in their face. I thought it was a joke. It was a good feeling to me. . . . Why? I don't know. I guess it goes back to my childhood, when I'd seen my father do the same thing to my mother" (qtd. in Sussman and Bordwell 119). "Sal" commented: "A rapist is one that takes it all—has no limits, takes what he wants. He doesn't give a damn about the person he's taking it from" (qtd. in Sussman and Bordwell 65).

Stranger rapists' satisfaction derives largely from the interpretation that they have exercised nearly absolute control over an unwilling, sensate person, forcing them into a humiliating, intimate act. Objects experience neither humiliation nor intimacy. Thus, it is as important to maintain the perception of the victim as human (i.e., not to dehumanize or objectify the victim totally) as it is to keep that relationship impersonal and on a class representative level, so that the rapist does not empathize or risk personal involvement with the suffering victim or begin to perceive him or her as a unique individual. "Julio" volunteered: "It wasn't so much that I was in it for the game or the enjoyment of the game. I found that I actually liked it when I'd force a woman to have sexual intercourse" (qtd. in Sussman and Bordwell 47). When asked if raping a woman made him feel "powerful and in charge," "Julio" clarified that, for him, it was less about the pursuit than the triumph by superior force: "It wasn't a machismo, chauvinistic type of thing. I just enjoyed the fact that it was done by force" (qtd. in Sussman and Bordwell 47). According to these rapists' discourse, succeeding was empowering, partly because the loser was a sensate, animate adversary, not an object. "Dave" responded to the question of whether he felt powerful when he raped with: "Yeah. I felt like I had everything in the world. I could do what I wanted. When you rape these women—I really can't explain it—it makes your male ego really souped up. Like, if you had Superman powers, you know? But after it was over I felt ashamed of myself that I did enjoy it" (qtd. in Sussman and Bordwell 129). Failing means that the victim won, and others who have participated in the game might admire the winning prey and ridicule the losing predator. Drinnon's old homesteaders' delight at the "squaw" who outsmarted her potential rapist attests to the premium placed on the challenge of besting a competitor in a zero-sum game. But any respect at losing to a victim attaches only to that "atypical" individual representative of the target group and is not generalized to the group to serve as a future deterrent to predatory attack.

Rhetors Express a Desire to Physically Assert—and Take Pleasure in Exhibiting—Dominance and Superior Hierarchical Status

Establish Hierarchical Superiority to Prey/Victims. Sport hunting has come to be associated among most Americans not only with the exercise of lethal power—and competing with a peer group to be the most effective at it—but also with an assertion of traditional masculinity. For example, one respondent to Stephen R. Kellert's survey of hunters commented:

> An important drive in hunting is the maleness aspect of it—the machismo aspect. . . . I don't know if the gun is a phallic symbol or not, but it's certainly a symbol of maleness, of machismo, of strength. . . . Cats kill birds not because they want a bird. They kill it to confirm their prowess and ability. . . . I think they share the same exultation in their prowess as the hunter. . . . (qtd. in Kellert, *Policy* 13)

This speaker continues by speculating that, at least for him, the "real drive" to hunt "is the maleness" or the masculine performance of prowess and ability that successful sport hunting represents to him (qtd. in Kellert, *Policy* 13). A "dominionistic" attitude indicates that one derives satisfaction from mastering and controlling animals, usually in some sporting context; animals "are valued largely as challenging opponents, providing opportunities for the display of prowess, kill, strength, and often masculinity. The conquest of the animal demonstrates superiority and dominance—the human ability to confront wildness and render it submissive and orderly" (Kellert, "Perceptions of Animals in America" 9). Kellert's survey found hunters to be "consistently and significantly more dominionistically and utilitarian oriented than either anti-hunters or non-hunters" (*Policy* 28). Furthermore, there is a clear hierarchy ordering prey, in sport hunters' discourse, according to both gender and the challenge presented. Generally, rarer animal types and male animals are more prized—unless there is some special challenge involved in hunting a more common species or a female. To illustrate, hunter Mark Walters's characterization of his "taking" a doe with a pistol telegraphs both the usual prey hierarchy and the presence of over-riding factors inflecting its interpretive status: "The challenge of using the pistol made shooting this doe better than taking a buck with a rifle" (B6).

Dominance and pleasure in succeeding at dominating beings characterized as "Other" become almost inseparable in this symbolic context. One interviewee explicitly likened successful deer hunting to sexual release: "Deer huntin' is like the fever. It builds up all year long and then has to be released. It's like buildin' up for 'a piece.' Once ya laid one, you move onto the next one that may be harder" (qtd. in Marks 150). Usually both sex and violence both revolve around perceptions of a distinguishable "Other." Edmund Leach observed that "venery's" meanings are hunting and sexual indulgence (45). Wild animals especially aptly symbolize disorderly "alien others," and beasts of venery metaphorically facilitate discussions of human aggression expressed through hunting or sexual relations (see Leach 44–45, 54; Mechling and Gillespie 4). In the hunting camp, virile tales of sexual and hunting conquests often intertwine (Cartmill 233). The hunter quoted earlier in this paragraph also characterizes the buck's main vulnerability to hunters as his desire for sex: "[A buck's] slick, when they want to be, can't they? Yeah. But we always outsmart them for some reason. There ain't but one thing that takes a buck's mind off of a human being, or a gun, and that's a doe when he's in rut" (qtd. in Marks 151). Thus, the blurring of violence and sex and the sense that successfully dominating a prey demonstrates sexual virility flows readily from this interpretive frame.

In the discourse of "hate criminals," the connections between desire and taboo, attraction and repulsion, complement and contrast extend to blur distinctions between violence and sex (see Sullivan 56–57). Hatred is "a complex, affective state alloyed with aggression," and acting violently on it may be pleasurable, even "delightful," to borrow from Drinnon's stories; consequently, as Harold P. Blum explained, "Hatred is not the opposite of love, though hatred may be erotized" (20). In "hate crimes," including the "squaw" lassoing episode that opened this essay, discriminations between sex and violence, as well as correspondences between self and "Other," become ambiguous. McCall explicitly recalled reveling in causing a victim pain: "Fucking up white boys like that made us feel *good* inside. I guess we must have been fourteen or fifteen by then, and it felt so good that we stumbled over each other sometimes trying to get in extra kicks and punches" (4). Sullivan's own musing after studying "hate crimes" also suggests this fourth point of correspondence: harming a sensate being contributes to the perpetrator's sense of dominance and superiority:

> For all our documentation of these crimes and others, our political and moral disgust at them, our morbid fascination with them, our sensitivity to their social meaning, we seem at times to have no better idea now than we ever had of what exactly they were about. About what that moment means when, for some reason or other, one human being asserts absolute, immutable superiority over another. About not the violence, but what the violence expresses. (Sullivan 51)

Such passages reveal not only recognition of dominating a sensate being, but also some attractive interpretive meaning in the act of domination for the predator.

Andrea Dworkin explained her take on the convoluted dynamic that enmeshes hate, violence, sex, discourse, and dehumanization in a revised version of a speech given at the University of Chicago Law School:

> I am struck by how hate speech, racist hate speech, becomes more sexually explicit as it becomes more virulent—how its meaning becomes more sexualized, as if the sex is required to carry the hostility. . . . [T]he racist hierarchy becomes a sexually charged ideal. There is a sense of biological inevitability

that comes from the intensity of a sexual response derived from contempt; there is biological urgency, excitement, anger, irritation, a tension that is satisfied in humiliating and belittling the inferior one, in words, in acts. We wonder, with a tendentious ignorance, how it is that people believe bizarre and transparently false philosophies of biological superiority. One answer is that when racist ideologies are sexualized, turned into concrete scenarios of dominance and submission such that they give people sexual pleasure, the sexual feelings in themselves make the ideologies seem biologically true and inevitable. (Dworkin 184–85)

For instance, before leaving Matthew Shepard, their gay target, tied to a Wyoming fence, Aaron McKinney and Russell Henderson got into a fight with two Hispanic teenagers, whom they taunted with sexual and animalizing slurs such as "Fuck you!" and calling the teens "bitches." In his confession, McKinney also stated that he and Henderson had told Shepard that they were going to "jack him up" before beating him (Thernstrom 271). McCall's buddies referred to the boy they beat as "motherfucka" (3). As the statements from the "hate criminal" discourse quoted here show, the pleasures of sex and violence seem to bleed together until they are difficult to separate at an interpretative level.

For the stranger rapists whose discourse shows the same formal pattern, sexualized dominance obviously is a goal; rape is not about "power to" but "power over." "Chuck" clearly explained stranger rape's pleasure for him in terms of a symbolic show of dominance over an unwilling and anonymous relational partner who represented a specific class of people (i.e., women): "I wanted somebody to show me the fear and the hurt that I always had to show. It was a turn-on to see em' [sic] scared and me being in control for once. Rapists want to be in control. Somewhere in their life a woman destroyed their ego. Rape is a way a man rebuilds his ego, rebuilds his manhood. Shit like that" (qtd. in Beneke 79). As one who raped two or three times a month for two years, "Luke's" comments resonate with the theme that stranger rape is a sexualize act of dominance, in which much of the pleasure comes from the rapist's physical demonstration of supremacy and a victim's humiliated forced submission:

> It seems to me like every time something didn't go right in the crib, I'd leave and rape someone. It wasn't like no sexual urge that I gotta have some, 'cause I got some all the time with my little ol' girlfriend. . . . In a way it was a thrill for some reason because they were scared. You know—"I gotcha." They didn't want to do it, and that's what really turned me on. I was makin' them do something they didn't want to do. . . . If they cried it was just a bigger kick. (qtd. in Sussman and Bordwell 178)

Likewise, "Sal" commented: "I always had one thing in mind when I was younger—take advantage. You can't get it voluntarily, you have to take it" (qtd. in Sussman and Bordwell 59).

Just as sport hunters enjoy "taking" game, presumably against the prey's will, stranger rapists want to "take" women, not cooperate in consensual sex. For example, "Sal" never even seemed to attempt to "get it" voluntarily. In his first rape, he followed a girl home from school, peeped at her for a week in her first-floor bedroom, then broke into her bedroom, knocked her unconscious, tied her up, and raped her. Later in his interview, "Sal" asserts, "Of course it was my right. I felt that way. I figure if you're not going to give it to me, then it's my right to take it. So I took it any way I can" (qtd. in Sussman and Bordwell 64). "Ray" fumbled with the interviewer's follow-up question over why he never considered asking women to whom he was attracted out on a date instead of raping them: "I don't know. I can't answer that. If I would have tried I probably could have. At the time I just wanted her, and I took her" (qtd. in Sussman and Bordwell 116). Stranger rape is not just about sex, but about forcibly "taking" another person and forcing false intimacy on a member of the class one desires to dominate more generally.

Sometimes stranger rapists deny that their attacks harm victims in any way other than hierarchical subordination. "Ben," incarcerated in Louisiana's state penitentiary for rape, claimed that he "wouldn't deliberately try to hurt anybody. Even though I raped these two girls, I didn't hurt 'em in any way except just to embarrass them a little or hurt their pride" (qtd. in Sussman and Bordwell 105). "Luke," incarcerated in an Illinois prison, responds similarly to the question "So you liked the power over these women, is that it?":

> That was my goal. It was to humiliate them. That's what the goals of rapists are—to humiliate. To me it was more like a revenge type of thing. . . . I remember there was one or two women that seemed like they enjoyed it. They might've been faking it and tryin' to keep me from hurtin' them. And I really didn't get as big a thrill out of it. The ones that seemed really frightened is the ones that really turned me on. That's what I'd need, you know? (qtd. in Sussman and Bordwell 179)

Of his first "completed" rape, "Chuck" recounted, "When I first attacked her I wasn't even turned on; I wanted to dominate her. When I saw her get scared and hurt, then I got turned on. I wanted her to feel like she'd been drug through mud. I wanted her to feel a lot of pain and not enjoy none of it. The more pain she felt, the higher I felt" (qtd. in Beneke 74). "Quentin," too, answers simply the question of whether raping made him feel powerful: "Extremely so" (qtd. in Sussman and Bordwell 136). Even, maybe especially, in prison, rape is about establishing one's hierarchical position relative to the victim. "Willy," who claims that he tries to rape about three times per week in prison, constructs this practice as one that enhances rather than diminishes his "manhood": "When I do something like that there, it don't tear me down. It's making me feel bigger, stronger" (qtd. in Sussman and Bordwell 96).

Establish Hierarchy Among Peers. Although women's hunting participation increased by twenty-three percent between 1989 and 1999 to two million (Rupp 8), hunting of any sort is still predominately a male activity (Cartmill 233; Franklin 108; Vanden Brook, "Big" 6A). More significant, symbolically hunting is a "quintessential masculine activity," a way of defining, reinforcing, and extending a traditional construction of masculinity, gender roles, and power distribution (see Franklin 122). "Masculine," of course, denotes only a voluntary subject position; it can be assumed by men or women and not all men choose the traditional version of it with which hunting is associated. But, for many, hunting has become not only "a tried, proven, and proper way of becoming and being a man;" today it is also one way of affirming a particular traditional masculine identity "in a world where the lines of demarcation between the sexes are blurred and where the presumptions of male 'superiority' are being questioned" (Marks 6). One hunter interviewed described the symbolic context of hunting as it relates to gender politics and reasserting traditional male dominance as women gain greater power in society at large: "It's the politics of cunt and hunt!" (qtd. in Marks 161). In some hunting camps, peers humiliate hunters who miss a passing buck by cutting off their shirttails with a large hunting knife (Marks 140, 146–49; Yatzeck 101). The only photograph of the ritual that I could locate shows one hunter holding another's *front* shirttail out at waist height and chopping off a length of it while others look on (Marks 129). Failure to exploit successfully a killing opportunity results in what appears to be public ceremony of symbolic emasculation. Indeed, a neophyte's first successful kill, not first excursion or attempt, is the ultimate initiation into the hunting fellowship (Marks 72; see also Yatzeck 99–102).

By participants' own admission, sport hunting is not only about dominating a prey but also about demonstrating superiority to other sport hunters. For example, when a featured hunter on *Under Wild Skies* kills his first mule deer with a single shot, he inquires of his companion about an absent colleague, "I'm awfully excited not only about the stalk but the great hunt. Where is Tommy? I wanted him to see my first mule deer. . . . I wanted to brag a little about my shot, you know." The present companion already has acknowledged the shooter's prowess with the comment, "When he [the mule deer] went down, it was like you hit him with a sledgehammer." Even more telling is the procedure shown on *World of Ducks Unlimited.* The hunting guide dictates the turn-taking process: those hunters whom he perceives as most likely to down a prey will have the first turn, while the presumably less skilled hunters must not fire. Moreover, the favored hunters' "turn" lasts well beyond taking their first bird; they hunt without competition from the second group until each of them has collected many carcasses. Only then are the others allowed to step forward. Their success suggests that major skill differences was not strictly the issue. Now, one might attribute this choice to production value or economy, but I detect clear elements of asserting hierarchy. After all, the cameras keep rolling when the second spate of hunters finally gets their turn, and each second stringer successfully downs a bird on his first shot—in addition, editing easily could produce the desired final effect or omit this guide's decree from the final televised program. Consistent with Marks's arguments, hunters' own discourse suggests that they symbolize their relative status, standing, and distinction with respect to other hunters based on their demonstrated skill at downing game (Marks 77, 81, 269).

Judging from the discourse, for some, sport hunting not only serves to exhibit relative masculine prowess but also to express sexual dominance (see Marks 160–61). Trophy shots, in which the victorious hunter smiles as he holds up the head of the carcass that he or she created by conquering a living being—the bigger or rarer, the more admired and likely to be published—appear in virtually every issue of every hunting specialty magazine. Sexually suggestive article titles like "So You Want a Bigger Gun?" (Boddington)—complemented by trophy pictures of the relatively more impressive game (e.g., moose, eland, Botswana sitatunga, brown bear) that one can score with such weapons—are reinforced and contextualized through advertisements like these two recurring sexualized Dillon and European American Armory (EAA) Corp.'s ads. The former ad, captioned "Something Special from Dillon," features at center the photo of a voluptuous blonde with upswept hair in a strappy evening gown operating a shotshell reloading press and surrounded on all sides by (usually vertical) shooting equipment. The latter, EAA's "Delivering not Teasing" Bounty Hunter ad shows two women: one seated, barefoot, and dressed in an all-white, micro shorts and cowgirl hat ensemble with a cocked rifle over one shoulder and an ammunition belt encircling her torso and the other, crouched and clad in a bikini and high heels, who blows "pretend" smoke off the pistol she holds in one hand while caressing her own thigh with the other. The sexualization of violence hardly could be clearer in these ads, which appear in mainstream, "newsstand" magazines such as *Shooting Times* and *Guns and Ammo*.

According to this interpretive framework, hunting success hierarchically orders males who participate, and prowess at conquering game, or beasts of venery, also intimates sexual prowess. On numerous hunting programs, a successful shot often is acknowledged by hunting buddies with phrases such as "You are the man!" Hunters thus may use their sport hunting success to perform dominance over prey and other hunters, and also to represent superiority in relationships with intimates. Stuart A. Marks opened his ethnography of Southern hunting by observing, "The ways hunters, as individuals and as groups, relate to animals are keys that unlock some of the meanings in their social relations and in their lives" (3). Marks observed that, in white "non-pot-hunting" households, eating the game "frequently has important gender significance in marking the dependency of family members upon masculine abilities" (72).

"Hate crimes," which often involve multiple predators working together, also resonate with messages of demonstrating hierarchical status relative to one's peers, as well as the victim, via the assault. One might establish superiority among peers by the degree of callousness one can show toward the victim's suffering or the amount of pain and damage one is willing to inflict on a sensate being based solely on his or her group classification. As McCall recalled, "We walked away, laughing, boasting, competing for bragging rights about who'd done the most damage. 'Man, did you see how red that cracker's face turned when I busted his lip? I almost broke my hand on that ugly motherfucka!'" (McCall 4). "Hate crimes" committed by more than one individual sometimes are framed by participants as a "fraternal" ritual or "proving ground" for new initiates (Dees). The grisly beating and dragging death of African-American James Byrd, Jr., by three white Texans, for instance, was part of a bonding ritual for their emerging white supremacist group (Sullivan 50). And Russell Henderson's landlady remembered him as "pretty neutral—a follower"; he was a good student and an Eagle Scout, until he started hanging out with guys like Aaron and quit school (Thernstrom 270). Eventually Henderson assisted McKinney in Shepard's gruesome death. Group participation in a "hate crime" against some "Other" establishes a sense of group superiority as well as bonding and individual pleasure in domination (Sullivan 88).

When it comes to stranger rape, relative dominance over peers becomes an issue especially in gang rape. An anonymous stranger rapist described the synergy of having a partner predator: "Having a partner is like having something to drink. I felt braver. I felt stronger. This gave me the courage to do something I might not have done on my own" (qtd. in Groth 112). But with the empowerment of camaraderie comes the hierarchical pressure of peer competition. Men who participate in gang rape sometimes are goaded by peers into more drastic actions than they would take alone. "Norman" hesitated to follow his friend "Rick's" direction to have intercourse with their victim after "Rick" already had forced her to perform fellatio; but he complied once "Rick" called him "chicken" (qtd. in Groth 111). Sometimes stranger rapists engage in rape to be more like a higher status peer. For instance, all of "Kurt's" stranger rapes involved his friend "Pete." "Kurt" explained his perceptions: "I always looked up to Pete and felt second-class to him. I felt I owed him and couldn't chicken out on the rapes. I worshipped him. . . . Taking part in the sexual assaults made me feel equal to him. . . . He was five years older and almost like a father to me. . . . He made me a somebody. . . . We raped about eight girls together over a four-month period" (qtd. in Groth 113). Acceptance and recognition among peers whose approval affects one's relative status are intertwined with representatively dominating the victim and her class in gang rape. Sometimes the victim even is asked to "rank" the "performances" of her attackers. One anonymous rapist recounts, "I'm balling her, and she says to me, 'You're either good or it's been a long time since I've had it.' I said, 'Tell that to my cousin [the other participant in this rape].' After we had her, we asked her who was the best" (qtd. in Groth 116).

Establishing relative status among men may play a role indirectly even when a stranger rapist acts alone. "Tom" commented, "After I went to Stateville I got involved in group therapy. Through that I found out the reason I was doing it was proving to the men in my family that I was more of a man than they were, and proving to the women that I wouldn't be henpecked like the men were" (qtd. in Sussman and Bordwell 186). Although one might write this explanation off to Tom's therapist's successful projection, other rapists' comments are curiously congruent. As a child, "Ray" helplessly watched his father rape his mother with a Coke bottle; he attributes his loathing of his father's act to making him a rapist himself at fourteen. When an interviewer observed, "It would seem that what your father did would turn you off to men rather than women," "Ray" responded with an apparent *non sequitur:* "Right. It did. I wouldn't mess with a man. I wouldn't associate with them. . . . I was angry at my father. Being angry at him, being he was a man, I was angry at men. What I couldn't do to them, I would take out on a woman" (qtd. in Sussman and Bordwell 118). "Ray's" motive to dominate gets expressed via impersonal violence subordinating members of a weaker, wronged class rather than against either his father or a representative member of the father's gender.

Conclusion

Because they are inherently symbol users, humans—including those who repeatedly engage in impersonal violence—live, as Clifford Geertz put it, "suspended in webs of significance" that they themselves have spun (5). This piece reveals a recurring internal logic, evident when one examines a large set of sport hunters', "hate criminals'," and stranger rapists' discourse. Together the four premises discerned above form a widely recurring, cogent, and relatively complete motivational system. As my earlier work demonstrates, some accusations of illogic or disturbance are traceable to unrecognized differences in interpretive frameworks' assumptions rather than the processes by which their adherents build out from those assumptions (Olson, "Expanding," "The Role"). In practice, symbol users tend to move from an interpretive frame's assumed "premises to conclusion with the syllogistic regularity of a schoolman. . . . We may offer grounds for questioning the entire rationalistic scheme, as tested by our technique of testing—but we cannot call a man illogical for acting on the basis of what he feels to be true" (Burke, *Permanence* 85). However strongly our postmodern sensibilities proclaim an incoherent world, most people still function on a day-to-day basis *as if* in a coherent reality, which they help create by "making sense" using symbolic patterns from one or another of more-or-less internally consistent interpretive perspectives. For most humans, an interpretive perspective that makes one's violent actions justified—even praiseworthy or required—is a necessary, though not sufficient, condition for repeated acts of impersonal violence. Five significant conclusions emerge from the rhetorical homology observed in participants' discourse across impersonal violence different in preferred targets, situations, and physical expressions.

First, this study suggests that attending closely to individuals' discourse for the detected rhetorical pattern might alert a potential victim to discursive danger signs of impending impersonal violence and so coach self-protection. The same coherent interpretive framework underwrites acts of impersonal violence across various participants, most unknown to each other, and differing circumstances. As Brummett noted, "The ways in which wide ranges of bits might cohere meaningfully require an attention to unifying homologies, especially when the traditional unifying forms of discreet or specifically expositional texts are not relevant in the situation. . . . [I]dentifying a form that might have ordered such a situation is much of the news that a critic can offer" (*Rhetorical* 97). Burke's brilliant unraveling of the motivational structure of Hitler's rhetoric—originally published in 1941, long before the extent of its interpretively justified atrocities were known—teaches the prescience of observed symbolic patterns and the importance of attending to them as indices of future behavior (*Philosophy* 191–220). Not every person whose discourse exhibits this homological pattern may play it out violently, and those who do so may act through relatively socially acceptable violence (e.g., sport hunting) rather than socially unacceptable forms (e.g., "hate crimes," stranger rape). However, rhetoric that expresses the pattern indicates that the rhetor holds a worldview consistent with, and even justificatory of, impersonal violence. Detecting such a pattern is the first step toward both prediction and response.

Second, the homology's demonstrated reach across the discourse of sport hunters, "hate criminals," and stranger rapists suggests that similarity in *discursive form,* rather than *physically violent particulars,* may be the most fruitful conceptual entry point for studying impersonal violence. This homological analysis suggests that these three versions of impersonal violence are different individuations of a coherent motivational structure of the interpretive framework that itself invites impersonal violence in many forms and against a whole range of victims. "They are 'all doing the same'—they become but different individuations of a common paradigm. As so considered, they become 'symbolic' of something—they become 'representative' of a social trend" (Burke, *Philosophy* 19). My argument indicates that categorizing violent acts based on victim types or specific physical expressions may prevent researchers from seeing the forest for the trees. For instance, perhaps stranger rape has more in common with "hate crimes" and sport hunting than it does with rapes involving intimates. From an interpretive standpoint, sport hunters also may have more in common with stranger rapists and "hate criminals" than with "pot" hunters, and "hate criminals" with stranger rapists and sport hunters than with criminals who engage in "equal opportunity" murders, assaults, and kidnappings. Should that be the case, productive research must realign to reflect the realization that the common interpretive framework justifying and motivating all these violent individuations is the primary social threat; the particularities of its multiple violent expressions are secondary. Prioritizing the shared interpretive "why" rather than the diverse "who," "how" "where," and "what" particulars of impersonal violence represents a promising entry point for research as well as creative intervention. Effective intervention may require approaching impersonal violence not only at a different level (i.e., more social, less individual), but also with a different orientation (i.e., symbolic and interpretive) than currently used.

Equally important, the homology's presence in discourse by participants engaged in three very different types of impersonal violence implies a pressing need to examine critically discourse from perpetrators of other impersonal violence for the same pattern. For example, the demonstrated interpretive perspective might animate the discourse of "bullies" and so may enrich our understanding of and productive response to it. If the homological pattern manifests itself, what already is known about "bullying" conversely might refine understanding of the common interpretive framework, complementing what was learned through examining the initial three individuations. For instance, Richard J. Hazler observed that bullying victims who acquire power may become bullies themselves (10). Given the symbolic or physical improbability of hunting or rape victims identically mimicking their attackers' specific violent expressions of the interpretive framework, victims' post-attack motivation to replicate the interpretive perspective of their attackers in order to justify their own impersonal violence likely would go unnoticed without the additional "bullying" discourse set. Such possibilities deserve examination because they resonate with as-yet-unexplained details of the examined discourse sets, such as the fact that surviving classmates admit that Columbine shooters Dylan Klebold and Eric Harris (who fit the "hate criminal" definition) were themselves regularly harassed as "faggots" by schoolmates (Sullivan 57). Additionally, while this study explicitly limits itself to contemporary American discourse, it should prompt research into whether the identified homological framework extends into other cultures. For instance, Philip Gourevitch's chilling 1998 account of the symbolic build-up to Rwanda's 1994 genocide of the Tutsi minority contains tantalizing clues that the proposed homological pattern, or some variant of it, interpretatively may have facilitated these impersonally violent atrocities.

A third, and disconcerting, conclusion is that the homological pattern's existence in and through symbols makes it "communicable" in persuasive ways. In other words, the rhetorical homology indicates that, at least for these speakers, impersonal violence is neither random nor just individual idiosyncrasy; it is backed by a cogent, sharable interpretative framework that can be advocated and so to which other symbol users may be recruited actively. Gourevitch's account of official discourse preceding the Rwandian genocide highlights how an interpretive perspective that justifies physically harming an "Other" can be constructed and manipulated intentionally through rhetoric. A coherent interpretive framework justifying impersonal violence is especially attractive when material resources appear unequally divided. As Edelman suggested, perception of deprivation (whether of materials or status) is a function of social cues about what is to be expected and what exists, rather than directly resulting from "objective" conditions (107).

Even the comfortably situated may feel relatively disadvantaged and thus motivated to compete, using impersonal violence, to assert superiority. For example, in spite of his admittedly well-to-do adolescent existence, McCall recounted feeling relatively disadvantaged and so justified in physically attacking white strangers:

> Sometimes, when I sit back and think about the crazy things the fellas and I did [at fourteen and fifteen] and remember the hate and violence that we unleashed, it's hard to believe I was once part of all that—I feel so removed from it now that I've left the streets. Yet when I consider white America and the way it's treated blacks, our random rage in the old days makes perfect sense to me. Looking back, it's easy to understand how it all got started. (4)

Yet the fact that this homology justifying impersonal violence against various sensate beings is rhetorical and so symbolically transmittable carries hope for those who would like to stem certain types of impersonal violence. Symbolically grounded violence can be resisted with more persuasive counter-symbol use. Further hope for stemming impersonal violence comes from the homological analysis's demonstration that participants already see their victims as similarly sensate beings and relational partners, not objects. Perhaps these relationships can be recast symbolically.

A fourth conclusion is perhaps this study's most unsettling. From a rhetorical perspective, the interpretive framework uniting sport hunting, "hate crime," and stranger rape looks disturbingly like a *variation on* rather than a *deviation from* mainstream American culture's driving priorities. Though usually not acted out in such physically violent extremes as "hate crimes" and stranger rapes, capitalistic economies and democratic societies admire unfettered competition, sometimes even that in which one party goes out of the way to humiliate another. Aggressively asserting hierarchy over others is visible in stock trading, political elections, football end zone dances, and in-your-face basketball rim-hanging—and the popular culture that valorizes them. As evidenced by recent American leisure spectacles, new levels of actual physical pain and one-on-one humiliation by other competitors seems to boost the entertainment value of hierarchical contests (e.g., the Xtreme Football League, the Worldwide Wrestling Federation, and television programs such as *Survivor, Weakest Link,* and *Fear Factor*). Thus, the homological framework identified here may differ more in degree than in kind from one widely accepted in contemporary American society.

If the homology is either a reasonably close reflection or an outgrowth of values that mainstream America valorizes (e.g., competition, hierarchical superiority), this essay's results call for renewed self-examination at a social level.

Whether Burke is correct that hierarchy is inherent to language use or Suzanne Sievert correct in asserting that "it's part of human nature to be competitive" (12), both seem to be persistent motivations in contemporary American society. Regardless, neither competition nor hierarchy is *innately* immoral or anti-social; both can be powerful motives for common good. Their social desirability depends rather on their specific expressions. A viable, pro-social interpretive alternative to this homology would need to enfold motives of competition and hierarchy in a perspective that is at least as internally and externally consistent as well as motivationally compelling.

Fifth, and finally, is a time-tested, yet always radical, proposal for those committed to diminishing impersonal violence by addressing it at an interpretive level. As Rita Kirk Whillock and David Slayden recognized, suppressing speech that justifies impersonal violence is not the answer; rather, taking it seriously and analyzing it is the change agent's first productive move (xv). The foregoing homology argument further underscores the importance of such discursive openness. Censorship or subsequent penalties will not curb impersonal violence, but at most would restrict analysts' access to such discourse and how it appeals, thus obscuring early danger warnings. Additionally, trying to force an alternative interpretative framework (however socially positive) on people through a central authority or majority vote would be both unworkable and undesirable. Instead the task of those who want to break the hold of any socially threatening interpretive framework is to coach people's voluntary embrace of "some other kind of writing, of a different incantory quality" (Burke, *Philosophy* 123). Any persuasive substitute would have to be at least as coherent, comprehensive, and compelling in encompassing the key motivations (competition and hierarchy, played out in impersonal relationships) as the homology's.

I am tempted to end this piece right here, but two factors prevent it. The first is my own annoyance with criticisms that find only fault and make no effort to propose a better alternative course. The second is Burke's cautionary words: "If the reviewer but knocks off a few adverse attitudinizings and calls it a day, with a guaranty in advance that his article will have a favorable reception among the decent members of our population, he is contributing more to our gratification than to our enlightenment" (*Philosophy* 191). So, in the interest of rounding out this criticism on a positive note, let me sketch just one of many possible alternative interpretative frameworks: one derived from the words of Jesus as reported in the four Gospels, which has proved its persuasiveness across centuries and cultures. My reading finds in these words a coherent interpretive frame that encompasses, yet inverts the homology's hierarchical and competitive motives, with pro-social implications for behavior in impersonal relationships.

My hesitation to continue stems from the fact that it is not politically expedient in academic journals to include positive comments that hint at anything remotely religious. Such essays may be dismissed or systematically misunderstood.

That said, consistent with my argument's requirements for productive alternative frames, one already-formed alternative emerges from my reading of New Testament gospels. This frame certainly is not the only pro-social alternative, but is one that seems obvious to me and has proven inviting to millions. In 1939, T. S. Eliot argued for such an alternative in *The Idea of a Christian Society*. Eliot's controversial and often-distorted position was paradoxically revolutionary, yet moderate. He asserted the desirability of a hypothetical society that embraced Christianity's interpretive framework and the derivative social practices it justified, whether or not that society's members accepted or even were aware of Christianity's philosophical and theological tenets. Eliot carefully articulated his opposition to any imposition of an official religion or secular philosophy. Rather, Eliot's book merely imagines human interactions should a society's members choose to understand experience and act according to Christianity's interpretive perspective. In light of what this homological analysis reveals about that framework's integration of hierarchy and competition with impersonal relationships, Eliot's suggestion should provoke renewed interest among those dissatisfied with the current state.

Although my suggestion still is likely to be controversial, let me first offer a few caveats. Not all Christians would read the Gospels as accepting hierarchy and competition. Various Christian doctrines may refuse this notion outright. In fact, the hierarchy/competition angle is not even the primary way that I usually read the Gospels; but it is one of many textually defensible readings. Further, this reading presents an ideal; I am not claiming that Christians have realized it in practice. Across two millennia, people claiming to act "in the name of" Jesus have acted in ways more consistent with the impersonal violence homology than—even in direct violation of—the upcoming alternative interpretive framework and this article's requirement that any workable alternative be accepted voluntarily, not by force. Additionally, this reading draws only on passages that the Gospel writers attribute to Jesus as direct quotations. Finally, like Eliot, I imagine that people could embrace this Gospel-based interpretive frame, with its social behavioral implications, without religious conversion to Christianity. It is a coherent interpretive alternative coaching pro-social action in even impersonal relationships, whether one regards Jesus as divine Savior or merely a wise human teacher.

Christianity's theological and spiritual aspects aside, the basic interpretive framework, derived from the statements of Jesus as recorded in the Gospels of Matthew, Mark, Luke, and John offer a pro-social alternative encompassing both hierarchy and competition; it explicitly explains them with respect to impersonal relationships. I argue that hierarchy and competition are not eschewed by this framework, but embraced and inverted toward serving, not hurting, others, including others to whom one is not personally connected. Within this context, hierarchical aspirants are given clear directions for achieving relative greatness, even in earthly life: "If anyone wants to be first, he must be the very last, and the servant of all" (Mark 10:35); "For he who is least among you all—he is the greatest" (Luke 10:48b); and "So the last will be first, and the first will be last" (Matt. 20:16).[7] Jesus set himself up as the behavioral exemplar for such hierarchical achievement: "Now that I, your Lord and Teacher, have washed your feet, you also should wash one another's feet. I have set you an example that you should do as I have done for you" (John 13:13–14) and "You know that those who are regarded as rulers of the Gentiles lord it over them, and their high officials exercise authority over them. Not so with you. Instead, whoever wants to become great among you must be your servant, and whoever wants to be first must be slave of all. For even the Son of Man did not come to be served, but to serve and to give his life as a ransom for many" (Mark 10:42–45). This alternative enfolds human hierarchical tendencies (innate or learned) and harnesses them for loving service rather than violent impersonal relationships. Although these Gospel passages and others like them have additional importance if one embraces Christianity as a faith, alone they interpret experience in a way that encompasses individuals' hierarchical tendencies while coaching pro-social impersonal relationships.

According to Jesus's statements, to achieve greatness, one must act lovingly not only toward one's intimates but also toward those with whom one only interacts impersonally (e.g., those who might become one's victims under the homology's framework). The Golden Rule is the supreme standard offered by Jesus for laudable human interactions, whether in personal or impersonal relationships. After establishing a primary commandment regarding humans' proper relationship with God, Jesus continued: "The second [overarching commandment] is this: 'Love your neighbor as yourself.' There is no commandment greater than these" (Mark 12:31); "And the second is like it: 'Love your neighbor as yourself'" (Matt. 22:39); and "So in everything, do to others what you would have them do to you, for this sums up the Law and the Prophets" (Matt. 7:12). Jesus told the parable of the "Good Samaritan," perhaps the Gospels' best-known story, in response to the follow-up question, "Who is my neighbor?" (Luke 10:29–37). That story underscores how the same caring, serving behavior should extend beyond personal relationships to impersonal ones; the framework's logic is socially comprehensive (see Rom. 13:9–10). On another occasion, Jesus made the same point with respect to the hierarchical excellence of extending these norms to impersonal relationships less obliquely:

> If you love those who love you, what credit is that to you? Even "sinners" love those who love them. And if you do good to those who are good to you, what credit is that to you? Even "sinners" do that. And if you lend to those from whom you expect repayment, what credit is that to you? Even "sinners" lend to "sinners," expecting to be repaid in full. But love your enemies, do good to them and lend to them without expecting to get anything back. (Luke 6:32–34a; see also Matt. 5:43–47)

The interpretive framework simultaneously accounts for pro-social competition and tells interested competitors how to avoid humiliation:

> When [Jesus] noticed how the guests picked the places of honor at the table, he told them this parable: "When someone invites you to a wedding feast, do not take the place of honor, for a person more distinguished than you may have been invited. If so, the host who invited both of you will come and say to you, 'Give this man your seat.' Then, humiliated, you will have to take the least important place. But when you are invited, take the lowest place, so that when your host comes, he will say to you, 'Friend, move up to a better place.' Then you will be honored in the presence of all your fellow guests. For everyone who exalts himself will be humbled, and he who humbles himself will be exalted." (Luke 14:7–11)

Moreover, motivated competitors who adopt this frame will avoid judging others. Instead, they will direct such impulses toward re-examining, then positively and competitively revising their own behavior. Again, in the words of Jesus:

> Do not judge, or you too will be judged. For in the same way you judge others, you will be judged, and with the measure you use, it will be measured to you. Why do you look at the speck of sawdust in your brother's eye and pay no attention to the plank in your own eye? How can you say to your brother, "Let me take the speck out of your eye," when all the time there is a plank in your own eye? You hypocrite, first take the plank out of your own eye, and then you will see clearly to remove the speck from your brother's eye. (Matt. 7:1–5; see also Luke 6:41–42)

So, even when one rejects or brackets Christianity's spiritual and theological elements, words of Jesus offer one alternative interpretive framework that is well-equipped to re-encapsulate the hierarchical and competitive motives of the homology in a way that coaches more pro-social impersonal interactions. Within this framework, greatness is demonstrated by non-judgmentally loving others as much as (not "instead of" or "more than") one loves oneself, and superiority is enacted by loving and serving even those with whom one has no personal relationship. Social reformers interested in intervention might do well to advocate the broader voluntary embrace of this or other alternative interpretive frames that more pro-socially encompass the motives central to the impersonal violence homology. Especially in a free speech marketplace, interpretive frameworks grounded in, and so sharable through, symbols may be resisted or replaced by more persuasive counter-symbol use.

Notes

1. In self-reports, "pot" hunters, those who must hunt to survive, attitudinally construct their prey, motivations, and activities differently than those who hunt for "sport" as a leisure activity (see Kellert, *Policy*).

2. I focused only on discourse from admitted rapists and further only on the subset of those who raped strangers rather than (or occasionally in addition to) their romantic partners, friends, dates, or other familiar acquaintances. I assume that those who rape non-strangers might have different motives and symbolic interpretations than do stranger rapists, though that is an assumption worthy of further testing.

3. In this essay, the term "hate crimes" denotes physical violence against people perceived as different from the offender because of the victims' perceived racial or ethnic classification, religious affiliation, or sexual orientation. It is a rhetorical delineation that does not square consistently with the shifting legal definitions or other academic uses of the term, so I will put the term in quotation marks throughout my argument's text to remind readers constantly of this particular definition. Traces of the term's vigorously contested meanings can be found in Altschiller, Jacobs and Potter (45–64), Jenness and Broad, Levin and McDevitt, and U.S. Department of Justice.

4. Although readers readily may entertain the possibility of a rhetorical homology between "hate crimes" and stranger rape, they may bridle at any attempt to add the formal parallels of sport hunters' rhetoric to the group, even though sport hunting is a contested activity in contemporary America, objectionable to a large portion of the population. As early as 1978, Stephen R. Kellert noted "a very significant expansion in anti-hunting sentiment" accompanying Americans' newfound interest in wildlife (1). By the 1990s, only twelve percent of Americans (and only one to two percent of American women) engaged in hunting, and almost one-third of the population supported a ban on sport hunting (Cartmill 229, 233, 284–85; Franklin 108). An earlier study showed sixty percent of those surveyed as opposed to any kind of recreational or sport hunting (versus subsistence and need-based hunting), though participants relented somewhat *if* the hunter consumed the meat, even if the hunt was not motivated primarily by this utilitarian purpose (Kellert, "American" 101). Similarly, seventy-seven percent of a national sample denied admiring trophy hunters (Kellert and Berry 48). When non-hunters' needs temporarily coincide with sport hunters' goals—for instance, when proliferation of a deer population threatens humans through a rise in the related auto accidents and eco-damage—"hunters [become], if not heroes, then more widely accepted," according to Mark Damian Duda, executive director of Responsive Management (qtd. in Vanden Brook, "Deer" 17A). But, because such acceptance arises from pragmatic alliances rather than acceptance of the sport's intrinsic value, it is ephemeral. Sport hunters (as contrasted to "pot hunters" who need to hunt in order for their families to survive or "slobs" who kill wantonly or unsportingly, who waste the prey's meat, or who poach) particularly present themselves as under attack and on the defensive much of the time as a result of their sport (e.g., "Game"; Gresham; *Remington Country*, 7 Nov. 1999) and resent generalizations that indiscriminately lump together hunters who exhibit varying degrees of sporting behavior, especially those that treat the unsporting "slob" as representative (Marks 264–66).

It is crucial, then, to underscore that no evidence of which I am aware links hunters with an increased propensity to participate in any type of human "stranger" violence, which is the only type explained by the proposed homology. Thus, I hope to observe this homology in interpretive frame without condemning sport hunting or offending the many upstanding hunters whom I know from a lifetime residing primarily in the upper Midwest. I live in Wisconsin, a state in which one of every seven residents older than sixteen hunts deer (Vanden Brook, "Big" 6A) and to whose hunters "deer season . . . means more than Christmas" (Yatzeck 20), and have lived in Michigan's Upper Peninsula, where hunting is valued at least as highly. So, I have had many opportunities to attend to hunters' discourse as I try to better understand the attraction of blood sports and to sort out the highly-nuanced perspective on animal-human relationships that also made Wisconsin the first U.S. state to make deliberately torturing or sadistically killing an animal a felony ("Cruelty" 1).

5. Violence against intimates or acquaintances operates under a different set of social expectations than does impersonal violence. Rightly or wrongly, personal (vs. impersonal) relationships have more nuanced norms for and gradations of socially acceptable violence. A particular violent act considered socially unacceptable if directed at a stranger may be considered socially acceptable if one is "punishing" a child or pet or "defending" oneself or others against a person (e.g., abusive spouse or parent or acquaintance) who is not threatening harm at the moment of "defense," but who has a personal relationship with and history of violence against the "defended." Though beyond the scope of this essay, there may be observable homological patterns linking the discourse of those who engage in various types of personal violence. Ascione and Arkow's 1999 edited volume, together with their individual work (Arkow; Ascione, "Children," "Battered," "The Abuse"), their work with other coauthors (Ascione, Weber, and Wood), the work of numerous other scholars (Felthous; Felthous and Kellert; Kellert and Felthous), and applications of such conclusions ("Cruelty"; Lockwood; Lockwood and Church; Lockwood and Hodge; Smith; White and Shapiro) hint that a common interpretive frame may link personal violence against different classes of intimates, such as one's own significant other(s), children, and pets.

6. Sussman and Bordwell interviewed each rapist separately and at three different prisons in different parts of the country, so the similarity in responses was not produced by group interaction.

7. All biblical quotations are from the *Concordia Reference Bible*, New International Version.

6

Classy Morality

The Rhetoric of Joel Osteen

Luke Winslow

This chapter is about power—who has it and what they do to keep it. Who has the most power is not always determined by who has the biggest muscles or largest guns. Power is often obtained and reinforced through the evaluations and judgments we make about the people around us. These judgments help create distinctions that sort out who is powerful and who is not. For example, research on physical attractiveness says that we evaluate good-looking people more positively in a large number of areas, including judgments about intelligence, happiness, and marital competence (Cialdini 171). The physical makeup of an individual's face can thus influence how much power we perceive that person to have.

Class is another criterion we often use to make judgments about other people. Class is most often used to explain a person's economic situation, such as "she is from a middle-class family." But class also refers to the shared political and cultural characteristics that result from similar economic standing. Class-based judgments are important because they explain a lot, including our behavior, our assumptions, how we are taught to behave, what we expect of ourselves and others, our concept of the future, how we understand problems and solve them, and how we think, feel, and act (hooks 103). These class-based judgments do not stand alone; they are made when we connect class to other issues. In this way, class is used as a shortcut to other criteria we use to make judgments about other people. For instance, if I run into a man at the Department of Motor Vehicles who is of a noticeably lower class, I use his class standing to make broader judgments about other areas of his life.

This chapter looks specifically at the way class can be connected to morality to make these judgments. I analyze the rhetoric of Joel Osteen, a popular evangelical minister, to argue that he makes a connection between the traits assigned to class and the traits assigned to morality; in this way, Osteen can disguise morality within class. Four traits—marriage and family, hard work, appearance and decorum, and health—are used by Joel Osteen to explain why the poor are poor. These traits operate as a disguise because they are also the traits attributed to the moral. Using them allows Joel Osteen to disguise morality within class by connecting the similar traits.

To better understand these traits and how they can help disguise morality, imagine a family member or friend you may have who seems to know all there is to know about life and loves to tell you about it. I have an uncle who is this way. To my uncle, life is simple. Complex issues like class, for instance, are easily explained by attributing specific traits to the poor that make them that way. Think for a second about what those traits might be. Even without knowing my uncle, you may be able to guess some of them because, as untenable as these traits are, they are constantly being reinforced. The connection between these traits is what allows Osteen and my uncle to explain both class and morality and thus to disguise morality within class.

I support my argument by first explaining the way class intersects with religion. I then move on to the method used to detect a disguise before detailing the underlying form that links class to morality in Osteen's rhetoric. I will close the chapter by discussing some implications of that disguise.

More Than Class

Being a member of the upper class is usually accompanied by the expected trappings: nice homes, nice cars, and nice clothes, to name a few. But another benefit that is rarely openly acknowledged is the assignment of higher *moral* status to the upper class. In the same way that we connect good looks with intelligence, we make moral judgments based on class standing. This allows class standing to represent much more than just wealth.

The idea that class standing indicates morality is unsettling, as you've probably noticed. We never admit that the rich are of stronger moral cloth than the middle class and poor—that would be un-American. Can you imagine a presidential candidate reassuring his constituents of his upstanding morality by citing how much money he has in his bank account? The result would no doubt be outrage. We do not like to admit that class determines morality because the United States is supposed to be a classless society. The United States is where anyone can rise to the upper class, irrespective of his or her origins. This idea is important to the American ethos. We hold up Horatio

Alger–like stories and people like Oprah Winfrey and Donald Trump because they presumably were able to climb from a lower class. These stories capture the imagination of the American public because we do not want to let go of the myth that the United States is a classless society where all can rise (hooks 74). This idea restores our faith in our country and our way of life. Democracy and free market capitalism are credited with allowing people like Michael Irvin to go from being so poor that he had to eat ketchup sandwiches as a child to NFL stardom and upper-class status. With a little luck and a lot of hard work, everyone can be wealthy. Everyone can make it big.

Most of us quickly learn, however, that this notion is not true. Instead, the rich seem to get richer, and the poor seem to get poorer. The gap between upper and lower classes in the United States continues to widen like never before. When confronted with this reality, discussions about class become difficult. Leon Festinger's work on cognitive dissonance is helpful in explaining why. Many years ago, Festinger argued that, when we are presented with realities that do not conform to our existing worldview, anxiety (or dissonance as he called it) is created. For example, when a cigarette smoker is presented with a message about how bad smoking is for his or her health, that knowledge causes the smoker some level of discomfort. That anxiety can be eased in numerous ways. One of the most common methods is to avoid the issue. A smoker, for example, can change the channel to avoid the television commercial causing the anxiety.

I cite this example of cognitive dissonance because it helps explain how class is handled in the United States. Class segregation—the gap between the rich and the poor—does not fit within the worldview that the United States is a classless society. There is a street near the campus of the University of Texas at Austin where many homeless folks and transients ask passing students for spare change. Most cities have a street like this one. It is noticeably difficult for many middle- and upper-class college students to walk on this street, in part because dissonance is produced at the sight of the lower classes. One remedy many students choose is to simply avoid that street. We do the same as a society. Like the smoker who changes the channel, as a society we would prefer to avoid the class issue. bell hooks, in her book *Where We Stand*, argues that, nowadays, we would rather talk about race and gender than class. Class is a subject that makes us tense, nervous, and uncertain. I remember when I was a child being severely reprimanded for asking my wealthy aunt how much money she made. Children are taught at a young age not to ask such questions because they bring one's class standing into the open, and class is a taboo topic. Our societal aversion to class is an indication of the cultural force it has. If class were not a major issue, we would not have a problem discussing it openly; but it is, and we do.

One exception to this rule is religion. Christianity in particular is one area where class issues are openly discussed. Christian teachings have traditionally addressed issues such as greed, wealth, and the poor. Historically, Christianity took a sympathetic stance toward the poor. bell hooks points out that the Christian church played a major role in creating a compassionate image of the poor, as well as compassionate identification with the poor (87). In three of the four New Testament gospels, Jesus warns that each of his disciples may have to "deny himself" and even "take up his Cross." Generations of churchgoers have understood that being a Christian means being ready to sacrifice for the lower classes. Verses such as Matthew 6:19–21 are cited:

> Do not lay up for yourselves treasures on earth, where moth and rust destroy and where thieves break in and steal; but lay up for yourself treasures in heaven, where neither moth nor rust destroys and where thieves do not break in and steal. For where your treasure is, there your heart will be also.

Christianity extends a sympathetic view to the poor by assigning the lower classes a higher moral standing. Jesus says in Mark 10:24–26 that it is easier for a camel to go through the eye of a needle than it is for a rich man to enter the kingdom of God. The implication is that, to be rich, one must also be lacking in morality.

Beginning in the 1980s, however, a new brand of evangelical Christianity began viewing the class issue in a much different way. Prosperity Theology, also known under a variety of names—Word of Faith, Health and Wealth, Name It and Claim It—emphasized God's generosity in this life and the ability of His followers to experience that generosity through the accumulation of wealth and material possessions. Many in this movement point out that a God who loves you would not want you to be broke. A consistent theme in Prosperity Theology is that if you are wealthy you must be under the favor of God. This side of the issue cites biblical support as well—verses like John 10:10 in which Jesus said, "I have come that they may have life, and have it more abundantly," for example.

Prosperity Theology rose to prominence most recently in the 1980s, but its history stretches back much further. Sociologist Max Weber argued that, as early as the 17th century, Puritans sought salvation through economic activity. Puritans saw profit and material interests as a sign of their status among God's elect. Profit maximization was seen as a badge of virtue. Wealth provided believers an assurance that they were favored by an all-powerful and all-knowing God and would also inherit eternal life. Conversely, just as the crowning sign of God's favor was wealth, the universal sign of God's disfavor was poverty. Those unable to acquire material wealth were sinners, not favored by God and, therefore, not among His elect.

Early Puritans were concerned by the uncertainty that comes with a doctrine of predestination, so they created for themselves certainty of salvation through work and wealth. These religious beliefs directly associated psychological rewards with economic interest. Early Puritans solidified their faith through material possessions. We see here the beginning of the confounding of religion and class in the United States. One's wealth and one's salvation were seen as synonymous for early Puritans. Those who had wealth were among the elect, and those who did not were reprobates or unworthy of God's blessing.

Today, Prosperity Theology and the megachurches it has inspired reflect the theology Max Weber ascribed to early Puritans. One example of a proponent of this theology is Joel Osteen. Osteen is a popular television evangelist who relies on a consistently upbeat, health and wealth message that emphasizes God's favor on His people as exhibited through wealth and material blessings.

His message has found an audience. Since 1999, Osteen has risen from a college dropout running his father's television ministry to head pastor of the largest and fastest-growing church in North America. Lakewood Church of Houston, Texas, boasts a weekly congregation of over 45,000 adults and in 2005 moved in to the 16,000-seat Compaq Center, formerly home of the NBA's Houston Rockets, to accommodate growth. Osteen's television show is the highest-rated religious broadcast in the country, found on over 200 stations and reaching 225 million people in 150 countries. His 2004 book, *Your Best Life Now,* has sold over 3 million copies and became a number-one *New York Times* best-seller.

Joel Osteen's rhetoric is examined here to understand how class is used to disguise morality. Osteen would never preach a sermon on the immorality of the lower classes. Image is as important for a well-known religious leader like Osteen as it is for any Hollywood celebrity, and a sermon that directly denigrated the morality of the poor would certainly hurt his image. Instead, Osteen uses what I call an *underlying form* that connects the traits that make a person rich to the traits that make a person moral. The underlying form then allows Osteen to deliver moral instruction couched in language about wealth and class.

Form and Disguise

The disguise in Joel Osteen's rhetoric is based on an underlying form that connects class to morality. Understanding how form can be used to disguise will be helpful not only in understanding Osteen's message but, more importantly, in recognizing other messages that may come in under our critical radar. We are often influenced by subtle messages that sneak in when our defenses are down. Uncovering the underlying form in Joel Osteen's rhetoric is useful because it can show how form can cover up disguises. To understand the numerous disguises in our rhetorical world, let us begin by discussing what form is and what we should be looking for when attempting to uncover a disguise.

The best way to understand form is to think about it as a consistent structure or pattern found in the language of a text (Burke, *Counter-Statement* 31). The form is based on making a connection between two different things, such as class and morality. This connection is useful for criticism because it allows us to see "this" in terms of "that." In this way, form can act as a bridging device that passes content across different experiences (Brummett, *Rhetorical Homologies* 4). For example, I may have no experience with the drug dealing, gang violence, or police brutality spoken of in rap music, but it can still appeal to me because of a deeper, formal connection between how Jay-Z handles his authority problems with how I handle mine.

We often attempt to make connections between things we understand and things we do not. Most people are complex creatures and difficult to fully understand, but a good first step is to make a connection to a person's favorite book, how she spends the weekends, and her parents' occupation. Knowing those things provides insight into that person.

Form is used to make a connection between class and morality because most people can make class judgments quickly and with relative ease. We can usually identify who is upper and lower class in seconds. Salespersons make snap judgments like these daily to quickly evaluate who will lead to a sale with a sizable commission. Morality, on the other hand, is messy. It is much harder to make snap judgments about who is moral and who is not in the way class judgments are made. To remedy this problem, the form makes a connection between something we recognize (class) and something much more difficult to understand (morality). This is why Osteen's ability to guide his audience morally without ever mentioning morality is important. Morality is messy for a reason. The criteria we use to make moral judgments about someone have a huge impact on our overall evaluation of that person. If we are using the same criteria to make moral judgments that we are using to make class judgments without ever knowing it, we are in danger of simplifying a subject that is not so simple.

Now that we know what form is and what it can do, let's look more closely at some criteria that can be used to identify an underlying form. We will then apply these criteria to Joel Osteen, but keep in mind that their real value will be in allowing you to identify formal disguises in your everyday life.

The first thing to look for when attempting to identify an underlying form is unusual or unexpected ways of speaking. When analyzing a text, be aware of what is surprising about the language. What is surprising can often lead to a form that operates below the surface. For instance, there would be nothing surprising about a newspaper advertisement that read "10% off all furniture in stock!" There is probably no underlying form there. With Joel Osteen, on the other hand, we may raise an eyebrow when we realize that there is very little explicit moral instruction in his message. Osteen's avoidance of moral instruction is odd for a minister. Of all professions, the ministry would be the most obvious one for offering moral instruction. It is also surprising that Osteen talks so much about class issues. There is so much talk about class and so little talk about morality that words like abundance, wealth, and favor seem to stand in for day-to-day moral instruction.

Along with keeping an eye out for what is unexpected and unusual, it is important to be aware of how often a formal connection is made. Form gains its power from emphasis and repetition (Brummett, "Homology Hypothesis" 203), hence the consistency of the connection is significant. The connections we are concerned with here come in a disguised form, so an outright link is not forthcoming, but we can see the form develop when the traits of one thing are consistently connected to the traits of another. Joel Osteen never mentions morality, but he can instruct his audience morally by repeatedly lumping together the traits that constitute an individual's class standing with his or her morality.

It would be futile to argue for an underlying form if this connection only occurred a couple of times in the text. We have a methodological imperative not to manufacture evidence but instead to find enough evidence in the text that the connection is evident. Any pattern or form can be argued for, but its backing comes from the amount of evidence in the text. This evidence keeps us honest and prevents us from simply locating what we set out to find.

The third criterion we need to identify is called systematicity. Systematicity is concerned with the implications from one side of the form matching the implications from the other. Systematicity is like an alembic still or large pot that you put some kind of substance in, where that substance is refined or transmuted to become something else. Systematicity occurs in Osteen's case when traits of morality put into the pot come out exactly the same as what comes out when traits of class are put in. When the implications from both sides of the form match, we can say they are systematic and can further support the existence of an underlying form.

The fourth clue in detecting an underlying form is the relevance or significance of the issue. The existence of an underlying form used to disguise will be much more likely when the issue being discussed matters to our daily lives. This is especially true when we are studying popular culture because, as Kenneth Burke said, we use popular culture as the "equipment of living." What occupies our free time serves as equipment for living because it provides us with motives appropriate to our lives (Brummett, "Electric" 248). This is a large reason for popular culture's appeal and explains how texts become rhetorical. Barry Brummett used this illustration:

> Suppose a person goes to see a film about World War II and from it gains motives that help her or him to live through a protracted conflict with a neighbor. Perhaps this person turns the hero's grim determination to beat the Nazis into grim determination to confront the dragon next door. This disagreement with the neighbor is *not* World War II, but the two are formally linked by the structures of conflict and resolution, antagonist and protagonist, patterns of risk, defeat, and gain. ("Homology Hypothesis" 204)

Another reason that underlying form often disguises significant issues is because the magnitude of the subject matter is such that it needs to be disguised. In other words, underlying form usually disguises "big issues." In the example of

Joel Osteen, we are dealing with two significant and complex issues; morality is messy, and we don't like to talk about class. We can begin to see the purpose of a disguise here. If I wanted to talk to an audience about the NFL playoffs, would I need a disguise? Probably not. Although many people might not agree, the NFL playoffs are not a relatively "big issue." If I wanted to talk about the playoffs, I would do so on a content, or surface, level. I would not need a disguise.

Uncovering the form that can disguise big issues should fire you up. Big issues, like class and morality, reveal a grand engine of human motivation. Knowing how an underlying form can help cover a disguise can go a long way in explaining why we do what we do. That fires me up.

As you might expect, I will use these four criteria to uncover a disguise in Joel Osteen's rhetoric. In the next section, I analyze what is surprising, what is consistent, what is systematic, and what is significant in his rhetoric that disguises morality within class. Keep in mind as you read the upcoming analysis that, although these criteria are used to identify the traits in Osteen's rhetoric, they can also be used to identify the disguises in your own life.

The Underlying Form

To uncover the traits that link class to morality, a smart place to begin is to ask yourself what makes the poor poor and the rich rich. When you pass by a homeless man begging for your spare change or hear a story on the news about a welfare mother in the inner city, what traits are you or others assigning to them? These traits often have no grounding in reality. They are attributions that nevertheless seem to be common in our society. Recall my uncle and his explanation for why the poor are as they are. Because we operate under the premise that we live in a classless society where everyone can make it big, there must be some reason the poor remain poor. The same is true of the rich. When you hear about a multibillionaire on television or read about a rich person in a magazine, what traits are ascribed to that person? Of course, there are exceptions. People like Paris Hilton can be born into wealth without possessing any of the traits normally assigned to rich people, but we like to think those exceptions are rare. If they were not, it would hurt our concept of a democratic and classless society. In other words, it would be unfair. We assign specific traits to the rich and the poor because those traits help reinforce the idea of a classless society.

These attributions go deeper than surface explanations of class. The poor may be poor because they are on welfare, use food stamps, rent instead of own their homes, are unwise with money, and lack an education, but those explanations alone do not justify the plight of the poor. Something more accounts for their destitution. Likewise, the rich are not rich simply because they embody the antithesis of the poor person's traits, such as they own property, are smart with money, and are well educated. They are commonly perceived to possess traits that the poor do not; but these traits are disguised because they not only make the rich richer, they make them more moral.

In Joel Osteen's rhetoric, marriage and family, hard work, appearance and decorum, and health serve as formal underlying traits that connect class to morality. According to Osteen's message, the poor are poor and the rich are rich because of these traits. The traits are then connected to morality through Osteen's emphasis on God's blessing. God only blesses those who are moral, and He shows His blessing through wealth and material abundance. An in-depth analysis shows that God's blessings come only to those people with strong marriages and families and to those who work hard, dress well, and are healthy and in shape.

It is important to understand these traits because they are not unique to Osteen. A common justification for the poor being poor is that they come from broken homes. Another is that they are poor because they are lazy and refuse to work hard. They are often depicted as poor because they are unkempt and do not know how to dress and act properly and because they are unhealthy and out of shape, which adds to their shabby appearance. To identify and analyze these traits is not to endorse them as accurate but, instead, to expose the formal connection that links class to morality by way of a powerful disguise. These traits are usually reinforced whenever discussions of class come about. We learn from Osteen's work that these traits disguise moral judgments beneath class distinctions without ever having to mention them out loud.

MARRIAGE AND FAMILY

The first trait that makes up the underlying form concerns the marriages and families of the lower class. Like all four of the traits, the trait of marriage and family constitutes a formal connection in Osteen's rhetoric because it matches the previously established criteria. Although it is not unexpected for a religious leader like Osteen to talk often about marriage and family, for him to directly connect an individual's marriage and family life to his or her class standing is surprising. Osteen makes the connection consistently and often; it is a systematic connection because the implications of the trait match both class standing and moral standing; and, finally, marriage and family are significant issues.

Let's use my uncle as an example of how marriage and family can be connected to class standing. My uncle might argue that the poor come from dysfunctional, broken, nontraditional, and non-nuclear families. In other words, the poor are not being raised in *Leave It to Beaver's* house. The poor, instead, come from divorced families and out-of-wedlock parents. Fathers are often nowhere to be found, and children are given free rein to run the streets. These children never learn the behavior that can propel them into the upper class, and they never learn the lessons that can make them more moral. This theme is pervasive in Osteen's rhetoric as he connects class to strong marriage and families.

Osteen makes it seem very hard to be single and wealthy and, at the same time, single and moral. Family and work successes go hand in hand. Osteen tells his reader, "[God has] allowed people to cross your path who are far more successful than you are, who have stronger marriages, who are enjoying His favor in marvelous ways" (9). Whenever Osteen uses the term favor, he is connecting it to class. In this case, that success is also connected to people with strong marriages. He continues to make this connection by quoting people overwhelmed with troubles, who say things like, "Oh, I've got so many problems. My marriage is in trouble. My children won't do right. My business is going downhill" (14). Those who come under God's favor are able to change all this. Osteen says, "Start seeing that marriage as restored. See your business as flourishing. See your children as enjoying the good things of God" (63).

The single person is inadequate in Osteen's rhetoric because he or she (most often she) cannot experience the abundance of God. Osteen says many people sabotage their expectations by negative comments, such as, "I don't think I'll ever get married. I haven't had a date in ten years! I might as well file for bankruptcy; I'm so swamped with debt and bills, I can't see any other alternative" (17). Not being married is equated with filing for bankruptcy, which is terrible because it's an indication that you are outside of God's favor and, therefore, immoral. Osteen cites Darla as an example. She laments to Osteen,

> But Joel, everybody is getting so far ahead of me. When is it going to be my turn? All my friends are getting married; everyone I graduated with is making big money and living comfortably; everybody is being promoted in my company *except me*. (166, italics in original)

Osteen comforts his unmarried reader by saying, "If you are unmarried and are believing for a mate, you don't have to worry. You don't have to beg God incessantly. You don't have to pray every fifteen minutes reminding God to send you a mate" (196). Shelby is cited as an example of an attractive woman in her mid-30s who genuinely desires to be married. After 2 or 3 years without a date, God finally blessed her with a man, and she did not have to spend the remainder of her life as a single woman (199).

Denigrating single parents also helps establish this formal connection. Osteen cites a young woman who was saved at his church; she was previously suicidal because she was pregnant and not married (246). He also cites Phyllis, a 16-year-old who got pregnant, dropped out of high school, and eventually had to go on welfare. Phyllis was able to overcome, however, because she tapped into God's favor, and she eventually earned a master's degree and became a school principal. Osteen cites Phyllis because she "broke the curse of poverty and lack in her family" (27).

Osteen often supports his points by referencing his own family and marriage as models of what is possible by tapping into God's favor. His family life is the ideal to which we all aspire. He writes, "I was blessed to be raised in a good family. I had parents who were fine role models" (25). He says he saw the goodness of God modeled by his dad: "Nobody could have represented God any better to us Osteen kids than my dad did" (135). His dad was able to overcome a divorce in his first marriage and to raise Joel and his siblings despite the heartbreak and devastation. Osteen says that his dad "thought that his ministry was over, that God's blessings had lifted from his life" (176). It seems that divorce, or the lack of a strong nuclear family, indicates a deficiency in God's blessings on one's life. Although God's blessings account for class differences on the surface, we begin to see a deeper connection to moral failings, as well.

HARD WORK

The second trait comprising the underlying form concerns attributions about the work ethic of the lower class. My uncle might complain that the poor are lazy and refuse to work hard. He assumes that there are plenty of well-paying jobs available for anyone who will put in his or her time, yet the poor would rather live off welfare, food stamps, and the labor of his tax dollars. In Osteen's disguise, the inability to work also constitutes a moral failing, because it keeps the individual outside the favor of God.

For Osteen, God's blessings come to those who work hard. A hard worker is someone who "arrives at work on time. They give their employers a full day's work; they don't leave early or call in sick when they are not" (282). The person of integrity shows up to work 10 minutes early and stays 10 minutes late and doesn't call in sick to stay home and take care of personal business (287). He continues, "If you're taking home your company's office supplies, that's being dishonest. If you're not giving your company a full day's work, that's not integrity." According to Osteen,

> A lot of people show up at work 15 minutes late, then wander around the office, go get some coffee and finally get to their desk or worksite 30 minutes later. They spend half the day talking on the phone, playing games, or sending jokes on the internet, and then they wonder, *God, why don't You ever bless me? Why don't I ever get promoted?* (283, italics in original)

Osteen emphasizes hard work because hard work in your occupation brings blessings. He writes

> If you work outside your home, don't give you employer a half-hearted effort. Don't dawdle on the telephone, wasting your employer's time and money. If you are digging a ditch, don't spend half the day leaning on your shovel. Do your work with excellence and enthusiasm!

To the person who responds that his or her employer doesn't pay well enough to work that hard, Osteen says, "You won't be blessed, with that kind of attitude. God wants you to give everything you've got" (298).

APPEARANCE AND DECORUM

The third trait making up the underlying form concerns the physical appearance of the lower class. For instance, my uncle will complain about the disheveled appearance and improper decorum of the poor people he runs across. The adage "Cleanliness is next to Godliness" is appropriate here. The poor are poor partly because they are unclean and unkempt. They do not measure up to standards of appearance, so they cannot get well-paying jobs.

Osteen makes the connection between morality and class through appearance by asking his reader

> What would you think if I introduced our two children to you and they had holes in their clothes, uncombed hair, no shoes and dirt under their fingernails. You'd probably say, 'That man is not a good father. He doesn't take care of his children.' Indeed, my children's poverty would be a direct reflection on me as their dad. (87)

It seems there is no way Osteen can be a good father if his children's appearance is lacking. His children's unsightly appearance indicates their class standing, which disguises the moral failings of Osteen as a father.

Osteen advises his reader to start making excellent choices in every area of life, even the mundane. Good choices begin with appearance. Osteen tells his reader not to drive a car that hasn't been washed in weeks or that has sports equipment and office supplies scattered all over it. Driving these kinds of cars, for Osteen, represents God poorly. He says

> Many times before I leave my house, I'll take a couple of minutes and clean out my car, not because I want to impress my friends, but because I feel better driving a clean car. You need to take pride in what God has given you. (283)

If we take care of what God has given us, He is more likely to give us something better, Osteen insists. This treatment extends to our homes. He references one example that helps disguise morality beneath appearance:

> A while back, I was driving through a certain section of Houston and I noticed that many of the people didn't take care of their homes. The yards weren't mowed, the weeds were overgrown, and things were stacked and stored everywhere, on the side of the house, in the front yard, where ever space was available. The entire neighborhood looked messy. As I continued driving, I came to one particular house that stood out among the rest. The yard was mowed, everything was neatly in order, and the home looked beautiful. When I got to church, I commented about that house in that neighborhood. Somebody said, "The people who live in that house are some of our most faithful members." (283–84)

Osteen thus implies that the appearance of a house gives an indication of the faithfulness of the people who live there.

Osteen's grandparents are another example. Osteen says they kept their little wood-framed house spotless inside and out, maintaining the yard and bushes and reapplying the paint. "My grandparents did not have a lot of money," Osteen says, "but that didn't matter. They were people of excellence. They knew they represented God, and they were intent on being a positive reflection" (284).

Osteen says the same should be true for his reader. He says, "Because we were made in the image of the Almighty God, how you present yourself in appearance should not only be a reflection of how you feel about yourself, but also a direct reflection on God" (284). Osteen even says that God reprimanded him for going to the grocery store in workout clothes and messed up hair. God said, "Don't you dare go in there representing Me like that! Don't you know I am the King of Kings?" Osteen says he returned home, took a shower, combed his hair, brushed his teeth, and put some clean clothes on before returning to the store.

The reader can gather from these passages about appearance and decorum that God does not want people looking shabby and unkempt. We can begin to see what our response should be to shabby and unkempt people. Osteen is the model of morality, and if God spoke directly to him to improve his appearance, then those who smell like urine and alcohol, with torn and dirty clothes (much less post-workout clothes), must not be nearly the moral being Osteen is.

HEALTH

Think now about what my uncle might say about the health of the poor. In the same way marriage and family, hard work, and appearance and decorum contribute to class standing, so do health and physical fitness. This trait makes up the fourth and final one found in Osteen's rhetoric and that underlies his formal connection between class and morality.

In the Introduction to his book, Osteen prepares his readers for a life-changing experience. The reader's health is one area where drastic improvement can be expected. He says

> You may have been sick for a long time, but this is your time to get well. You may be bound by all kinds of addictions, all kinds of bad habits, but this is the time to be set free. You may be struggling financially, in all kinds of debt, but this is the time for promotion. This is the time for increase. (10)

Osteen continues to combine several negative traits into one struggling person by quoting three hypothetical examples of negative attitudes:

> "I knew my marriage wasn't going to work out."

> "I don't think I'll ever get out of debt."

> "I guess I'll just have to put up with this health problem for the rest of my life." (123)

Osteen cites Job, an Old Testament figure who, in less than a year, lost his family, his business, and his health (50). He also features Brian, who is able to serve as a contemporary Job. Brian's world fell down around him; he went bankrupt, lost his family through divorce, and his health deteriorated. He was no longer the extremely successful man he once was, until he again came under the favor of God. After that happened, Osteen says, "his health and vitality returned" (16). Osteen also cites Carly as an example of a woman who "should not have made it," in part because she was overweight, with one leg slightly shorter than the other as the result of a childhood accident (55). The health of Carly, Brian, and Job is cited as part of a larger picture of one's class standing. When health improves, class improves along with it. Health is then understood to be a moral trait because those who are healthy are also under the favor of God. The next section explains this idea in more depth by showing how the favor of God is used to indicate moral standing.

Moralizing Class

For morality to be hidden beneath class status makes sense for an American product like Joel Osteen. Osteen takes sacred principles and wraps them in a veil of wealth and poverty to present a new form of the "Capitalistic God," suitable for an American society permeated by economic motives. Osteen's disguise accurately summarizes the foundation of American culture. Kenneth Burke points out that, if a tribe living by a river had adapted their entire way of life to the condition of that river, it would be understandable to sum up the tribe's motives in a name Burke calls "River God" (*Rhetoric of Motives* 111). Burke says that worshipping a "River God" gives realistic and materialistic justification to the tribe's traditions and recognizes the material conditions responsible for its way of life. Those who preach Prosperity Theology have devised a monetary motive and transformed it into what Burke calls a "secular analogue" (*Grammar of Motives* 44). Osteen brings together multiple interpretations of morality under a monetary motive and deploys an action that can unite many different understandings of what constitutes moral living.

Osteen devotes a large part of his book to describing the class implications that come with abiding by his teaching. Osteen says, "God wants us to be constantly increasing, to be rising to new heights. . . . God wants to increase you financially, by giving you new promotions, fresh ideas and creativity" (5). Like others who teach Prosperity Theology, class standing is an important indicator of one's relationship with God. Osteen says

> God doesn't want you to drag through life, barely making it. He doesn't want
> you to have to scimp and scrap, trying to come up with enough money to pay

for food, shelter, transportation, to pay your bills or worry about how you are going to send you children to college. . . . Start believing for increase and abundance. (77)

At one point, Osteen writes to his readers, "Don't just say, 'God, can I have a bigger apartment?' No, God wants you to own a house" (35).

Osteen is also very clear about what lower-class standing reveals about one's faith. He uses his own family as an example. Before his father was saved, he suffered from what Osteen calls a "poverty mentality" that kept him from fully coming under God's favor. Osteen's father came from one of the poorest of the poor cotton-picking families during the Great Depression. Osteen's dad often went to school hungry, with holes in his pants and shoes. The most dangerous aspect of his dad's life, Osteen claims, was that he came to expect poverty. He was not able to accept God's blessings awaiting him.

Osteen says that the poverty mentality is not glorifying to God. He says, "God is not pleased when we drag through life, defeated, depressed, perpetually discouraged by our own circumstances. No, God is pleased when we develop a prosperous mindset" (87). When Osteen's dad became a Christian when he was 17 years old, he was able to lose the poverty mentality and take on a prosperous mindset, thus coming under God's blessing. His dad broke the "poverty curse" in Osteen's family because he believed God had more in store for him (25). He quit seeing himself as a poor, defeated farmer's child with no hope, no education, and no future (64). He discovered God was a "God of increase" and was able to offer a multitude of advantages to Joel. The result of breaking the poverty curse is that Joel Osteen is now the head pastor of what *Forbes* magazine named the largest church in America and a powerful television ministry, and is a number-one best-selling author.

Osteen devotes so much of his message to class because class represents morality in disguise. The disguise is completed as these traits are assigned moral qualities. The poor are poor because they do not have these traits, and the rich are rich because they do. The traits become moral traits when the class status that produces them become qualifications for God's blessing. Those who possess the traits that lead to improved class also possess the traits that lead to God's blessing. We know that God would not bless the immoral, so we can deduce that the traits comprising class standing also comprise moral standing without ever having to mention morality.

Conclusion

The purpose of this chapter goes beyond the rhetoric of Joel Osteen. Understanding the criteria that can be used to detect a formal disguise will hopefully equip you with the necessary tools to see these disguises in your own life. Being able to understand such disguises allow for a greater understanding of our rhetorical world. The messages that influence us are not limited to pure persuasive attempts, like a television commercial or a presidential debate. Persuasive messages often come in indirect forms, hence we are not able to recognize and defend ourselves. Recognizing more nuanced forms of persuasion—those that come in the form of a disguise—can contribute to a greater understanding of why we make the decisions we make.

When Joel Osteen connects class to morality, he reassures his audience by granting its members moral permission to pursue material wealth without guilt. Wealth can be used to reassure people that they are among God's elect; it thus offers a measuring stick of morality. My cars, clothes, and bank account are symbolic of God's favor on me and my membership in His elect. But I am also offered a way to measure the morality of others with this economic measuring tape. For the complicated construct of morality, Osteen offers a simplified meter.

Of course, this chapter cannot reveal everything about the intersection between class, morality, and religion. Joel Osteen cannot represent all those who profess Prosperity Theology, much less religion in general. I would also be hesitant to claim that the four traits uncovered here that connect class to morality are the only traits that make this connection. But this chapter can contribute to our understanding of the many forms rhetorical messages can take, in part, by introducing questions for future research.

An IBM commercial states that the best ideas are sometimes the ones that give other people ideas. The same is true with scholarship. As the introductory paragraphs in this chapter state, power is played out in numerous forms. Sometimes those forms take on disguises that make them hard to recognize. Like the other chapters in this book, this chapter contributes to a larger understanding of the disguises those power plays can take.

Ultimately, Joel Osteen's message affirms, perpetuates, and reinscribes existing class structures in disguise. To argue, explicitly or implicitly, that the rich are under God's blessing and the poor are not is a form of domination and control of the powerful over the powerless. Disguises often exercise a formal muscle in that they work below the surface, are not easily identified, and can result in the reinforcement of a hegemonic social order. The formal disguise is the key to the rhetorical perpetuation of inequalities that are unquestioned because they are disguised in the religious language of God's blessing. Osteen reinscribes a way of thinking that aligns his congregation with power over "the lesser beings" (the non-elect), who are destined for an impoverished life.

This message has important class implications. Accepting morality on class-based terms gives the prosperous, like Joel Osteen, justification to discount the fundamental inequalities at the root of poverty. The ideology allows those who subscribe to it to assume the best about their own possibilities, as well as their social, cultural, and economic context. Not surprisingly, those with decidedly less optimistic assessments of broader social structures find much to disagree with within the tenets of such an ideology, because the message serves as a mask to preserve the injustice condemning the non-elect to nonexistence. It serves as an instrument of power for those who "have." To reinscribe the idea that money is a blessing of God is an ideological ruse for maintaining the existing social order. It takes a deft rhetorical critique, however, to uncover hegemony in taken-for-granted, superficial rhetoric that can be hidden behind a folksy demeanor, innocent smile, and uplifting message.

Finally, this chapter has shown how power management on a formal level can provide justification for class divisions that empower some and disempower others. Religion is powerful not because it is a mystic, supernatural phenomenon; rather, it is powerful because it can be an ordering device that tells us who we should be and how we should respond to other people. Despite the many prosocial functions religion can serve, when it is used to divide classes, it lends support to Karl Marx's claim that religion is the opium of the people. Religion can be used as a drug that allows many to tolerate the abysmal conditions of the world. Religion can be a tranquilizer so we do not become upset about injustice. And religion can aid and abet people in power who want nothing more than to conserve and preserve the unjust status quo that is so profitable and comfortable for those on top of the class hierarchy. Recognizing how disguises are formed will allow you both to combat them and to identify other disguises that may creep in under the radar.

7

The Re-visioned American Dream

The Wildlife Documentary Form as Conservative Nostalgia

Angela J. Aguayo

My intention was to tell the story in the most simple and profound way and to leave it open to any reading.

—Luc Jacquet (Director of *March of the Penguins*)

The way conservatives tell it, the restless homosexual menace is taking over America. . . . Rest assured, Middle America, help is on the way. There, on the ice! It's a bird! It's a plane! No, it's God in a tuxedo waddling across an iceberg! Or put another way, Emperor penguins are the new Jesus—or so you'd think listening to evangelicals swoon over the hit documentary, March of the Penguins.

—Patrick Letellier (*Lesbian News*, December 2005)

In the summer of 2005, a sentimental wildlife documentary was the sleeper hit of the movie season (Puig 1). *March of the Penguins*, made by a French documentary team and packaged specifically for U.S. distribution, follows the mating and birthing season of Antarctica's fierce emperor penguin. To the surprise of many in the film industry, *March of the Penguins* grossed over $75 million at the U.S. box office (Scott, "Hollywood" 74) and ranked second behind

Fahrenheit 9/11 as the top grossing documentary of all time (S. Smith 12). The typical audience for wildlife documentaries is much more modest (Pounsett 33); given the typical ho-hum appeal of nature documentaries and the ever-increasingly competitive summer movie market, what exactly brought audiences to the box office in droves?

Typically, wildlife documentaries are not considered box office sensations. However, 2 years prior to the release of *March of the Penguins,* Sony Pictures released *Winged Migration* with moderate but unprecedented success. The documentary was a spectacular tale of the migratory patterns of birds, shot and edited from the point of view of the animals. *March of the Penguins* was the second installment in a recent Hollywood trend, widely distributing a high-profile wildlife documentary to compete in a bustling movie market. The resounding success of *March of the Penguins* and the magnitude of its popularity reverberated in the box office sales, in the media, and on the Internet alike.

The film was advertised as an epic wildlife documentary with a heart; however, the subtle but familiar subtext produced public speculation about a political agenda in disguise. For the vast majority of the public, the documentary was another spectacular wildlife film, an episode in a recent movie trend. For a very particular audience, the rhetoric of *March of the Penguins* circulated as a narrative that naturalized a Christian fundamentalist political agenda. Conservative critic and radio host Michael Medved was quoted in the *New York Times* as supporting the documentary: "the motion picture of the summer that most passionately affirms traditional norms like monogamy, sacrifice and childrearing" (J. Miller 2).

After the release of the documentary, the political and religious right as well as some members of the mainstream press began to regard the penguins as a paragon of family values and an ideal example of monogamy, not to mention a pretty strong case for intelligent design. As articulated by a news columnist, some fans regarded the stars of the documentary "as big-screen embodiments of the kind of traditional domestic values that back-sliding humans have all but abandoned, as well as proof that divine intention, rather than blind chance, is the engine of creation" (Scott, "Reading" 1). The depiction of the penguin's life cycle in the documentary, according to this view, encourages audience members to naturalize particular lifestyle values such as monogamy and/or heterosexuality. For audiences who have an interest and investment in the public anxiety over the values surrounding sexuality in contemporary society, *March of the Penguins* was a flashpoint, a kind of evidence used to inform several contemporary political controversies. The box office success of *March of the Penguins* was unexpected; however, the political firestorm that was ignited by this inconspicuous wildlife film around fervently contested social norms such as heterosexuality, mating, marriage, and monogamy was especially unusual.

Cultural texts such as movies, music, magazines, and television occasionally do important political work in disguise. It is not unusual for popular cultural texts to engage vital political issues of the time directly and explicitly. Whole genres of cultural texts have evolved from this phenomenon, from protest music to activist documentary. In fact, in moments of political and social upheaval, these overt acts of cultural politics are frequent and compulsive. What is more subtle and studied less frequently is the manner in which cultural texts engage the political process covertly and in disguise. The influence of these kinds of texts is significant given their tendency to exist in the sphere of the trivial, frequently consumed without much critical attention to a subtle political subtext. As film scholar Mas'ud Zavarzadeh suggests, "The trivial is the space in which the daily is negotiated; it is the space that is represented in the common sense as 'real,' 'natural,' and as such, it must be denaturalized by ideological criticism for social transformation" (xi). For cases like *March of the Penguins*, it is not enough that these kinds of covert rhetorical acts mask subtle political subtexts; those subtexts must also strike a cord with a particular audience(s).

The appeal and popularity of the conservative nostalgia present in *March of the Penguins* are no coincidence. Lingering from the post-2004 election cycle, social anxiety over sexuality, coupling, and mating in the United States marked the year 2005. Political pundits across the spectrum and anti-gay advocates claimed that the gay marriage issue cost John Kerry the election in 2004. Coined as the presidential election that mobilized the Moral Majority, 11 anti-gay marriage amendments were passed, including one controversial ballot initiative in the battleground state of Ohio. Greg Quinlan of Ohio's Pro-Family Network, a conservative Christian group, remarked, "Now that we've defined what marriage is, we need to take that further and say children deserve to be in *that* relationship" (quoted in Curtis). The very illusive notions of family, love, coupling, and parenting are hotly contested constructs in contemporary American society.

On the surface, *March of the Penguins* is a glance into the lives of the emperor penguins' adaptation to the harsh and changing environment around them. On the formal level, the film narrative, framing, content selection, and editing techniques encourage the audience to read connections between the lives of penguins and humans. This form in wildlife documentaries encourages the audience to read these films in a manner that attributes human characteristics to natural phenomena and animals. It is not unusual for cinematic wildlife films to encourage identification with animals in human terms. The Animal Planet's wildly popular show *Meerkat Manor* routinely attributes rational intentions and human emotion into the plot narratives explaining the social and communal structures of the African meerkats. Beloved animal lover Steve Irwin's series of shows—which continue to air after his death—are built around explaining animals in human terms, so much so that very little physical distance exists between human and animal. However, using the wildlife documentary rhetoric as justification for human behavior is a unique feature of this cinematic identification. As one reviewer noted, "This hugely successful French documentary . . . yields itself so readily to anthropomorphic reading that it's hard to say where bird ends and man begins" (Denby 58). The result is a discourse on a wildlife documentary disguised in the framework of conservative nostalgia and promoting a new evangelical American Dream. This new American Dream, however, is a conservative narrative that accepts and accounts for the shifting traditional gender roles in society. In this chapter, I will begin by talking about the formal aspects of wildlife documentary, followed by the analysis of *March of the Penguins* as human exploration and finally as an articulation of documentary discourse in the framework of conservative nostalgia.

Wildlife Documentary Form as Human Discovery

Words we hear and images we consume usually have multiple meanings and resonances. Sometimes movies, television shows, political speeches, and music carry in disguise certain thoughts, attitudes, and social conventions. As stated in the introductory chapter of this book, "Language and images are unruly, sending tentacles out beyond their immediate locations, connecting to wide ranges of issues beyond the conscious intentions of creators and users of messages." That is to say, a text or message may seem to be about one thing on the surface but is actually disguising a social or political contestation or an affirmation of deeply rooted normative values. One way in which this work is accomplished is through patterns of form.

Form, or a pattern embodied in many different texts, is a powerful mediator between the message and the audience. Form carries with it expectations and preferred reading constructions. For example, when we recognize a cultural text as a documentary, audience members expect to learn something and thus read the text within particular logics of objectivity and reality. In the United States, the public memory of documentary film and video has strong ties to the standards of news journalism. Beginning in the 1950s and before the development of portable recording equipment in the late 1960s, the most visible documentary work was housed in network news departments. The documentary form already lends itself to the assumption that reality and truth are being revealed through the genre, and the historical control of popular documentary content by network news departments from the 1950s until the late 1970s reinforces public expectations that documentary is an objective enterprise. In a recent news report about documentary trends in popular culture, one expert argued, "If you want to see good documentaries, look at *Frontline* on PBS. That is serious documentary making. Documentaries should be trying to get to the truth, not obscuring the truth for the political message" (O'Donnell, Colgan, Myers, and Scarborough). When a political cause is embedded in the form of the documentary without disrupting the illusion that the documentary is functioning objectively, partisan politics have the potential to slip under the radar.

It may be difficult to theorize how major genres of cultural texts such as music or film create expectations and preferred reading formations, given the multiplicity of these texts. Yet subgenres like blues music or wildlife documentary may be less illusive and more easily distinguishable as a reoccurring form. As suggested by film scholar Scott MacDonald, scientific wildlife films reflect the expectations of the documentary genre and are read with "an aura of objectivity that is confirmed by the cinema's ability to make indexical, seemingly objective, record of sensory phenomenon" (5). In other words, the audience consumes images as though the action is happening right before their very eyes. In that moment, the camera's eye becomes the human eye, and the images function as sensory evidence.

The wildlife documentary, in particular, is reliant on formulaic patterns of narrative structure. In his seminal article on wildlife documentaries, Derek Bouse argues that, after years of exposure, audiences have developed certain expectations about films depicting the behavior of animals. Wildlife filmmakers are therefore obligated to play into these conventions. The result is a distinct film genre with its own recognizable patterns and codes (120). Scholars have recognized several patterns within wildlife documentaries, from the reliance on narration to adult themes of violence and death. Perhaps the most interesting and powerful of these forms is the importation of human family systems, emotions, and relationships into the animal kingdom. Put another way, this particular manifestation of the documentary form is an attempt to understand wildlife exploration as an insightful meditation into human nature.

Form is a complicated pattern that must also be understood in terms of its function. In his book *The Philosophy of Literary Form*, Kenneth Burke suggests that form is designed to "do something." An important aspect of investigating form, therefore, is to address how and to what ends a formal equation is serving particular interests, or, as Burke suggests, "we seek to discover the functions which the structure serves" (101).

In the case of *March of the Penguins*, the film narrative, framing, content selection, and editing techniques encourage a cross-identification of species in a particular manner. The form of wildlife documentaries, specifically the importation of human family systems, emotions, and relationships upon the animal kingdom, encourages the audience to read these films in a manner that attributes human characteristics to natural phenomena and animals. The wildlife documentary is thus understood as providing a peephole into understanding human nature. These formal aspects of the wildlife documentary were present in *March of the Penguins* and ignited a controversy over the film. Subtly and in disguise, the documentary served as a springboard for the public to negotiate the contemporary controversy over normative notions of marriage and childrearing in the United States. The formulaic equation present in *March of the Penguins* functioned to affirm competing ideological values by developing an identification between human nature and the environment. The following sections will explore the rhetorical devices used to develop these connections.

Personified Natural Phenomena

In the opening sequence of *March of the Penguins*, the documentary is labeled by the narrator as a tale of survival but, more specifically, a story about love. As the metaphorical voice of God, actor Morgan Freeman is the narrator and voice of the natural habitat we are about to discover. The first shots of the documentary are stark, with images of Antarctica's glaciers. We are told of a land once teeming with lush forest and life, now dense with ice and uninhabitable temperatures. Here we are introduced to our first character, the physical environment, for every great love story is not complete without overcoming tremendous odds. Blockbuster documentaries like *March of the Penguins* often supply "the emotional and narrative satisfaction associated with popular commercial cinema, mining its material directly from the real world rather than synthesizing it according to screenwriting formulas" (Scott, "Hollywood" 74). In this particular narrative, the environment is cast in the role of fierce and indiscriminate predator, the primary barrier to overcoming the odds of survival. Within the context of the film, the physical environment is referred to as the "great white expanse."

The film attributes human characteristics to natural phenomena such as wind, temperature, and ice formations. As a result, natural phenomena are explained through the lens of human experience and interaction. The opening moments of the film begin with an explanation of the environment in terms like that of a leading character, which will then act upon the animal population. The voice-over narrative implies intention and agency for the "great white expanse" by suggesting the purposeful creation of an inhabitable living space for anyone but penguins.

The physical environment functions much like an antagonist to the many penguins seeking to reproduce the cycle of life. The antagonistic environment is characterized as violent and deadly. In describing the more than 70-mile journey that the emperor penguin must undertake to reproduce, the narrator explains:

> By May the light will nearly disappear from the sky and the temperature continues to drop. And for those who began their march too late or have fallen behind because of weakness or hunger, hope of survival is now remote. The lone penguin has no chance against the winter's cold. It will simply fade away, absorbed by the great whiteness all around it.

This narration is accompanied by images of a lone penguin traveling across the ice, followed by wide, expansive images of the glaciers. The images are desolate, absent of life or community, and represent the perspective of the lone penguin. When the narrator alludes to a "great whiteness," the audience is asked to gaze upon several closely framed images of the sharp and deadly landscape.

The attribution of human characteristics to natural phenomena in *March of the Penguins* results in the characterization of the physical environment as a formative antagonist in the lives of the emperor penguin. Understanding the physical environment through the human experience does not end with the anthropomorphism of natural phenomena, however. The animal environment is subjected to a similar description.

Penguin as Biological Blueprint

Within the documentary text, the penguins function as the protagonist of the story and are strongly attributed with human characteristics. As stated by Mark Gill, president of Warner Independent Pictures in the *Wall Street Journal*, "They [penguins] feel a lot like an adorable version of humans" (Lippman W6). The penguins are frequently depicted as possessing logical intention, participating in the emotional process of falling in love, acting out socially constructed concepts such as monogamy, and engaging in familiar human courting rituals. The result is an attribution of human characteristics that naturalizes a particular depiction of family life for penguins and possibly their wayward human counterparts.

In an effort to explain the harsh and relentless natural environment of Antarctica, the narrator explains

> As for the former inhabitants, they all died or moved on long ago, well almost all of them. Legend has it, one tribe stayed behind. Perhaps they thought the change in weather was only temporary or maybe they were just stubborn. Whatever their reasons these tallward souls refused to leave. In some ways this is a story of survival. A tale of life over death. But it's more than that really; this is a story about love. And like most love stories it begins with an act of foolishness.

The language and images used in this sequence are pointed, for several human attributes are being assigned to penguin behavior. The word tribe, commonly used to depict a form of human collectivity, is used to describe penguin migratory patterns. This description is accompanied with beautiful expansive shots of the sculpted, icy typography, edited with images of tiny migratory dots. The indistinguishable moving beings stand in for the particular (penguins) but simultaneously represent any tribe that weathers difficult climates in the name of love.

Some of the more interesting human attributions to penguin behavior involve the unlikely identification of emotional states. In the example above, the narrator explains the isolation of the penguin population in Antarctica as a possible form of stubbornness as opposed to environmental evolution. A framework of human dating and mating is evoked from the penguins' reproductive patterns, resulting in an insinuation that penguins actually fall in love.

The documentary attempts to understand penguin reproductive behavior in terms of heteronormative typology and courting. While the film shows images of penguins walking around and bumping into each other, the voice-over narrative explains the sexual politics of the alleged male and female penguins. The overt connections made between love and the "natural" outcome (that is, reproduction) are routine. The film is a gesture toward a particular kind of love story, one that resonates with all of us because it is tattooed into our collective moral unconscious, not because it is "natural" or represents a universal experience. Within the framework of traditional gender norms, the voice-over depicts the penguins as heterosexual, monogamous beings and describes the resulting fierce competition involved with finding a mate. The narrative storyteller concludes, "They are not that different from us; they pout, they bellow, they strut and occasionally they will engage in some contact sports." The story directly invites the audience to consent to the likeness between the social behavior of penguins and humans. In this rhetorical move, any dominate thematic value reflected in the lives of the animal stars is naturalized because the patterns simply exist in nature without the tainted intervention of human reason. In other words, "the film instructs the audience on how to make sense of the global reality of the culture" (Zavarzadeh 8).

The most striking visual montage is the wildly constructed sequence of penguins falling in love with one another. There is a significant intervention of poetic and creative license in the filmmaking process here, where images—with the help of narration—are used to form an identification with the penguins by showing mating and reproduction as an act of heterosexual love. Slow, romantic music plays in the background while images of smitten penguins, with their heads hunched and close to one another, rub their beaks together and find love. These images are close shots of the penguins; the audience is given a tight gaze into the eyes of the penguins, their touching beaks, and selective body parts. The formulaic equation of this scene vaguely mimics a PG-13 love scene, where the audience is left to assume sexual intercourse has occurred although the film does not directly show the act. In other words, as one reporter noted, the scene is focused on some demurely photographed funny stuff. These close images not only create a sense of intimacy between the penguins but also a kind of intimacy that the audience is encouraged to reflect upon. As one reporter noted, "The penguins love and yearn, they hope and have courage, all without saying a word" (Reyes 22). These human attributions are not isolated occurrences but rather an integral part of the fabric of the documentary narrative.

The overtures toward heteronormative conceptions of love and coupling are so pronounced that two scientific magazines, New Scientist and Scientific American, dedicated editorial space to setting the biological record straight. Fraught with concerns about the misconceptions propagated by the documentary, these articles attempt to counter the heteronormative agenda present in the depiction of penguin life. One writer in the *New Scientist* explains, "Penguins, you see, are not quite the straight-loving creatures you might suppose. For a start, a lot of penguins singularly fail to uphold traditional family values. Around fifteen per cent of adult emperors change partners every year. And some penguins engage in homosexual activities" (Walker 17). The article, like many in its vein, disputes the narrative form of the documentary and the connection of penguin social patterns with prescribed human behavior, but it does not impugn the importance of the penguins themselves.

The New Evangelical Fundamentalist American Dream

The identification of animal behavior and natural phenomena with human behavior allows for a reading of the film as an exploration into naturalized coupling and mating behavior. Given the social and political landscape in which the film was released, it's not difficult to understand how *March of the Penguins* functioned to naturalize an emerging fundamentalist American Dream. By the term fundamentalist I mean "the affirmation of religious authority as holistic and absolute, admitting of neither criticism nor reduction; it is expressed through the collective demand that specific creedal and ethical dictates derived from scripture be publicly recognized and legally enforced" (Lawrence 78). I am not suggesting that *March of the Penguins* directly and overtly projects a fundamentalist agenda; however, a naturalizing narrative of conservative nostalgia can be extrapolated from the identification encouraged by this particular wildlife documentary form. Coupled with the increased political anxiety over gay marriage and normative conventions of human mating, the conservative reading of the documentary circulated in the media and at the pulpit.

In the documentary, divine intervention in the framework of faith is introduced as a natural phenomenon. Penguin migration is interpreted as being guided by some unknown force. The narration of the documentary explains how the penguins annually migrate to birth their young:

> The destination is always the same, their path however, is not. The ice on which the birds travel never stops shifting and changing. New roadblocks will appear to baffle them, every year. We are not exactly sure how they find their way. Perhaps they were assisted by the sun or the stars. Or maybe having taken this march for thousands of generations they are guided by some invisible compos within them.

Although vague, the explanation that penguins are led by some unknown compos could be interpreted as guidance by the spiritual realm. As an investigator in the *New Scientist* reported,

> Penguins may be the models of upright social behavior—in the biochemical sense. But some members of the Christian Right in the US are going much further. . . . They see the bird's arduous annual migration across the shifting ice floes of the Antarctic as an allegory for the Christian spiritual journey and suggest that birds should be held up as role models for human behavior. (Walker 17)

In other words, the narrative has been embraced as a parable of steadfast faith. Ben Hunt, a minister at the 153 House Churches Network, commented, "Some of the circumstances they [penguins] experienced seemed to parallel those of Christians. The penguin falling behind is like some Christians falling behind. The path changes every year, yet they find their way, is like the Holy Spirit" (J. Miller 2). At the very least, the documentary depiction opens up the interpretive space to understand unknown phenomena within the framework of salvation through faith. It is these vague spiritual references coupled with a reinforced American Dream mythos that triggers a social pressure point.

The documentary evocation of the American Dream is particular and pivots the nuclear family structure. Although the documentary records the reproductive life cycle of thousands of penguins, the movie trailer explains the documentary as "one family's journey to bring life into the world." This strategic labeling is focused on the great mythos of the individual family weathering the odds of survival. There is also a thematic motif of weathering storms and surviving great odds. As a result, there is a recognition that the physically weaker penguins will not survive, will fade away and be absorbed into the great whiteness around them. As Pete Porter suggests, "[T]he narrator consistently invites the audience to invest in the penguin goals of propagating the species and survival, both of which are continually under threat" (205).

One of the most interesting aspects of this new fundamentalist American Dream is the implied formation of a new nuclear family structure. The male partner becomes an integral, at times the primary, caregiver to the young. As the narrator explains,

> And now begins one of natures' most incredible and endearing role reversals. It is the penguin male who will attend to the couple's single egg. While the mother feeds and gathers food to bring back for the newborn, it is the father that will shield the egg from the violent winds and cold. He will make a nest for the egg on top [of] his claws, keeping it safe with a flap of skin beneath his belly.

This image makes for a powerful re-visioning of the American Dream that accounts for shifting gender roles in society. It justifies the social space where men are the caregivers and women are the metaphorical breadwinners. Although the social roles may be re-visioned, however, the basic structure and moral fabric of the family are kept intact.

As the female penguins leave their partners and eggs behind and head for the sea to nourish themselves, the male penguins are left to take on "the most difficult task." The voice-over narrative hierarchically places the sex roles in order of importance by suggesting, "As the winter progresses, the father will be *severely* tested. The mother will be tested as well." The language of the narration subtly preserves the masculinity of the new male role as both nurturer and protector. This male position is continually reinforced with language that connects the nurturing role with great acts of bravery. When describing how the male penguins keep the eggs warm during the cold winter months, the narrator characterizes their task as balancing "their egg [on their feet] like tight rope walkers."

A Clash of Civilized Values

These formal aspects of *March of the Penguins* ignited a controversy over the reading of the film in the news media and popular culture. The discourse on the documentary in magazines, television, the Internet, and the popular press reinforced the documentary as a springboard into discussion about preferred lifestyles for humans. As explained by entertainment writer Richard Schickel in *Time* magazine,

> We also learn from Luc Jacquet's *March of the Penguins* that they [penguins] are, like an ever increasing number of humans, serially monogamous. Every year emperor penguins meet, mate and remain faithfully bound—at least until their single offspring is walking and squawking. But these are animals that suffer for their families. (68)

Conservative groups have incorporated this unsuspecting wildlife documentary and "its stirring depiction of the mating ordeals of the emperor penguins into an unexpected battle anthem in the cultural wars" (J. Miller 2).

Given the trends in the mass media environment, one method for contemporary documentary is to "go popular." This strategy is not without its concerns and cautions, but it does open up new avenues of public advocacy through the means of documentary discourse. That is, when documentary functions as an event film, the discourse circulating in the public sphere and elsewhere becomes a gateway into a number of taboo and not so taboo political discussions.

After the release of the documentary, the political and religious right began to regard the penguins as paragons of family values and ideal examples of monogamy (A. Miller 13). Conservatives on the Web site WorldNetDaily.com extrapolated a pro-life reading of the movie, stating that it verified "the beauty of life and the righteousness of protecting it." Rich Lowery, the editor of *National Review*, remarked, "You have to check out *March of the Penguins*. It is an amazing movie. And I have to say, penguins are the really ideal example of monogamy. These things—the dedication of these birds is just amazing" (J. Miller 2). The documentary essentially functioned as a vessel to collect the coordinates for contested issues revolving around sexuality and marriage.

Three months after the box office opening, and in an unlikely reflection of animal life imitating art, FOX News reported that two male penguins at the Central Park Zoo, who "incubated an egg together during a six-year relationship," broke up when one mated with a female (Breznican 6). These infamous gay penguins, Roy and Silo, presented a perplexing antidote to the raging debate concerning penguins' behavior, human relations, and the normative prescriptions of sexual behavior. Responding to the controversy over the film and New York's famous gay penguins, one editorial argued

> Those who start looking outside the human family for old-fashioned values, in fact, will need to quickly narrow their search terms. They will surely want to ignore practices observed in animals like dolphins (gang rape), chimpanzees (exhibitionism), bonobo apes (group sex) and Warner Brothers cartoon rabbits (cross-dressing). ("Penguin Family Values" 11)

Given the polarized manner in which the conservative adoption of *March of the Penguins* was received, the element of form, as Kenneth Burke suggests, must be understood in terms of its function.

Conclusion

Objectivity could be considered *the* problematic term of our time. Objectivity demands that impartiality be embedded into our social fabric. As much as we are fragmented as a society by new technology and mass information, we are bound by ghostly values deemed necessary for the development of human understanding. We expect our news reporters to be objective. The core of the scientific method rests on the rock of objectivity. In the search for justice in our legal system, the proceedings are flush with creating an objective judgment process. The artistic and creative form of film is expected to adhere to objective methods of production and editing when labeled a documentary. Given the analysis of *March of the Penguins,* however, it is important to question whether the perception of objectivity is serving a particular interest.

The formal structure of the documentary produces a public discussion about political issues beyond the movie itself. In the process, the wildlife documentary form, which imposes the framework of human family systems, emotions, and relationships upon the animal kingdom, constitutes a space where public anxieties over human sexuality, family, and mating can be negotiated.

Every historical moment is a playground of contestable subjectivities. As Zavarzadeh suggests, "Films are not merely aesthetic spaces but political ones that contest or naturalize the primacy of those subjectivities necessary to the status quo and suppress or privilege oppositional ones" (5). The tale of the brave male penguins weathering Antarctica's most fierce environmental elements is a classic American Dream narrative of the nuclear family surviving against all odds. In this dream, however, the male penguin is allowed to play the role of both protector and nurturer, and the female penguin is allowed to be the metaphorical breadwinner. Not surprisingly, this new American Dream subtext mirrors the escalating shifts in the labor force in regards to gender. According to the U.S. Department of Labor, participation rates among women in the human labor force will continue to rise, whereas rates for men will edge down: "As more women are added to the labor force, their share will approach that of men. In 2008, women will make up about 48 percent of the labor force and men 52 percent. In 1988, the respective shares were 45 and 55 percent" (Bureau of Labor). In other words, the American Dream narrative in *March of the Penguins* naturalizes (among other things) a female subjectivity as hunter and breadwinner, reflecting the inevitable trends in human social patterns. As Zavarzadeh suggests, film has the potential and aim to naturalize subjectivities necessary for the status quo.

The film thus projects a new pattern for sex roles in the family structure, yet that new formation does not dismantle masculinity or question heterosexuality. In this new American Dream framework, heterosexuality is preserved—there was no mention of those pesky gay penguins that exist in nature—while the male nurturing of children is cast as an act of survival and bravery. In our contemporary times, these kinds of politics in disguise are not obscure popular culture puzzles:

> Hunting for ideological subtexts in Hollywood movies is a critical parlor game. . . . Now, thanks to the culture wars and the Internet, the game of ideological unmasking is one that more and more people are playing. With increasing frequency, the ideology they are uncovering is conservative, and it seems to spring less from the cultural unconscious than from careful premeditation. (Scott, "Reading" 1)

Sex roles in families may be in flux, but a fundamentalist Christian ethic is not disturbed and the masculinity of the male is reinforced within the American Dream mythos.

8

Weathering the Storm

Pirates of the Caribbean and Transnational Corporatism

E. Johanna Hartelius

Since 2003 a sensational pirate theme has spread through popular culture. It began with *Pirates of the Caribbean: The Curse of the Black Pearl*, the Disneyland adventure-ride turned action movie trilogy. After its success and massive media attention, audiences were thirsting for more. In July of 2006, the sequel, *Dead Man's Chest*, followed, breaking box office records. It rapidly became part of a promotional pirate frenzy. But why something so seemingly obsolete as pirates? What is it about pirates that speaks to the American audience? Are they the Disney version of James Bond or Indiana Jones? If audiences simply want to experience the thrill of a big-budget action film, what accounts for the failure of the third *Mission Impossible* film, which opened only a month before *Dead Man's Chest* (*DMC*)?

The reason for the recent popularity of pirates may be more complex than a secret yearning for wenches and rum. It is not as simple as "everyone wants to be a pirate." In an era of declining governmental power and growing corporate influence, the *POC* films formally reflect how Americans are managing everyday life. This current climate of transnational corporate expansion places us in a difficult position. We struggle to find our own place in a world where the same products are sold in Los Angeles, Rio, and New Delhi, where the boundaries of trade and politics are becoming blurry. Even though most Americans grow up learning about democracy—how politicians are elected, how a bill becomes a law, and so on—the actual government often seems a far cry from our daily lives. We don't know who our representatives are, and we may not care. Every sixth grader has heard that democracy means "rule by the people," yet, by the time we reach college, we may wonder how much "ruling" the people do. When Congress's policy initiatives seem light-years away and impossible to understand, our attention turns to other things: buying an *iPhone*, dressing like the stars, and watching Bravo's newest reality show. We grapple with identity and purpose in the midst of a global tug-of-war, the national government on one side and the transnational corporations on the other.

Rather than simply assume that American audiences secretly wish to be pirates, this chapter posits that the *POC* narratives are homologous to a real-life experience. A homology is a pattern connecting different kinds of experience. The pattern operates at the level of form rather than content, which means that the particular details of the homologous experiences vary. Just as the pirates' triumphant survival depends on their besting both oppressive aristocracies and greedy trading companies, so, too, does the American spirit's endurance depend on the ingenuity of its people against the government and transnational corporate interests. By examining specifically the construction and confusion of the characters' identity, the objects that render their owners uniquely powerful, and the narrative's unstable sites, one can identify several homologous relationships between the films and the experiences of modern Americans. In the end, the films' message is clear: the free and entrepreneurial individual in the end outsmarts larger forces. Thus, the films prescribe appropriate strategies for living through a struggle that happens beyond our control.

The chapter begins with a brief synopsis of the first two films' plots. Following the synopsis is an overview of the historical relationship between the nation-state and corporate expansion. This section introduces a shift in power between national governments and increasingly international business. The analysis then focuses on three specific aspects of the homology: the construction of identity, the negotiation of place and space, and the manipulation of power-objects such as money and other resources. For example, the way in which the films' main characters struggle with identity ambivalences is formally homologous to the same struggle for contemporary Americans. Complications arise in this process, for the characters as much as for the audience. The concluding section addresses the functions of formal "disguises" and suggests implications of this sort of popular culture analysis for pedagogical purposes.

Synopses

PIRATES OF THE CARIBBEAN: THE CURSE OF THE BLACK PEARL

This first film inaugurated the season of pirate enthusiasm. It is an impressive display of special effects and performances by well-known actors including Johnny Depp, Orlando Bloom, and Geoffrey Rush. The drama begins when

Captain Jack Sparrow comes to the Caribbean town of Port Royal, home-away-from-home for British governor Swann and his daughter Elizabeth. On the day of Sparrow's arrival, there is a promotion ceremony for a soon-to-be commodore, Norrington, a close friend of the governor and the presumed future husband of Elizabeth Swann. Norrington attempts a marriage proposal following the ceremony but is interrupted when Elizabeth's tight-fitting gown causes her to faint and fall off the wall into the waves below.

Sparrow rescues Elizabeth and is captured by Norrington's men. Charged with piracy, he is put into the town jail overnight, awaiting the gallows. During the night, however, the *Black Pearl* and its crew come into Port Royal. They plunder the city and capture Elizabeth, who is brought on board and taken to meet the infamous Captain Barbossa. The two bargain for the gold medallion that Elizabeth has kept hidden since the day she stole it off young Will Turner's neck. Taking the medallion and Elizabeth hostage, Barbossa and his men sail for the Isla de Muerta, the island of death, where they hope to dispel the ancient curse that plagues them.

Will Turner is the young man who has grown up to become infatuated with Elizabeth. He seeks Jack Sparrow's help in rescuing her in exchange for springing him free from the jail cell. At this point in the film, Will is still unaware of his pirate heritage. He and Sparrow agree to commandeer one of the Royal Navy's ships, sail to Tortuga to collect a crew, catch up with Barbossa, and save Elizabeth. What Will does not know is that Jack plans to give him over to Barbossa in exchange for the *Black Pearl*. Sparrow realizes that only the blood of Bootstrap Bill, Will's estranged pirate father, can repay the debt and break the curse.

Through a series of sea battles and sword fights, Will learns the truth about his family, Elizabeth is rescued from Barbossa, the curse is lifted, and all of "the good guys" return to Port Royal. The only one who does not fare as well is Sparrow, who in the final scene stands to be hanged in a public ceremony, paralleling the one at the beginning of the film. At the eleventh hour, Sparrow is rescued by Will, who finally embraces his identity and loyalty to pirates. Despite her promise to Norrington, Elizabeth admits that she is actually in love with Will, and the film ends on their sunset kiss. Sparrow, in turn, swims off to his beloved "Pearl," which has finally come back to him.

PIRATES OF THE CARIBBEAN: DEAD MAN'S CHEST

In this second film, the returning characters are joined by a few new ones, and the plot becomes, if possible, even more tangled. It begins with the ruined wedding ceremony of Elizabeth and Will. The East India Trading Company (EITC) has arrived in Port Royal in a scene that looks strikingly like military forces storming a beach. The head of the EITC, Lord Beckett, places Elizabeth and Will under arrest for aiding the escape of a convicted felon, Jack Sparrow. A warrant is also out for the arrest of Commodore Norrington, but we learn that he resigned from his post and left town a few months earlier. All three are to be executed, but Beckett offers Will a pardon for himself and Elizabeth if he can retrieve Jack Sparrow's magic compass. The compass would grant Beckett power over all the seas and their commercial dealings, including piracy. Will accepts, leaves Elizabeth in a jail cell, and sets off to find Sparrow.

When Will catches up with Sparrow, he agrees to help him find the key to the chest that holds Jones's heart in exchange for the compass. Will does not know that Sparrow plans to use the contents of the chest to call off Jones's evil "beastie," the Kraken, in order to avoid his debt. During a haggling scene, Jones insists that he hold Will ransom until Sparrow delivers 100 souls. Sparrow and his crew head for Tortuga, where presumably souls would not be missed. Here, they are reunited with Norrington, whose appearance and demeanor have changed since the first movie. He is angry and bitter and looking for revenge. He joins the crew.

Back in Port Royal, Elizabeth has escaped and bargained with Beckett for her and Will's pardon. Along with the pardons is a letter of marque, which would render its keeper a privateer in the Crown's service, for Sparrow. She sneaks onboard a merchant ship and hitchhikes to Tortuga, where all are convened. Using Sparrow's compass, they find the island where the chest with the heart is buried. At the same time, Will arrives on the island with the chest's key. All are now joined by Jones's crew of monstrous sea creatures. After lengthy sword-fighting scenes, everyone in the crew except Norrington escapes. He gives up the chest to the monsters on the island but keeps the heart, which, at the film's end, he delivers to Beckett.

The crew makes it back to the *Black Pearl*, but now Kraken is after them. They prepare to abandon ship, but at the last minute Elizabeth realizes that Kraken only wants Sparrow. She gives him a passionate kiss, all the while handcuffing him to the mast. Wielding a drawn sword, Sparrow goes down with his ship. The heart-broken survivors now head "up river" to the lair of Tia Dalma, a sort of oracular good witch, who suggests that there may be a way to save Jack Sparrow, if only they are willing to "sail to the ends of the earth and beyond." In the film's final minute, Barbossa appears in the witch's hut and becomes the rescue mission's new captain.

Transnational Corporatism

The U.S. government has long been struggling with its own EITC: Microsoft. For decades, federal courts have attempted to stem Microsoft's influence, accusing it of violating antitrust laws. A settlement in 2002 was harshly criticized for being too lenient on the corporate giant. This issue with Microsoft raises many questions: Is it possible to break the law if your business has already surpassed its parameters? If a corporate entity like Microsoft ultimately benefits the American economy, should it be charged with an economic crime? When Microsoft produces and supplies the very information system that government agencies depend on, what happens to relations of power (Murray)? This section of the chapter introduces the idea that economics hold an increasing primacy over politics in global corporatism. It demonstrates the formal patterns of experience that characterize Americans' struggle with forces beyond their control. The goal is to identify an important tension between national governments and transnational corporations—one in which the former increasingly dictates the terms of coexistence—that presents a considerable challenge for citizens.

In modern history and throughout the first half of the 20th century, nation-states were the major site of power from an international perspective (B. Anderson; Hobsbawm). They were the obvious basis for conducting most exchanges between different cultures. More specifically, trade and economic interactions were under the states' auspices. One culture's political dominance over another was traceable to a government power; this was the format for both British and French imperialism and colonialism. In times of heightened intensity, such as war and economic downfall, nationalism surged. Outwardly, the state was a people's representative to the world; inwardly, it was the mechanism for national coherence and identification.

But gradually, the cultural and political circumstances for nation-states have changed. This is particularly true regarding dominance over corporate interests. No longer does a country's government oversee the business conducted within its borders with complete control. The nation-state can no longer be described as an all-encompassing managerial umbrella under which businesses operate just like any other local enterprise. Masao Miyoshi offers a critical interpretation of the development of international trade:

> First, domestic companies simply undertake export/import activities, linking up with local dealers. Then, the companies take over overseas distribution and carry out their manufacturing, marketing, and sales overseas. Finally, the transnational corporations denationalize their operations by moving the whole business system including capital, personnel, and research and development. This final stage is reached when a corporation promotes loyalty to itself among shareholders, employees, and clients rather than to its country of origin or host countries. (736)

Miyoshi reveals a significant tension between decision-making powers, one that is at the heart of this chapter. When a corporation functions almost independently of its national home base, there is a hierarchical ambiguity between business and government. This ambiguity is particularly poignant from the citizen-consumers' perspective. We are the ones at the conflict's epicenter. If the decisions that have the most impact on our lives are made by CEOs rather than prime ministers and political parties, where does international power really lie? What has happened to traditional understandings of a representative democracy with popular influence? Today, the most influential transnational corporations have operating budgets matching that of small nations. Think of those organizations that create an entirely new scale of revenue: General Electric, Exxon Mobil, Wal-Mart, Time Warner, and so on. Their top-level executives travel the world and make deals that easily rival international policy treaties in terms of scope and importance. But unlike the political officials that are elected by a citizenry, the CEOs are uninhibited by mandates of public service when choosing a course of action. Check and balances do not necessarily factor into the corporate efficiency rationale. To the citizen consumers, it almost seems like these executives are untouchables, free to make up their own rules.

Another way to think about this power struggle is by focusing on relevance. To produce a profit, corporations go to great lengths to make their products and services relevant and intelligible to popular culture and everyday life. To examine this notion, ask which is more socially relevant to Americans' lives: an appropriations bill finally passing a congressional vote or a new Pixar film? Which is more likely to be talked about at the water cooler? Being interested in the film is easier, quicker, and more fun. At the same time, we're constantly obligated to appear politically informed. So, while the corporations invest money in making themselves relevant, the government spends energy in making politics a moral mandate. Who, for example, hasn't been told that voting is a civic duty? We are torn between being consumers and citizens.

The producers of popular culture have the people's attention in a different way than do the institutions of traditional politics. On an international level, consider for example the "Americanization" phenomenon. Americanization—the global marketing and suffusion of American culture in other places—does not mean that people in Sweden and Japan are suddenly preoccupied with American politics. Certainly, the dominant presence of the United States in world politics is not lost on the Swedes or the Japanese, but Americanization primarily means that they are wearing Nike, eating Big Macs, watching Disney movies, and listening to Usher and Kelly Clarkson. They are torn between different identities and loyalties. Popular culture's inseparability from global corporations is thus an important part of the tension between national governments and transnational corporations.

These tensions create popular ambivalence and anxiety. When one source of collective identification gradually loses power, it undermines that collective. Those who used to identify as members become unsettled; they have to find a new stable center. The next section of this chapter is a close analysis of the *POC* films focusing on three important narrative dimensions: identity, space, and powerful objects. The depiction of these experiences and objects is homologous to a real-life experience of change and instability. The formal pattern linking cinematic narrative and reality advises audiences on how to respond in their everyday lives to the "same" phenomena they see on the big screen.

Homologies in *Pirates of the Caribbean*

The tension between real-life transnational corporations and national governments is formally illustrated in the films by the East India Trading Company (EITC) and the British government. As a commercial center, Port Royal represents European colonialism; the importation not only of goods but of English customs and hierarchies is portrayed in both films. As the trilogy progresses, royal privilege is threatened by the independence of the EITC's business. The second film in particular features the company as a major "bad guy" character. It is a real menace, both for the government and for the 17th-century version of a small business owner. For example, a scene onboard an independent merchant ship tells us that "honest sailors" are hard-pressed to survive the EITC's competition.

The EITC is represented primarily by Lord Beckett, whereas the British government is represented by Governor Swann, Commodore Norrington, and their men. In the opening scene of the second film, the two forces illustratively collide. Governor Swann has prepared a lavish wedding for his daughter only to have it spoiled by the rude and brutal intrusion of the EITC. The old and cherished customs of the British aristocracy are left in the rain and mud; in all their dressy glory, its representatives are chained and imprisoned. Elizabeth and Will demand to know what authority Lord Beckett has to arrest them, whereupon he presents a warrant. This becomes somewhat confusing when Elizabeth angrily reminds him that Port Royal's citizens are under the rule of the king's governor. It is word against word as to whose power is mightier, the governor's or the EITC's. When the company's ships come into shore during this opening scene, the flags bearing its emblem are strikingly similar to pirate flags with the familiar skull and crossbones. This similarity may signal a likening of the company to pirates, but not to the sort of pirates with which audiences are invited to identify. In other words, the invasion of Port Royal is a crime comparable to that of piracy. The people responsible for it, however, are not the good-natured pirates that the movie depicts as heroes.

The *POC* films feature both good and bad pirates. Although the good guys clearly are pirates, not all pirates are treated equally in the plot's distinction of good and evil. For example, in the *CBP*, Sparrow's Tortuga crew faces Barbossa's cursed pirates. The former are shown as slightly inebriated but good-spirited men with a healthy sense of humor. The cursed pirates, on the other hand, are meaner and less inclined to spare a life. After all, they were the ones who marooned Captain Sparrow and who seek to sacrifice Bootstrap's offspring as payment for their wrongdoings. The audience can read this ambivalence in two ways: we can face the dual nature of humanity and recognize the potential for greed and sin in everyone, or we can divert the issue by delineating good and bad even within the group with which we identify. In other words, pirates represent ordinary people in the midst of larger forces, governmental and corporate. The films' depiction of pirates is thus formally homologous to the place audience members occupy in their own reality. Within the category of pirates, however, there may be less appealing factions of which the good guys must be wary.

The power of the EITC is shown as something dangerous but seductive. Several of the characters are tempted by its riches, but the audience understands that any pact with the company means "selling out." As mentioned above, Beckett offers Will a deal in exchange for his and Elizabeth's pardons. According to the terms, Will must serve as an agent of a "business transaction" by finding Jack Sparrow, stealing his compass, and persuading him to accept a letter of marque. When Will asks if he is to recover the compass "at the point of a sword," Beckett smugly says, "Bargain!" thus illustrating his commercial orientation. He proceeds to explain to Will that "the world is shrinking" and that "the blank spaces on the map are vanishing." Meanwhile, a cartographer is hard at work on a giant map of the world in the background. Beckett calls Sparrow a "dying breed" who must "join the new world or perish." A bit later, he has much the same conversation with Elizabeth, to whom he announces that "Currency [not loyalty] is the currency of the realm!" From the EITC's perspective, transnational business is the way of the future, and its expansion is unstoppable.

And yet the EITC needs some measure of support from the old order. Beckett tries his persuasive tactics on Governor Swann as well, after his attempts with Will and Elizabeth. He offers the governor the same letters of pardon. (Notably, when he addresses Swann as "mister," Swann corrects him by saying, "It's Governor Swann still!") In exchange for the safety and freedom of Swann and his daughter, Beckett asks for "your authority here [in Port Royal], your influence in London, and your loyalty to the East India Trading Company." Evidently, the company's growing wealth and international influence are not quite enough, and the audience recognizes the legal system and political history that still occasionally give the government's representative the upper hand. When Swann agrees to the deal, Beckett announces that "everyone has a price."

Norrington's fall from grace is a similar illustration of declining governmental powers. In *CBP,* he is a well-respected member of Port Royal's British aristocracy and about to be promoted. His main adversaries are the Caribbean pirates, whom he has managed nearly to eradicate. Norrington's responsibility to the Crown, moreover, is highlighted in the final scene where Sparrow awaits execution. To justify the seemingly harsh sentence, Governor Swann explains to his protesting daughter: "Commodore Norrington is bound by the law, as are we all." This scene's connection between the enforcement of law and order and the maintenance of royal power is clear.

In *DMC*, Norrington's star has fallen, and his relationships to pirates and authorities have been inverted. Having lost Elizabeth to Will, he evidently resigned his post and left Port Royal. He turns up again in Tortuga, the films' version of Sodom and Gomorra, with a soiled uniform and a half-empty bottle of rum. Elizabeth poignantly asks: "James Norrington, what has the world done to you?" The answer gradually unfolds through the rest of the movie as Norrington's nobility is tested. Even though he joins the pirates, he acts honorably in the bleakest moment and leads Jones's sea monsters away from the cast. In the end, however, he uses the captured booty—Jones's heart—to "buy his life back" from Beckett. When Beckett calls this act the "dark side of ambition," Norrington counters by describing it as "the promise of redemption." In other words, the Crown's redemption and survival depends on its obedient acceptance of the company's conditions.

The characters in these films are complicit in their own fates. They chose sides in the conflict, and their actions have direct impact on the plot. For example, Governor Swann and Elizabeth both choose to cooperate with Lord Beckett, potentially compromising their loyalties to the Crown. Likewise, the EITC chooses to trust the governor and depend on his long-established political influence. The same could be said for modern Americans. Our choices and priorities shape power struggles between the government and the corporations that challenge it. Because business needs consumers and political leaders need followers, we are in a uniquely influential position. More and more often, our loyalties are to the businesses that we patron; we are Saab drivers, Mac users, and Visa-card holders. Occasionally, however, we choose to exercise our nationalist identity. We rally ceremoniously around being American. Whenever the consumer impulse takes precedence over Americanism, the tension between national government and transnational corporations increases.

IDENTITY CONSTRUCTION AND CONFUSION

At the height of the nation-state's power, nationalism was the primary resource for collective identification (B. Anderson). To identify as an American was both necessary and sufficient for constructing social membership and purpose. But, as Peter Marden notes, the decline of the nation-state has had a profound impact on the stability of national identity. "[T]he forces of globalization are making us re-think our old ideas about democracy, sovereignty, citizenship and the state. As traditional allegiances are put aside, new ones are formed that have profound implications for political practice" (4). Institutions of all kinds are established ways of feeling connected. When any of them falter, including the state itself, it throws off processes of collective identification.[1] Identifying with one's social group is a fundamentally human gesture. It does not disappear because the terms of identification change. Put differently, the instability of national identity does not amount to an "identityless" people. Literature suggests that a new generation of Americans are discovering alternative bases for creating community.

One such alternative framework for identification is consumption. Rather than identify primarily with those who share the same nationality, Americans might identify with those who share the same consumer preferences. It may, in other words, be more telling to reveal one's choice of car than one's political orientation. For example, certain automakers have begun to promote their vehicles with clubs and vacation retreats exclusively for owners. Owners of, for example, Saturn get together and socialize based on the bond of driving the same brand of car. So whereas our parents' and grandparents' generation considered themselves Americans first and motorists, film buffs, or clotheshorses second, this generation may do the opposite. If so, it is indicative both of the diminishing effectiveness of the nation-state and its government in generating identification and of the increasing role of corporate influence on social connections.

The plots in these films are convoluted, partly due to the characters' identity-related confusion. For example, Norrington has a rather ambivalent relationship with pirates that features centrally in *CBP*. His actions toward them suggest a sort of subconscious indecision. In the first scene onboard the ship from England, Norrington has just commented on his plans to exterminate all pirates when young Will is rescued from the waves. Will, it turns out, is a pirate's son. Later, during a confrontation, he orders the men to hang Sparrow, despite the fact that Sparrow just saved Elizabeth from drowning. At the end of the film, he gives Sparrow a two-day head start before he sends his men after him and the *Black Pearl*. Norrington is obligated to persecute threats to the Crown; he is also a good and forgiving man. This conflicted relationship with pirates shapes Norrington's character throughout the films.

To analyze the films' construction and confusion of identity, I examine how each of the main characters grapples with identity issues. Because the films rely rather heavily on character development, I spend time on each person individually. Note that the portrayals of Will Turner, Captain Jack Sparrow, and Elizabeth Swann illustrate how identity is subject to external circumstances; that is, the films depict how tensions between the British Crown and the EITC influence the characters on a personal level. For the audience, this functions as a source of identification with the fictional characters. There is a formal homology between their struggles to find themselves and our likewise tumultuous search for identity. Because our experiences are homologous, we are invited to see ourselves in the characters.

Will Turner

Between the opening scene where Will is rescued and the morning of Norrington's promotion ceremony, 8 years pass. We infer that orphan Will was taken in as an apprentice by a blacksmith in Port Royal under whose guidance he now makes swords. Will does not seem to fit in anywhere, however. Before the ceremony, he is summoned to the palace to deliver a new sword that the governor has commissioned as a gift for the commodore-to-be. It is evident that Will is out of place in the fancy palace and awestruck by the beautiful but unattainable governor's daughter. He does not quite fill the role of suitor, though, just as the life of the high class is beyond his reach.

Much of the first film is thus focused on Will's self-discovery. When he enters the drama as a little boy, the pirate medallion around his neck is confiscated by his hostess Elizabeth. Not until much later does he learn of his father, Bootstrap Bill, and his pirate heritage. Sparrow, who breaks the news, assumes a kind of older brother role. It is his responsibility to teach young Will the ways of the sea and a pirate's morale. The blacksmith workshop is the stage for a particularly illustrative scene between Will and Sparrow, in which the latter is on the run from Norrington's men. Will, whose feelings for Elizabeth seemingly translates into civic duty, challenges Sparrow, thereby keeping him in the shop long enough to be captured. The dialogue between the two men reveals that Sparrow recognizes Will based on his resemblance to his father. Will rebuts in a scornful manner.

Sparrow: "You seem somewhat familiar; have I threatened you before?"
Will: "I make it a point to avoid familiarity with pirates!"

Sparrow acknowledges Will's fencing skills, but the fight has a noticeable sense of brotherly tutorial rather than confrontation. For example, Sparrow tests Will's footwork while teasing him about "finding himself a girl."

The pirate lessons continue onboard the *Interceptor* when Sparrow and Will are on their way from Port Royal to Tortuga. Sparrow claims that there are only two things to consider in life: what a man can do, and what a man can't do. He tries to get Will to accept that his father was both a pirate and a good man and that "pirate is in your blood." He asks Will, "Can you sail under the command of a pirate, or can you not?" This choice, for Will, becomes definitive of his identity. If his father was a pirate and he himself awaits the same fate, his affectionate bond with Sparrow is permissible. But the intense negotiation of righteousness and loyalty carry through both films for Will.

Will is in many ways the quintessential young man character. His background is ambiguous, which causes problems for him particularly in terms of class. His fatherlessness leads him to seek other male role models, in this case Sparrow. He is infatuated with a woman, but his insecurities prevent him from pursuing her. In fact, the American film audience frequently is encouraged to identify with exactly this form of the young male hero. We have seen movie after movie with basically the same figure in different circumstances and time periods (*Good Will Hunting, Save the Last Dance, Almost Famous, Wonder Boys,*

Scent of a Woman). In each film that features this character, some aspects of the form are present, and some are left out. The important thing is for the audience to experience the cinematic homology and relate its own versions of the fictional challenges.

Captain Jack Sparrow

Sparrow is at once an underdog and a legend. When he docks in Port Royal at the beginning of *CBP,* his vessel is a leaky old dinghy. Introducing himself as Mr. Smith—a nobody—he does not have the demeanor of a scary pirate or a mighty captain but, rather, a prankster. Nonetheless, he is emphatic about his captain title even without a proper ship. As Norrington, upon realizing that Sparrow's effects consist of a gun with no additional shots or powder and a compass that does not point north (see below), announces: "You are by far the worst pirate I've ever heard of!" To this, Sparrow replies with glee: "But you have heard of me!"

Sparrow's reputation precedes him. For example, when Norrington rolls back Sparrow's sleeve and spots a bird tattoo, he immediately identifies him by name. The films reinforce this legendary impression of Sparrow many times. One segment of *DMC* depicts Will looking for Sparrow through a sort of interviewing montage. A series of people tell Will when and where they last saw Jack Sparrow and the circumstances of their relationship. Most of the stories are less than flattering, but no one is confounded by the pirate's name. In another segment, Elizabeth and Sparrow swim ashore the very same island where Barbossa once marooned Sparrow. She wants him to get them off the desert isle the same way he did the last time and exclaims: "You're Captain Jack Sparrow! You vanished from under the eyes of seven agents of the East India Company! Are you the pirate I've read about or not?!"

Sparrow of course deliberately perpetuates his own mythical status. Upon reencountering Barbossa and the *Black Pearl* crew, his mutinous former confederates, he proclaims: "When you marooned me on that godforsaken spit of land, you forgot one very important thing, mate. I'm Captain Jack Sparrow!" Sparrow may be an institution of pirate lore, but, as one of the pirates says, "Not much is known about Jack Sparrow before he showed up in Tortuga." The mystery is part of his appeal and a major feature in the plots; no one seems to be able to figure him out. He is either a good man who happens to steal things for a living or a bad pirate who occasionally does the right thing. He has no solid connections to the other characters, which is how he manages the freedom to appear and disappear in the story. Sparrow's identity, in other words, is a strategic puzzle.

This may be the character with which the audience wants to identify. We see him on the screen and wish that our own lives were more like his: exciting, dangerous, and full of adventure. If so, it is this desire that inspires us to be extra sensitive to formal homologies linking Sparrow's reality and our own. When these become salient, the content-based details are less important; we can see past the eye liner, the pirate ship, and the accent. Instead, we may focus, for example, on Sparrow's continuous survival and triumph in the face of his enemies. Those audience members that fancy themselves underdogs who beat the odds can relate to the form of Sparrow's identity. Moreover, they may experience this form as a way of dealing with uncertain external circumstances. The form of Sparrow's character becomes a response to external tensions.

Elizabeth Swann

Elizabeth has a strange attraction to all things having to do with pirates. The audience learns this about her in the *CBP*'s opening scene, when a ship's fore is shown emerging in the fog. A little girl stands at the railing singing the emblematic pirate tune: "Yo-ho, yo-ho, a pirate's life for me." As mentioned above, Elizabeth keeps Will's pirate medallion. On the morning of the promotion ceremony, she sneaks it out of a hidden drawer and puts it around her own neck. When the *Black Pearl* pirates attack Port Royal, her pirate knowledge actually saves her life. She is captured but invokes the prisoner's right to parlay: "According to the Code of the Brethren, set down by the pirates Morgan and Bartholomew, you must take me to your Captain. If an adversary demands parlay, you can do them no harm until the parlay is complete." Her fascination with pirates is drawn into her own identity. Even Sparrow calls her a pirate at the end of *DMC* when she cuffs him to the mast and sacrifices him to Kraken.

Another aspect of Elizabeth's identity ambivalence is her romantic conundrum. This is portrayed as a thoroughly classic choice: the "smart match" with Norrington or the puppy love she shares with Will. Notably, this confusion comes up when Elizabeth is captured. To avoid becoming the pirates' hostage, she introduces herself as Elizabeth Turner, using Will's name and claiming to be a maid in the governor's household. Of course for the pirates, the name Turner suggests that she might be the offspring of Bootstrap Bill, whose blood they need to break the curse. Since the pirates think she is Bootstrap's child for a good portion of the film, her plan ultimately backfires.

Additionally, Elizabeth's identity construction is a matter of gender. In the second film, she disguises herself as a man to sneak onboard the merchant ship to Tortuga. Her abandoned dress is discovered by the other sailors, who make up a story about a woman's ghost haunting the ship. Elizabeth's sexual ambiguity, moreover, stretches beyond her appearance. In Tortuga, for example, there is a bar brawl in which her sword fighting ends up saving Norrington. He has foolishly challenged half the town folk to a duel in his drunken stupor. Her "skills with a blade" continue as a theme through the movie. Thus, Elizabeth's character oscillates back and forth between the hyper-feminine aristocratic lady and a pirate-like tomboy.

Elizabeth is the only heroine, which means that she is the female audience's only source of identification. Her struggles to find herself and negotiate her romantic relationships are featured as major elements in the plot. At one point or another, she has romantic affairs with all three major characters: Will, Norrington, and Sparrow. She is torn between suitors of different calibers, which contributes to the sense of tension in the films. One important formal aspect of Elizabeth's personality is her attraction to the films' "bad boys." Both as a girl and as a young woman, Elizabeth is drawn to pirate lore. For the female audience, this allure of forbidden love becomes a potential homology and a point of identification. The films ask, Who hasn't been tempted by the wrong kind of romance? In response, we may consider how our own identities are a function of the tensions going on around us, many of them fueled by romantic interests.

Negotiating identity is a challenge for these characters, especially because the external circumstances constantly change. This is part of the homology between their fictional selves and the audience's real experiences of change. For example, Elizabeth's identity construction is shaped by her father's predicament in Port Royal. When his position of power there is threatened, so is the stability of her origin. The second dimension of this chapter's analysis, in fact, concerns the impact of unstable spaces. In the following section, I discuss how the sites for the plot contribute to the impression of tension and change. Particularly noteworthy is the homology between these fictional spaces and the real-life spaces wherein the audience experiences the same thing.

UNSTABLE SPACE

Saying that the world is shrinking may be to resort to cliché, hence insisting that it is "under construction" is more helpful. Geographical space does not have the same meaning to contemporary Americans as it did for our predecessors. It is not as stable or absolute. If you are born and raised in the same town where you later work, marry, bear children, and live out your old age, your personal experience of space is rather restricted. Chances are good that most of the people you interact with share the same experience. Your bond is affirmed by a perspective on the world that rarely if ever is challenged. A challenge only occurs if a stranger comes to town, if the familiar space is infiltrated by foreign persons or symbols.

The scenario I described above is true for fewer Americans today than historically. Urban areas are becoming international metropolitans, and small towns are going out of business, for better or worse. In short, people are encountering cultural diversity (in friends as well as music, food, and religious convictions) and are experiencing space as something considerably more pliable. For example, a truly exotic vacation destination today may be Thailand or

Australia, whereas 50 years ago the equivalent may have been London or Paris. International travel has become faster, cheaper, and more convenient. This, in turn, alters the way we think about space—both when we are staying in one place and when we are in transit. No place is as permanent as it was when you knew you might only leave it once or twice in your life.

Tortuga

In the *POC* films, space becomes another variable for the heroes to negotiate. At times, it almost becomes a character in itself. For example, Tortuga represents all that is pirate. It is a no-man's-land, a place literally off the map, where misfits and rejects convene. The scenes set there construct it as a cross between a battlefield and a brothel, where danger and pleasure exist in a tumultuous mix. This mixture is not entirely objectionable; Sparrow mentions to Will that, if every place on earth were like it, no man would ever feel unwanted. In a sense, Tortuga and Isla de Muerta are depicted as interchangeable. They contain extremes—in gold or in hedonistic decadence. Both occupy a plot position that might be described as "pirates'/criminals' lair away from safe places like Port Royal." The description of Isla de Muerta as a spot that "cannot be found except by those who already know where it is" might be applied to all pirate lairs. They are mystical and not entirely physical spaces.

The Ships

Much of the *POC* plots take place onboard either pirate ships or navy ships, which illustrate the films' incorporation of unstable spaces. For both camps, a ship is much more than "a keel and hull and a deck and sails." As Sparrow explains to Elizabeth, those are the things that a ship *needs*. He insists that a ship really *is* freedom, suggesting that the audience's hope to be free does indeed depend on something quite unstable. This image is reinforced in the *CBP* jail scene. Sparrow, who has a unique relationship with his ship, hears its cannons in the distance and says that he "knows those guns." He then announces: "It's the *Pearl!*" For Sparrow, the *Pearl* means relief from the shackles of civilization. For the audience, a ship represents the independence and self-sufficiency that require mobility. We are discouraged from committing to a fixed spot, like a port or a home. Being free, the films insist, means negotiating the unsteadiness of a ship and the proverbial rough waters surrounding it.

A ship like the *Black Pearl*, moreover, epitomizes both freedom and danger. Perhaps its very allure lies in that threat. One of the early Port Royal scenes shows two navy men describing the myth of the *Black Pearl*: a ship with black sails that is crewed by the damned and captained by a man so evil that hell itself spat him back out. It is supposedly "non-catchable," which refers to the military's inability to bring it to justice. Another myth about the ship is that it "never leaves any survivors." What becomes confusing for the audience is the interchangeability of the ships throughout the plot's twists. It is difficult to keep track of whose ship is overtaken by whom, and which ship is the stage for each new battle scene. This adds to the general impression that ships are indeed unstable spaces.

POWERFUL OBJECTS

In a discussion of corporate globalization, money is of course a principal motivating object. Moreover, a struggle between national government and transnational corporations makes money an accessible symbol. As such, it is "a universal media of exchange and is 'passed around' transferring value from context to context, without regards to specific local settings" (Marden 6). Of course, resources like oil, land, and infrastructure are other examples of powerful objects, but in a capitalist system, these are by definition measured in terms of potential for profit.

Although it means belaboring the obvious, it is important to mention money as a pawn in the game between corporate and governmental interest taking place both nationally and internationally. Doing so draws attention to the basic form of a powerful or desired object around which competition is organized. This form recurs throughout the *POC* films, as I shall discuss in more detail below. Audiences thus recognize the powerful-object pattern and activate their experience of being in the midst of a tension that can in effect be reduced to that object. In other words, the experience of the films' powerful objects and that of the powerful objects in the real-life struggle resonate with one another.

To analyze the formal homology between these films and a growing influence of transnational corporatism, it is important to emphasize certain objects of power. As explained earlier, a capitalist system requires that transactions be reducible to a common denominator or currency. In the films, currency assumes several different forms. Put differently, there are a number of objects around which the plot revolves. These objects motivate the characters and become the victors' spoils. They are thus presented as homologous to whatever objects motivate the audience.

The Gold

As formal recurrences go, this may be the films' most thinly disguised theme. The gold, especially central in the *CBP* story, illustrates our simultaneous attraction and aversion to wealth. In the *CBP*, the gold is not just any gold but the cursed treasure of Cortés. Barbossa tells Elizabeth the story: The treasure contains 882 pieces of Cortés's gold. As a punishment for his cruelty against the Aztecs, the heathen gods placed on the treasure an evil curse. Any mortal who removes a single piece from the stone chest must suffer eternally; anything bought

with the cursed gold brings misery. The cursed pirates, Barbossa laments, are neither living nor dead. They are doomed to hunt for the last remaining pieces of
the treasure and return them. Barbossa explains, "Compelled by greed we were,
but now we are consumed by it."

The "undead" pirates are irresistibly drawn to the gold. Whenever a piece
is in the open, the ocean quells, and the winds turn, presumably as a sort of
beckoning for the pirates seeking to restore the treasure. This beckoning signifies our preoccupation with the accumulation of wealth. As one of the pirates
says, "The gold, it calls to us!" The curse, on the other hand, represents the pursuit of something that cannot be definitively gained. Consider the homology to
an American audience. For a true capitalist, there is no such thing as enough
money. More is more. Accumulating money is an inexhaustible enterprise.
Barbossa describes how the pirates cannot enjoy the gold but also cannot stop
seeking it. They are controlled by a greater force. Because this force is present
in the audience member's lives, its irresistibility resonates. We understand how
the cursed pirates must suffer and how their actions seem beyond their own
control. But there are "objects" other than gold that motivate men, in the films
as well as in real life. . . .

The "Girl"

Sparrow says to Will when he accuses him of being well on his way to becoming a pirate: "You're completely obsessed with treasure." When Will objects,
Sparrow smiles and replies: "Not all treasure is silver and gold, mate," and they
both turn to admire Elizabeth. In the *POC*, two different storylines characterize
a woman as a treasure or, in this analysis, as an object of power—that is, a woman
is the object of others' actions. In the first film, Norrington and Will compete for
Elizabeth's heart and hand. In the second film, Sparrow half-heartedly joins this
competition as well. Elizabeth, however, is the films' only active female, which is
to say that she is the only heroine among the main characters. Thus, she is both a
subject and an object. In some ways, she pursues the men in the films; ultimately,
however, her role conforms to being that of a "treasure."

Another woman plays an important role in the second film, but this character is notably absent. When Tia Dalma tells the tragic story of Davy Jones, it
turns out to be one of unrequited love; he succumbed to "that which vexes all
men"—a woman. Tia Dalma explains that he fell in love with a woman "as
changing and hard and untamable as the sea" and, when she betrayed him, cut
out his own heart. He put the heart in a chest, buried the chest on a deserted
island, and now always carries the key to the chest. According to this story, a
woman is to blame for Jones's evil character, which makes him seem more
humane and his actions more intelligible. Such an "off-stage woman" may be
more of a cause than an effect in the plot, compared to Elizabeth, but she is

nevertheless an object of power. In short, she generates power for others' benefit instead of her own.

Sparrow's Compass

This object of power appears several times in the films, but its centrality in *DMC* warrants separate treatment. The trick to this magic compass, which originally belonged to Tia Dalma before Sparrow bartered for it, is that it only works if its keeper knows what he/she seeks. When the crew travels upriver to the witch, she immediately notices that Sparrow does not know what he wants. To some, then, the compass appears to be useless and broken, since it does not point north. But, as one of the pirates knowingly points out: "We're not trying to find north, are we?" The compass leads to whatever you desire most, which causes many twists in the plot.

The significance of such a compass is potent. For instance, it is of no help to those who are truly lost. In a sense, it is an insider's trick. Just as the Isla de Muerta can only be found by those who already know where it is, the compass can only be used by those who already know what they want. This object befits a culture that nurtures mystery. As stated, tension between the national and corporate interests creates a confusing environment for ordinary people; this confusion, which is exceedingly mysterious in itself, is exacerbated by the fact that navigational aides only serve those who do not really need direction. In reality, people without Sparrow's confidence and certainty have no help, the film suggests. They would simply misinterpret the compass and remain lost.

Davy Jones's Chest

This object and the key that opens it are the central power sources of the second film. Whoever has it and/or the magic compass controls the sea. The entire plot thus becomes focused on bargaining and trade. To name a few examples: Beckett offers to grant royal pardons to Elizabeth, Will, and Norrington in exchange for Sparrow's compass. He of course wants it for the EITC's commercial benefit. Will agrees to help Sparrow find the key to Jones's chest in exchange for the compass, which he will then give to Beckett to free Elizabeth. Sparrow wants the key to use Jones's heart against him and cancel his debt. Bootstrap Bill commits himself to an eternity of service to Jones in exchange for his son's freedom. And, finally, Norrington delivers Jones's heart with the promise that he will be readmitted into the British establishment.

The subject of trade is prevalent in the first film as well. Elizabeth uses the pirate medallion as a bargaining chip to negotiate "cessation of hostilities against Port Royal." Sparrow wants to trade Will with Barbossa for the *Black Pearl.* Barbossa, in turn, wants to offer up Will to break the curse of the Aztec treasure.

The rapid exchange of one thing for another may complicate the plot, but it nevertheless underscores the films' main theme—the expansion of commercialism and international trade. This theme is the ultimate foil for the characters' challenges and triumphs.

Conclusion

I argued in this chapter that *Pirates of the Caribbean* offers a pop culture lesson in one of our time's most important political changes—the shifting powers of national governments and transnational corporations. The films instruct American audiences on how to negotiate our place amid these great forces, whose struggle is carried out largely beyond citizens' control. I focused especially on three themes—the construction and confusion of identity, the pursuit of empowering objects, and the manipulation of unstable space—to demonstrate a homology between the films and real-life experiences. This analysis showed that identity is a highly fluid construct in a culture that has relinquished the traditional institutions around which citizens form social networks. The films, I argued, reflect this ambiguity in their treatment of the characters' identities, many of which change in various ways throughout the story. Further, I illustrated the pattern of behavior that is centered on valuable objects and indicated how this struggle is shaped by the mobile sites that serve as context.

There are alternative ways of discovering this connection between the life of a pirate and the complex position of modern citizen consumers. Indeed, drawing attention to the recurring homology throughout different texts substantiates the argument linking discourse and experience. Consider, for example, the use of the term "piracy" to describe the illegal downloading of MP3 files (Spitz and Hunter; Taylor). As the introductory chapter of this book explains, language is one of the most important means of disguising social issues, whether intentionally or not. Choices in vocabulary reveal a lot about social attitudes toward the issue being disguised. Thus, using a phrase like "online piracy" suggests how the film and music industries conceptualize this phenomenon. By comparing such a term to the homology identified in this chapter, we might recognize the tension between federal laws regarding intellectual property on the one hand and large media conglomerates on the other. While the former decides what is legal and what is not, the latter has staggering control over popular culture and its profitable dissemination. Between the two interests are the consumers. In short, the term "piracy" here buttresses my analysis of how Americans behave when subjected to larger forces and the underlying forms that express those behaviors.

It is worthwhile to inquire about the benefits of this disguise in the first place. What is the point of a film about pirates if it is really about ordinary people? The introductory chapter describes how disguises sometimes offer a way of dealing with issues that are particularly painful or dangerous. A film's specific content, for example, can be a disguise for something with which audiences would have a difficult time engaging. In the *POC* trilogy, displacement is a protective strategy of disguise. The plot is set in a fictitious past far from the audience's real lives. As long as the bad guys are the stuffy British aristocrats and the East India Trading Company, the film is harmless. Americans have no reason to fear oppression from either one. A film about pirates thus poses no threat. No one is going to see the films and riot against the government or even the corporations that the EITC represents because manifestly they are simply fictional.

It would be preposterous to claim that *POC* teaches modern Americans to be pirates; rather, the reading I offer in this chapter suggests that there are formal ways of being a pirate that are profoundly influential to the American audience. Such formal patterns offer audiences "equipment for living." They instruct us on how to live in the midst of conflict. According to Kenneth Burke, symbols are our arms against perplexities and risks (61). When it provides means of handling difficult situations in everyday life, art, including movies, protects us against the unfamiliar.

Each time a story is told, the content or information is poured into certain formal patterns. Burke explains, "A given human relationship may be at one time named in terms of foxes and lions, if there are foxes and lions about; or it may now be named in terms of salesmanship, advertising, the tactics of politicians, etc. But beneath the change in particulars, we may often discern the naming of one situation" (302). The point is this: In the *POC* films, the particulars are pirates with eye patches, cursed Aztec treasure, and giant, tentacled sea monsters. These are not the circumstances of modern America, yet the situation has clear relevance. Like the pirates, we are encouraged to struggle against oppression, whether aristocratic or corporate. The films imply that we must always embrace our individualism, cherish freedom, protect our treasured things, and strive to maintain a sense of humor in the face of adversity. "Don't let 'em getcha down!" is the trilogy's Burkean proverb.

In closing, let me underscore an important implication of this rather celebratory analysis. To be sure, the justification for studying artifacts of popular culture has been made many times; it need not be reiterated here, except to note the pedagogical value of taking seriously a film about pirates. For many students of cultural criticism, detecting formal recurrences is a difficult and sometimes painful lesson. They are discouraged by the realization that popular texts (television, music, film, advertisements, etc.) often perpetuate the mainstream negative attitudes of racism, sexism, and so on. This in turn generates a reluctance to think in depth about everyday texts and experiences. Without diminishing the importance of critical insight, we must allow for other, more positive discoveries in cultural analysis. We might remind ourselves that being a critic means paying attention not only to the destructive characteristics of popular texts but also to their productive potential. Others might then consider them instrumental rather than simply entertaining and pursue cultural criticism more vigorously in the future.

Note

1. Of course, nationalism is not gone as a resource for identification. In fact, as Miyoshi argues, the myth of the nation-state remains vital long after the reality has lost its force. The point here is that, while "Americanness" may still connote a variety of symbolic resources for constructing identity, other symbolic systems are competing with it at greater rates than previously. There are more systems of identity to choose from today.

intense witch-hunt ever to occur in the New England colonies. In the panic that ensued, nearly 200 people, mostly women, were accused of practicing witchcraft. When the hunt was finally ended by Governor William Phips in October of 1692, 19 victims (14 women, 5 men) had been executed, one man had been pressed to death by stones, and three women, one man, and several infants had died in prison (Karlsen 40–41; Norton 4).

More than 300 years have passed since the witch-hunt of 1692, yet Salem is still haunted by the events of its past. In spite—or, rather, *because*—of Salem's notorious witch history, the city has become a popular tourist destination that each year hosts close to 1 million visitors looking to bump up against the past of the "Witch City." The official visitors' guide for the city of Salem advertises an eclectic menu of touristic fare, from the sensational (the Salem Wax Museum of Witches and Seafarers, the Witch Dungeon Museum) to the solemn (Nathaniel Hawthorne's House of the Seven Gables). Although a large portion of the booklet relates in some way to the 1692 hunt, absent from its 48 pages is any mention of the events that marked the hunt's 300-year anniversary or the memorial constructed to honor its victims. In 1992, Salem commemorated the tercentennial with the construction of the city's first memorial to the 20 victims who were executed or died under torture. Despite protests by the area's local Wiccan community in the months leading to the memorial's dedication, on August 5, 1992, the $100,000 project supported by grant money from the National Endowment for the Arts was dedicated by Nobel laureate and Holocaust survivor Elie Wiesel. The Salem Witch Trials Memorial, located adjacent to a historic cemetery where one of the original trial judges is buried, mirrors the Vietnam Memorial in Washington DC in its invitation to quiet contemplation, the victims' names etched in solid granite. In an interview prior to the ceremony Wiesel called the witch-hunt the result of "fanaticism," and in his public address at the dedication he compared the violence of colonial Salem to the Los Angeles riots and the Balkans (Brown F1).

Wiesel's evocation of the Salem witch-hunt to critique contemporary forms of violence and persecution underscores the political and symbolic power that the witch continues to invoke today. Although the 17th-century signification of the word "witch" has shifted in the realm of popular culture to artifacts like Halloween costumes, black cats, and *Sabrina the Teenage Witch*, people are still fascinated by witches. They are a powerful symbol (or category) with a wide range of meanings for diverse groups of people throughout history, and Wiesel's comparison is a perfect example of what historian and literary critic Diane Purkiss describes as the evolving "signification of the witch, and the way that her continued meaning is the product of the present" (31). For Europeans and New England colonists during the early modern period, witches were a pervasive threat, practicing black magic and making pacts with Satan; they were the ultimate enemies of the Christian God (Levack 32–51).

For young fans of author J. K. Rowling's popular *Harry Potter* series, the witch may represent a form of escapism and empowerment (Gunn 224–25). Such a complex and changing symbol, like the penguins, pirates, and superheroes explored in this book, has *rhetorical* power—it may serve as a site of identification, shape worldviews, or articulate certain understandings of gender, race, and class. The question one must ask, then, is what sort of rhetorical work is getting done when someone is called a witch?

Arthur Miller had an answer. In 1952 he wrote a play called *The Crucible* in which he used the Salem witch trials as a sort of parable for the anti-Communist sentiment of McCarthyism in the 1950s. In the play, Miller does not reference the congressional hearings that took place to oust suspected Communists on U.S. soil. Instead, he disguises a condemnation of U.S. policy in a play about a colonial witch persecution, and in doing so he offered an important argument for how "witches" continue to be pursued today. The "witch" label, so often used as a discursive marker to identify the so-called "monsters" of society, functions as "an approved mechanism for the *disguise*, and discharge, of social violence" (Ingebretsen 45, emphasis added). Calling someone a monster, a witch, or any label that denotes monstrosity or "Otherness" does far more than place that person in an undesirable category—it often leads to serious real-life effects like persecution, alienation, and violence. The Salem witch trials of 1692 are a poignant example of this result, but the present-day discourses that frame experiences of witch-hunt tourism in Salem avoid discussing it in many ways. Posing as authoritative historical explanations, Salem tourism hides the complex relationship between capitalism, patriarchy, gender, and witch-hunting—as well as the violent atrocities that were committed against the women and men accused. They hide this violence by encouraging visitors to understand colonial witchcraft as a form of clinical hysteria.

This chapter is divided into three parts. First, I examine the rhetorical function of various popular witch-related museums and attractions that typify much of Salem tourism. I also analyze the tercentennial memorial and its counterpart in the neighboring city of Danvers, arguing that both monuments complement the central narratives that frame touristic experiences of Salem witch history by disguising essential aspects of that history. To do this, I use texts gathered from Salem's official visitors' guide and tourist office, as well as from Web sites for the city's most popular tourist attractions, and examine the dominant narratives that frame them. A dominant narrative is a privileged story, account, or way of understanding that is produced by an authority. In some cases, as with museum exhibits, that authority may be an identifiable individual (e.g., a curator); in other cases it may be disembodied or more abstract (e.g., the Salem Office of Tourism and Cultural Affairs). These narratives are called "dominant" because they are often produced with the voice of authority and by those who occupy positions of privilege and power, and because they can encourage people—often times unconsciously—to understand the world in ways that help maintain those positions of privilege and power.

In the second section of the chapter, I turn to an example that opens a potential space for counter-memories of the 1692 hunt. The 1992 protest by Salem's Wiccan community against the Salem tercentennial memorial suggests possibilities for how alternative approaches to remembering can contest institutional control over the past. Finally, I conclude with a discussion of the ideologies that Salem tourism disguises—capitalism, patriarchy, gender—and their relationship to violence, arguing that this disguise is not constructed by accident. Rather, it serves a strategic function by obscuring the way the Salem witchhunt was a violent response to (1) the transition to mercantile capitalism and (2) perceived threats—namely by women—against the patriarchal order in colonial New England. This disguise situates the Salem hunt as an historical anomaly, an event that happened to "those" people, back "then." In doing so, it liberates the modern tourist from the burden of confronting the way naming and violence work hand in hand for social and political ends, not only in 17th-century New England but today as well. Salem tourism discourages visitors from understanding how the conditions that led to Salem's hunt continue to operate, albeit in different forms, here and now, and that the search for the witch, the Other, continues under different disguises today.

(Dis)Covering Salem History

History sells . . . and we have a lot for sale.

—Stanley Usovicz, past mayor
of Salem (quoted in Giordano G1)

*Throughout the world, Salem is most widely known for the witchcraft
trials of 1692. The legendary witch history makes Salem the undeni-
able place to be to celebrate the Halloween season.*

—Kimberley Driscoll, current mayor of Salem

The motivations behind our forays as tourists are many and varied. Often the goal is simply to enjoy a bit of leisure time, to "get away from it all." This was what my parents had in mind when they packed me and my two younger sisters in the family car each summer and set out on the road for a long day of driving along the coast of California. We would spend the weekend ordering takeout and relaxing poolside. The pleasure we experienced from the trip came more from the act of getting there, despite my and my sisters' constant protests (are we there yet?), and had little to do with the actual activities we took part in once we reached our destination. The exact opposite was true when I visited Madrid during a semester spent studying abroad in Spain. That excursion was prompted by my desire to experience a bit of Spanish history and culture, to see works of art from masters like Picasso and Dalí, and to sample the city's traditional culinary fare. Defining the modern tourist and uncovering the motivations behind tourists' excursions have played a central role in the academic study of tourism for many years. Much of tourism research to date, as Michael Bowman points out, has favored a polarized view of tourists as either passive sightseers or consumers and tourism as a "disembodied practice," at the expense of investigating what touristic experiences might signify to the tourists themselves (103–4).

Tourists, however, are not always disembodied consumers in search of authentic, unmediated encounters with other cultures and ways of life, doomed to experience what MacCannell calls "staged authenticity," or the type of faux-reality that one might encounter at, say, Disneyland (597). Writing on the nature of tourism in 1973, MacCannell expresses an elitist conception of tourism. "The touristic experience that comes out of the tourist setting," he writes, "is based on inauthenticity, and as such it is superficial when compared with careful study; it is morally inferior to mere experience" (599). However, this is not necessarily always the case. Recent research indicates that tourists seek out distraction, pleasure, and escape over objective authenticity (they are on vacation, after all) and, moreover, that these types of experiences do not inhibit opportunities for critical engagement with the narratives that frame them (Bowman 128). Jennifer Iles, for example, found that pilgrimages to World War I battlefields on the Western Front often take the form of intensely personal performances that "subvert and challenge" the dominant narratives of tour guides (177). Similarly, in Bowman's reflections on his personal experiences visiting battlefields of the American Civil War, he recognizes "gaps, interruptions, and distractions" and "tentative, fleeting moments of improvised resistance" that result in departures from the routine, scripted norms tourists are expected to follow (126). A vacationing tourist in a foreign country might notice a gap and seize it if she decides to abandon the official itinerary prepared by her travel agent, opting instead to embark on her own unplanned excursion. The tension, then, "between unreflexive and reflexive dispositions" is the defining characteristic of the modern tourist, a sojourner who at times "share[s] conventional ways of doing and thinking in relatively unchallenging contexts" and, at others, "seek[s] to test conventions" (118).

Despite recent attempts by city officials to "re-brand" Salem and shift focus away from its international reputation as the Witch City, the area's notoriety as the geographic site of America's most intense witch persecution remains the central draw for visitors to the region. Salem tourists who choose to begin their journey by perusing the city's official visitors' guide open their experience with a great tension between two central aspects of Salem's history: violence and capitalism. The discourses that frame this tension work their rhetorical magic by disguising the root causes of Salem's violent past, even as they openly discuss its effects.

After turning past an invitation to "experience the unexpected," the reader learns that, in the 17th century, the area was named "Salem" from the Hebrew *shalom*, meaning "peace" (Salem Office, "Salem Visitors Guide" 4). The brief historical vignettes that follow detail a past saturated with turmoil and violence that seems anything but what one would expect from a "City of Peace": political unrest, violence between Puritans and Quakers, torture, executions, occult practices. Yet, rather than account for the contradiction between the etymology of the city's name and its violent past, the unidentified author of the text immediately shifts the narrative from a "City of Peace" to a "City by the Sea." The reader discovers Salem's "glorious maritime past," that it was once one of the most profitable ports on the eastern seaboard and "one of the richest cities in America" (5). Violence emerges in the narrative as a threat to Salem's prosperity and good fortune. The "French and Indian Wars" disrupt the city's "lucrative trade"; later, the American Revolution interrupts "the town's shipping business" (5).

This discourse continues in the historical overview offered on the tourist office's official Web site. There one learns that "there is much more to Salem than the trials of 1692." The site describes industries like "fishing, shipbuilding, [and] overseas trade" and the "millions . . . made by Salem sea captains!" as noteworthy milestones in Salem's progression away from the senseless violence of the hunt and into mercantile capitalism (Salem Office, "History"). "America's first millionaires," the narrative continues, offer living proof of Salem's transformation: "The legacy of their wealth lines Salem's streets in the forms of incomparable architecture and unique museums. Their legacies can be witnessed at the Peabody Essex Museum, the House of the Seven Gables, the Salem Maritime National Historic Site and the Stephen Phillips Memorial Trust House." These historical and cultural sites share no obvious relation with the events of Salem's witch past (aside from the Peabody Essex Museum, which houses some of the original historical documents from the hunt); instead, they serve as living reminders of how Salem has overcome the legacy of violence that visitors associate with the city.

The tension between violence and commerce that defines Salem's history in the narrative provided by the city's official tourist literature disguises the agents of violence by focusing on the effects of the violence. Violence is constructed as an external threat to, as opposed to a product of internal tension in, the community. War, revolution, and witch-hunting become outside obstacles that impede Salem's natural progression to a modern, capitalist community. But what if that causal relationship was reversed? What if the conflicts that caused so much of the tension within the Salem community stemmed from the move to a commercial, market economy that was taking place throughout the New England colonies, as some historians have argued? Tourist literature in Salem does not entertain that possibility; instead, it disguises the connections between Salem's violent past and capitalism and ignores the role that gender, class conflict, and religion played in that violence.

Historians Paul Boyer and Stephen Nissenbaum addressed the tensions that defined life in colonial New England in their influential 1974 study *Salem Possessed,* discussing at length how the changing economy in the colonies was an important precursor to the witch trials. They examined the sociological foundations of the Salem hunt, locating them in the "dangerous conflict between private will and public good" that existed between the agricultural community of Salem Village (now known as Danvers) and the commercial merchant community of Salem Town (present-day Salem) (105). The trade that resulted from Salem's status as one of the primary colonial shipping ports "had polarized the distribution of its wealth" so that, in the decades prior to the 1692 hunt, 62% of Salem's total wealth was controlled by only 10% of the population (86–87; see also Levack 116).[1] This "commercial development," Boyer and Nissenbaum argue, "represented a looming *moral* threat with implications of the most fundamental sort" (105, emphasis in original). While the violent witch persecutions that emerged as a weapon to fight that moral threat may have disrupted (temporarily) the area's commercial pursuits, as the Salem tourist literature offers, it is important to recognize that they were born out of the many pressures affecting 17th-century New England society. Not least of those pressures was Salem's new role as one of the most important commercial ports on the East Coast.

Like the work of Boyer and Nissenbaum, the history lessons provided by Salem's visitors' guide and the tourist office's Web site also prompt tourists to think of the city's violent past in terms of the movement of capital and goods, but in a very different kind of way. Violence is positioned as an *obstacle to* Salem's transition from an agriculture-based economy to mercantile capitalism rather than the *result of* the tension and conflict caused by that transition. The tourist literature thus exercises rhetorical power by disguising (or simply not acknowledging) the religious and political leaders who orchestrated the witch persecutions in 17th-century Salem, as well as the social and economic conditions that made those persecutions possible. Absent these important historical foundations, the Salem tourist is primed to understand this particular style of violence—witch-hunting—as a "normal" step along the way to a better, more prosperous community. A danger inherent in messages like these lies in their ability to make complex forms of violence appear as natural and self-perpetuating and, therefore, impossible to prevent.

Much larger than the space dedicated to Salem's history, however, are the two sections of the guide that detail the museums, tours, and attractions that tourists may choose from. Of the 21 pages that compose this portion of the guide (nearly half the total number of pages), 18 make reference to Salem's witch history or advertise an activity that clearly alludes to that history (Spellbound Museum and Tours, for example, offers displays of "authentic supernatural curios and oddities" and "unearthly fun" in its Victorian-era ghost parlor [28]). Attractions associated with witches, ghosts, and the occult clearly emerge as the central sources for diversion and entertainment over the area's gastronomy, art galleries, and boat tours.

That the occult (and attractions related to it) is at the center of touristic experiences in Salem should come as no surprise for readers of this book. The appeal of occultic texts stems from their ability to disguise, or what Joshua Gunn identifies as the "logic of secrecy, interpretation, and discrimination" that characterizes occultic texts in a postmodern era (xxiii). In other words, they are attractive to visitors because they seem to conceal some hidden mystery. For tourists not familiar with the complex history of Salem witchcraft, witch-hunt tourism offers the opportunity to unlock the secrets of that dark past. As stated in the visitors' guide, one of the features of the Witch History Museum is the grisly "untold stories of 1692" that will be "revealed" to visitors (23). The Salem Witch Village promises guests will "understand the truth behind the legends" (26), and the Hocus Pocus Evening Walking Tours invites adventurous individuals (if they dare) to "experience Salem's dark shadows" as well as "uncover" the "simple scary truth" behind the "myth, magic, and legend" of Salem's past (32). Even one of the city's key architectural treasures, the famed House of the Seven Gables, features a "secret staircase" among the "house's many surprises" (16). These tourist attractions and many others like them tempt guests to take a peek behind the curtain, to uncover the Truth behind one of history's most complex and misunderstood persecutions. However, as Gunn argues, occultic texts must be viewed in the economic context of late capitalism, where their apparent secrets often take a backseat to fancy packaging. They become fetishized commodities imbued with seemingly "magical" powers, meant to "entertain and titillate or to quell widespread anxiety about this or that crisis stimulus" (203). More important, these attractions complement dominant historical accounts of Salem's past by promising "the answer" to questions about a historical period whose complexities have challenged witch-hunt historians for decades.

What sorts of stories do those secrets tell? What is the answer they provide? In the museums, tours, and attractions that dominate witch-hunt tourism in Salem, hysteria is offered as the central focus of the hunt of 1692. This psychological disorder (now recognized by the medical community as "conversion disorder") was for many years used to explain a wide array of physical symptoms including amnesia, nervous breakdowns, or erratic displays of overdramatic behavior. In the discourses I now examine, the victims of the Salem witch-hunt are described as suffering from hysteria. The larger hunt is explained as a hysteria itself. "Hysteria" works as a disguise when the trials become a product of individual and communal madness, thus hiding the architects of a political and religious-sanctioned persecution and making the accused witches active participants in their own victimization.

Both inside and outside academia, one of the most-discussed aspects of the 1692 hunt is the strange conduct of many of the accusers. After exhibiting behavior associated with demonic possession, a growing number of young girls and women were believed to be suffering from attacks by local witches. Early writings by Cotton Mather detail some of the afflictions one group of children experienced:

> Sometimes they would be deaf, sometimes dumb, and sometimes blind, and often all this at once. One while their tongues would be drawn down their throats, another while they would be pulled out upon their chins to a prodigious length. They would have their mouths opened unto such a wideness that their jaws went out of joint, and anon they would clap together again with a force like that of a strong spring-lock. The same would happen to their shoulder blades and their elbows and their hand wrists and several of their joints. . . . They would make most piteous outcries that they were cut with knives and struck with blows that they could not bear. . . . Thus they lay some weeks most pitiful spectacles. ("Memorable" 263)

Why the women and children acted this way has been the subject of much speculation and study. One explanation commonly offered is that the accusers suffered from hysteria, a form of clinical illness historically associated with women as far back as 2,000 years before Christ (Veith 2).

The association between witchcraft and hysteria is not a new one. As early as 1677 the physician and skeptic John Webster wrote "The Displaying of Supposed Witchcraft," in which he condemns his contemporaries' witch beliefs and offers natural causes to explain behaviors associated with witchcraft or Satan. Although Webster was writing in England over a decade before the Salem hunts, parts of his treatise address behaviors that bear remarkable resemblance to those exhibited by the "possessed" in Salem: "passive delusion," "depraved fancies," "idle, foolish, false and impossible" confessions that are "falsely ascribed unto demons," and so on (Webster 308–9). He ultimately concludes that such afflictions are not caused by organized sects of witches but rather "melancholia figmenta," in other words, hysteria (308). Two centuries later, famed psychoanalyst Sigmund Freud was expressing an interest in demonic possession, hysteria, and witches. In an 1897 letter to his close friend Wilhelm Fliess, Freud even mentioned that he had ordered a copy of the *Malleus Maleficarum,* a notorious 15th-century witch-hunting manual, that he planned on studying "diligently" (Masson 227). In 1923 he published the essay "A Neurosis of Demoniacal Possession in the Seventeenth Century," where he argued that "what in those days were thought to be evil spirits to us are base and evil wishes, the derivatives of impulses which have been rejected and repressed" (436–37).[2]

Salem authorities considered the "afflicted" individuals' behavior as evidence of witchcraft, not some psychological illness, although their unusual behavior has prompted several historians to offer explanations for what that behavior signified. Historian Mary Beth Norton explores the subject in the final pages of her recent study on Salem witchcraft, *In the Devil's Snare.* She offers that the accusers may have suffered from a form of post-traumatic stress disorder (the parents of some had been killed in wars with Native Americans and the French), and that the similarities between different individual accounts of witches' torments were the result of "prearranged collusion" (307). But, she warns, the authorities who coordinated the persecutions were ultimately the ones responsible for the imprisonment, torture, and execution of the women and men accused. Historian Carol Karlsen addresses gender directly, arguing that how one labels the behavior of the women and children is less important than what the behavior was a response to. "When possessed," Karlsen argues, a woman "could rebel against the many restrictions placed upon her, she could dismiss the kind man in the black robe who himself symbolized her longed-for independence and power and tell him what a rogue she thought he was" (247). Although ultimately (and tragically) unsuccessful, possession was an attempt to invert the patriarchal gender hierarchy that restricted women's lives to the domestic, private sphere in colonial Massachusetts (248). Associating such actions with the demonic, Karlsen argues, "only tells us how certain cultures resist the knowledge of female dissatisfaction and anger with their condition" (251).

For visitors to present-day Salem, hysteria stands out as the central focus of the hunt of 1692. In some cases the word "hysteria" is used to signify mass panic, turning the witch-hunt into a type of witch-*craze*, a term historian Brian Levack cautions against because it wrongly suggests witch-hunting was the product of mental disorder (2). This explanation is the one offered in the historical overview on the tourist office's Web site: "[Salem] was where the infamous Salem Witch Trials of 1692 happened. It all began in the winter of 1692 when some girls *fell ill* and blamed members of the community for their *affliction*. Hundreds of innocent people were accused during the *hysteria*, and ultimately nineteen men and women were hung and one man was pressed to death" (emphasis added). Note that, in addition to the association between witch-hunting and hysteria, the violence is not attributed to any agent except the "ill" girls themselves. Absent are the political and religious authorities who played a prominent role in the trials and executions.

The homepage for Salem's Wax Museum also hystericizes the hunt by referring to it solely as an "hysteria." The site references the tercentennial memorial, "erected in memory of the victims of the Hysteria of 1692," and displays the wax figure of an accused witch "who helped fuel the hysteria" ("Salem Wax Museum"). The museum also offers a "Hysteria Pass" for purchase (only $9.95!) that gives visitors discount admission to both the wax museum and the Salem Witch Village. Although the village is operated in collaboration with Salem's local Wiccan community, it, too, slips into the realm of the hysterical and the spectacular. The village's homepage references the "medieval hysteria" of the past, and the village doubles as a haunted neighborhood during Salem's popular "Haunted Happenings" celebration each October ("Salem Witch Village"). Not least among the numerous other examples of hystericized tourist attractions is Mass. Hysteria Haunted Hearse Tours, which offers visitors a driving tour of Salem in, well, a hearse.

By hystericizing witch-hunting, witch-hunt tourism in Salem forwards a medical explanation for why the hunt happened and couches it firmly within a tradition of discourses that rhetorical scholar Dana Cloud calls "rhetorics of therapy." In her book *Control and Consolation in American Culture and Politics*, she talks about this therapeutic rhetoric as a type of discourse that shifts responsibility for political and social ills away from their larger root causes (such as racism, homophobia, or classism) and onto individuals and their families. The oppressed and downtrodden become responsible for their own victimization and are encouraged to accept their lot rather than attempt to change it (10). As a strategic pattern of messages often deployed in moments of social conflict— like the witch-hunts or their present-day commemoration—therapeutic rhetorics "encourage citizens to perceive political issues, conflicts, and inequities as personal failures subject to personal amelioration" (3). When expressed through this type of discourse, Salem's witch-hunt history becomes witch-hunt *hystery*, and a complex state-sponsored persecution with profound gender and class implications becomes the product of individual or collective psychosis. Witch-hunters were nothing if not rational, and they often pursued their victims with the most calculated methods (not to mention the backing of legal machinery designed specifically to address the crime of witchcraft). Suggesting that Salem's witch-hunters were hysterical or crazed denies their responsibility for the persecution, and claiming that the victims suffered from mental pathology (or were poisoned, as some historians hypothesize) disguises how violent campaigns employed in the hunt for social deviants throughout history are inextricably bound to issues of power.

The Salem and Danvers Tercentennial Witch Trials Memorials

The memorial is surrounded on three sides by a granite wall. Inscribed on the threshold are the victims' protests of innocence. This testimony is interrupted mid-sentence by the wall, symbolizing society's indifference to oppression. Locust trees represent the stark injustice of the trials. At the rear of the memorial, tombstones in the adjacent cemetery represent all who stood in mute witness to this tragedy. Stone benches within the memorial perimeter bear the names and execution dates of the victims.

—Message at the entrance
to the Salem tercentennial memorial

The engraved granite block that marks the entrance to the Salem Witch Trials Memorial invites visitors into an experience markedly different from the spectacle of the shops, tours, and museums in downtown Salem. The memorial's setting is one of quiet serenity. Three solid granite walls enclose a small shaded, grassy space. Jetting from the walls are large stone blocks, each showing the name of one of the twenty victims. The memorial bears a striking resemblance to the Vietnam Veterans Memorial, not in its architecture but by the way in which it draws attention to the finality of the persecution. The Salem memorial unmistakably evokes death: it is flanked by one of the city's oldest cemeteries, where one of the trial judges is buried; the manner in which each victim was executed is engraved beneath her or his name; locust trees, the same species of tree from which the victims were supposedly hanged, line the memorial on all sides (and allude to Gallows Hill, a city park in the neighborhood development "Witchcraft Heights" that some believe lies near the execution site of the hunt). Another powerful reminder of the finality of the hunt is the granite threshold at the memorial's entrance. Engraved in the stone are actual pieces of testimony from the women and men accused of witchcraft. As the entrance plaque describes, the words are cut off mid-sentence, emphasizing not only that their pleas were not heard but that they never will be. The monument is, as others have pointed out about the Vietnam Veterans Memorial, a memorial for those who were killed (Carlson and Hocking 205; Foss 335).

The narrative that frames the tercentennial memorial differs from that of the attractions analyzed above, yet the centrality of the physical body as a site of violence and identification also prevents it from offering a nuanced critique of the persecution. According to the tourist office Web site, the memorial is meant to serve "as a reminder of the lessons of tolerance and understanding learned from the Salem Witch Trials," a "contemplative environment in which to evoke the spirit and strength of those people who chose to die rather than compromise their personal truths" ("Early Salem"). This statement is consistent with the message on the plaque at the memorial's entrance, which calls it a symbol for "society's indifference to oppression." An extra burden is thus added to the memorial's role, for it is meant to signify not only the violence of 1692 Salem but violence across societies and throughout history. When Elie Wiesel spoke at the memorial's dedication, he called on his audience to consider this dual role. "[F]anaticism is the greatest evil that faces us today," he said, "for today, too, there are Salems" (*Witch City*). The committee that approved and commissioned the memorial essentially created a monument that promised to remove the disguise operating in the museums, tours, and attractions of Salem. If Wiesel was correct, then this memorial would prompt visitors to think about the "fanaticism"—political, religious, social—that caused the Salem witch-hunt and, more important, to recognize that similar fanaticisms operating today create the conditions for future persecutions. This experience is a markedly different one than that provided by, say, the Salem Wax Museum, which encourages tourists to see the hunt as an historical anomaly born out of hysteria and madness.

Of course, few visitors to the Salem memorial were present at the dedication ceremony held in 1992. Most never got to hear Elie Wiesel's moving speech, hence they must make the connections between the 17th century and the present on their own. The memorial does not offer a detailed history on witch-hunting or other forms of persecution; instead, tourists must bridge the gap between past and present through what Diane Purkiss calls the "suffering female body" (14). This body, and the violence that was used against it, is represented throughout the memorial in the engraved granite blocks and their details of torture and execution and in the presence of the locust trees used to hang the victims. The stories that the memorial tells do move visitors to seek an empathic connection with the witch, but they do so by offering "an instructive spectacle of violation and dismemberment, offering no opportunity to the reader who wants to know" them (14). "Empathy differs from understanding," Purkiss explains, and discourses of execution and torture, with their emphasis on the suffering human body, do little to illuminate the causes of violence and witch-hunting (14). As long as death remains the central motif of the Witch Trials Memorial in Salem, it will only contribute to the multitude of discourses that disguise the complex roots of the witch trials and the possibility that Wiesel really is right—that today, too, there are Salems.

Another memorial to the hunt's victims that is not frequently mentioned in the Salem tourist literature was also erected in 1992, but in the neighboring town of Danvers. In 1692 Danvers was known as "Salem Village," a rural settlement directly north of present-day Salem. Several of the victims of the 1692 hunt were from Salem Village, making Danvers an appropriate site for commemorating the persecution. Like its sister memorial in the city of Salem, the Danvers memorial displays the names of the victims and the manner in which they were executed. It differs in several respects, though. The three large granite panels that compose the majority of the monument add a degree of historical specificity that the Salem memorial does not. Included are an additional four names of individuals who died while in jail, and the memorial indicates the town or settlement that each victim originated from. The center panel is flanked by two smaller, angled panels, each bearing the words of four victims, as well as the date and source of their testimonials. Although the Danvers memorial appears to present a slightly more nuanced commemoration of the 1692 hunt (especially in its geographical specificity, an allusion to the complex tensions between 17th-century Salem Village and Salem Town), the large granite pulpit that faces the victims' names frames the memorial with precisely the same narrative that dominates much of witch-hunt tourism in nearby Salem. The inscription engraved on the face of the granite reads, "In memory of those innocents who died during the Salem Village witchcraft hysteria of 1692." Hysteria, or a witch-craze, is again evoked as one of the defining features of the largest witch-hunt to occur in colonial America.[3]

Counter-Memory, or, Resisting the Disguise

Tourists who encounter the dominant narratives that frame Salem's violent history are encouraged, but not forced, to accept them. Acts of remembrance and commemoration, commercialized or not, can be reappropriated as sites of struggle when individuals and groups contest authoritative, institutional control over public remembrance. Such is the implicit argument throughout rhetorical scholar Barbara Biesecker's analysis of World War II popular memory texts, such as Steven Spielberg's film *Saving Private Ryan* or Tom Brokaw's book *The Greatest Generation*. In her essay she describes the way these texts function as "civics lessons," helping those who consume their discourses to organize a sense of national collective memory and, in the process, come to a better understanding of what U.S. identity and Americanness mean today (394). However, although these World War II texts exercise a powerful rhetorical influence on the public, Biesecker is careful to point out that their effects are never predetermined or forced on audiences. The political consequences of collective memory, she argues, "are an effect of *what* and *how* we remember, and the uses to which those memories are put" (406, emphasis added). Indeed, this is what I have attempted to show with my analysis of touristic texts in modern-day Salem. The meanings they communicate are not so potent or convincing that they are impossible to contest. Given that the dominant narratives that run through Salem's tourist attractions disguise the complex religious, social, political, and gendered aspects of witch persecutions, do some visitors choose to refuse that narrative, enact different scripts, or remember the hunt of 1692 in a different way? Are some able to see through the disguise?

For the answer to this question, I turn to a struggle that happened over the construction of the Salem Witch Trials Memorial. Like most texts of public and popular culture, monuments like this one can mean many different things to different groups of people. Their meaning is never static. On the contrary, monuments are dynamic sites of remembrance where public memory is continually contested and negotiated, even (especially) after a monument's construction and formal dedication (Blair, Jeppeson, and Pucci 277). Take Blair, Jeppeson, and Pucci's description of the Vietnam Veterans Memorial, for example: "[It] both comforts and refuses to comfort. It both provides closure and denies it. It does not offer a unitary message but multiple and conflicting ones" (281). Monuments do not operate as solitary, autonomous texts disconnected from any context or history; they share relationships with other monuments, museums, and souvenir shops, exercising their rhetorical power in the memories, fantasies, and lives of the tourists who come to experience the past through them.

Monuments can therefore serve as a site of intervention for what George Lipsitz calls "counter-memory." Counter-memory is an important strategy that underprivileged, disempowered groups can use to get *their* history heard. This is especially relevant in the context of Salem's tourist industry because, as Lipsitz explains, "counter-memory looks to the past for the hidden histories excluded from dominant narratives" (213). By "supplying new perspectives about the past" that give a voice to the voiceless, people can use monuments and memorials as opportunities to accept, engage, negotiate, or refuse dominant narratives and the histories they disguise (213).

Such was the case in 1992 when members of Salem's sizable Wiccan community protested the tercentennial memorial. Laurie Cabot, Salem's "official city witch," along with other practicing witches objected to the memorial's use of the word "witch." "Visitors to Salem will take away that witches are evil, Devil worshipers and Satanists," she said, and "it's against our civil rights, bordering on hate crime" (quoted in Brown F1). Following the lead of other oppressed communities who have fought to reappropriate and subvert the semiotic value of labels previously used against them, Salem's Wiccans assert ownership of the word "witch" and distinguish its modern meaning (a practitioner of a peaceful religion) from its early modern connections to *maleficium* (harmful magic) and Satanic pacts. For Cabot, what appears to be at stake is not the commemoration of the Salem trials but, rather, the right to self-definition. "Our enemies have defined us and have for many hundreds of years," she said, adding that "to have your enemies define you is the worst thing that can happen to a group historically" (F1).

Cabot's protests seem to have fallen on deaf ears among members of the tercentennial memorial committee. Linda McConchie, the committee's executive director, called Cabot's claims of discrimination "reprehensible and appalling" and said the committee was not responsible for promoting the Wicca religion (quoted in Brown F1). Another group unsympathetic to the Wiccans' message included Christian fundamentalists, who staged their own protests against the community of witches residing in Salem. In one example that bears a troubling resemblance to the public accusations common during Salem's 1692 hunt, a group of Christians encircled a woman on the street, grabbed her, raised her into the air, and called her a "witch" (F1). Evangelical minister Kevin Steigler, in remarks made about the Wiccans' protests, said that "they want to make sure that the tercentenary of the trials is in the news by saying that it is still happening, that there is intolerance today. Not true at all" (F1). Much like the dominant narratives of Salem tourism, the rhetoric of religious authorities like Steigler asserts that witch-hunting in Salem is a thing of the past and that even its modern-day manifestations have nothing to do with religious intolerance, violence, or power.

Clearly, the focal point for the tension between Salem's modern witches, Christian fundamentalists, and the tercentennial committee was religion and the struggle over the symbol "witch." What that highly charged word means, and who gets to determine its meaning, were central issues for the three groups that clashed in the months prior to the memorial's dedication. Given the numerous

levels on which the Wiccan community could have engaged the planned commemoration of the hunt's victims, it is interesting that they chose religion as their
point of entry. The dogmatic beliefs of Christian fundamentalists and the legal
restrictions that constrained the tercentennial committee's ability to recognize
established religions suggests that an alternative platform may have been more
effective. Regardless, it is an excellent example of how underprivileged groups
can assert their own stories and histories to the greater public. The Wiccan community in Salem exposed the way witchcraft accusations continue to sanction
and disguise violence, even now, more than 300 years after the 1692 hunt.

Toward a "Better" Tourism

Who am I to say "no" to tourism?

—Elie Wiesel, at the Salem
tercentennial memorial dedication (*Witch City*)

The purpose of this chapter has not been to present an indictment of the tourist
industry in Salem, Massachusetts, nor is it to suggest that Salem should stop
using the witch-hunt as a basis for inviting visitors to the city. Rather, I have
examined the dominant narratives that frame touristic experience in Salem to
show how they shape what the witch and witch-hunting mean for those who
visit the city. These narratives describe the persecution as the result of psychopathology and irrational hysteria and, in doing so, effectively disguise some
of the most important aspects of the Salem witch-hunt: first, that the trials and
executions were caused at least in part by tensions stemming from the transition to mercantile capitalism in the colonies, and second, that the "unruly"
women accused of witchcraft were threatening to those who held positions of
privilege and power in the patriarchal system that structured Puritan society in
17th-century New England. The narratives that Salem tourists encounter disguise
the relationships between patriarchy and gender, and capitalism and violence,
relationships essential for understanding why the hunt happened.

   This disguise has important implications for the modern tourist visiting
Salem today. The disguise is pervasive, working actively in museums, evening
walking tours, and monuments throughout the city. It hides the complex nature
of the 1692 hunt. It covers up the historical foundations of the trials even as it
entices visitors with the promise to reveal the secrets of the witch persecutions.
But that is not all that Salem tourism does. The true power of the discourse lies
in its ability to disguise the way the violence of 17th-century Salem is part of a
long tradition of monster-making in human history. In his book *At Stake:
Monsters and the Rhetoric of Fear in Public Culture*, Edward J. Ingebretsen argues

that societies seek out and label people as "monsters" because they believe that, in doing so, these less-than-humans can then take the responsibility for our own downfalls and weaknesses. "Monsters," says Ingebretsen, "are those who test the lines, those who fail to stay within the bounds of neighborliness—the ones who, for whatever reason, we no longer want. . . . Monsters cannot be allowed to live because they allow our slip to show" (204). They present a frightening vision of ourselves, and when language fails to offer a satisfactory explanation for social, economic, or political turmoil, the word "monster" is often used to bridge that gap, to explain the unexplainable (38). It then becomes a cover for doing all sorts of political work, oftentimes in violent, oppressive ways.

I agree with Purkiss in that those who create authoritative accounts of witch-hunting, like those offered in contemporary Salem, act "as if witchcraft were over and done, a marker of our difference from the past" (31). Witch-hunt tourism in Salem frames the 1692 hunt as a specific, hystericized phenomenon— something that happened to *those* (crazed) people, back *then*. It refuses to consider how much in common the modern tourist has with the victims who were persecuted three centuries ago. It denies, as Ingebretsen would say, that "the monster *is* us: bone of our bone, wish of our wish, or even ourselves, slightly out of focus—or maybe frighteningly focused" (203, emphasis in original).

While many historians argue against using the term "witch-hunt" to describe persecutions other than those that occurred in Europe and colonial America between 1450 and 1750, others have argued persuasively that the search for "witch-substitutes" continues today. Levack, for example, has described the unsettling similarities between Salem's hunt and Senator Joseph McCarthy's search for communists during the Red Scare of the 1950s, and how the current War on Terror has created the conditions for another witch-hunt (292–94). Levack even described the witches' sabbath, a sort of orgiastic party carried out by witches and demons that played a role in many witchcraft accusations, as "a universal nightmare that haunts people whenever the social order appears to be in danger" (303–4). Witch-hunt tourism in Salem denies this universality, thus giving the tourist an encounter with history that disguises how that history connects to his or her life, right now.

Dominant narratives and the stories (or histories) they disguise do not have to be definitive. Even dominant narratives are full of gaps that enable tourists to engage, resist, and reappropriate them. It is with this in mind that Bowman argues that "the remedy for 'bad' tourism isn't *no* tourism but *better* tourism" (105, emphasis in original). Touristic frames that hide notions of agency and the gendered, ideological nature of witchcraft persecutions (both past and present) do not, and should not, have the final word. One challenge, then—for both tourist and critic alike—is to engage the forces that shape public remembrance and to inject empowering counter-memories during the performances, discussions, even those quiet, introspective moments that characterize modern-day acts of tourism and commemoration. Disguises like the ones I have examined in this chapter might be operating in places tourists least expect them. Museum exhibits, art galleries, and heritage tours; visitors' information centers, travelers' guides, and tourist maps; amusement parks, film festivals, and town celebrations— each of these diverse, disparate elements that a vacationer might encounter tells a story. They are framed by a narrative, or narratives, that do rhetorical work leading to real-life consequences. A witch-hunt historian once wrote that "the witch may be the other, but witchcraft beliefs are in *ourselves*" (Briggs 411, emphasis added). This proposition may be difficult to accept because it encourages a degree of reflexivity that many find troubling, but it is that reflexivity, which can be developed through a critical awareness of the texts one consumes when adventuring in unfamiliar lands, that can open up the meaning of hidden messages and enrich one's experience as a tourist.

Notes

1. These statistics are remarkably similar to those cited by Dana Cloud in the introduction of her book *Control and Consolation in American Culture and Politics*. In 1994, the wealthiest 10% of the population controlled 66.8% of the nation's wealth (xi).

2. For a detailed critique of Freud's assertion that those who experienced demonic possession suffered from hysteria, see Heinemann 103–6.

3. Richard Trask, a historian and town archivist for Danvers who chaired the committee for the Danvers Witch Trials Memorial, also believes the hunt of 1692 was the result of what he calls a "massive clinical hysteria" (Trask). Two of his ancestors were executed in the 1692 trials.

10

Outing the Marlboro Man

Issues of Masculinity and
Class Closeted in _Brokeback Mountain_

Teresita Garza

I n December 2005 the film _Brokeback Mountain,_ a dramatic story of forbidden love between a Wyoming ranch hand and a rodeo bull rider, debuted in the United States. In Hollywood circles, the screenplay adaptation of Annie Proulx's 1997 short story was known as "the greatest unproduceable screenplay ever written" (Schamus quoted in "Sharing the Story"). Seven years passed before a willing director would bring the screenplay to life. Often referred to in the popular press as "the gay Cowboy movie," the film quickly became embroiled in controversy. Debates surrounding the film were fueled by disputes taking place over proposed public policies, state supreme court rulings on same-sex marriages, and the proposed federal marriage amendment.

In spite of such controversy, _Brokeback Mountain_ garnered fiscal success with U.S. box office returns estimated at $83 million, worldwide profits of $178 million, and $1.4 million in sales on the first day of its DVD release ("Brokeback Mountain"; Arnold). The film was nominated for eight Academy Awards and won three for best-adapted screenplay, best original score, and best director. Ang Lee became the first Asian to win an Academy Award for best director ("Taiwan Cheers"). At the 17th annual Gay and Lesbian Alliance Against Defamation (GLAAD) Media Awards, Lee accepted the top honor for best wide-release motion picture (Michaud).

Contentious situations often require filmmakers, authors, politicians, artists, community leaders, and so on to make rhetorical choices regarding how, or whether, to express particular attitudes, opinions, or perspectives on political or social issues. Social pressure, fear of repercussion, or uncertainty often contribute to the decision not to deal with social issues directly. Disguising or obscuring remarks or commentary through the use of metaphors, analogies, allusions, turns of phrases, catchwords, narratives, depictions, representations, topical substitutes, and other means becomes a common way to contend with controversial social issues. Sometimes disguising social issues functions as a way of reinforcing dominant attitudes. At other times, the concealment offers the rhetorical potential to promote critical engagement.

Given the social and political climate during the making of *Brokeback Mountain,* broader questions and conflicts regarding homophobia, classism, and cultural hegemony required careful rhetorical treatment by the filmmakers. Audiences mired in the daily discursive tinder of war, corporate scandal, and shrinking personal liberties were likely to have little tolerance for social sermons or cultural admonishment. Rather than deal with all of the potentially inflammatory social issues outright, *Brokeback Mountain* tells its story through layered and coded messages. Similar to the practice of signifyin(g) found in African American narratives such as Brer Rabbit or Native American stories of Trickster Coyote, the film relies on the audience to decipher the coded meanings and disguised social messages.

The layered or coded messages function as a hidden rhetoric. In place of explicit statements, *Brokeback Mountain* conceals or disguises arguments about social issues in a subtext underlying the primary storyline. However, the notion of hidden rhetoric should not be confused with the pseudo theory of subliminal advertising or the dubious marketing practice of product placement, which are premised on the unfounded claim that, by intentionally interring repetitive messages in texts, people can be made to react in a desired way (i.e., eat more popcorn or consume particular products). Rather, the coded messages or disguised social issues carried in hidden rhetoric require that both rhetoricians and audience members engage as active participants in a meaning-making process that is at once multifaceted and complex.

Homological Analysis

In his book, *Rhetorical Homologies: Form, Culture, Experience,* author Barry Brummett offers a pertinent explanation of the concept of homology. He describes a homology as "a formal resemblance, . . . a pattern that orders the content or physical manifestation of the message" (1, 3). In other words, homologies underscore the direct content of a message. Homologies are to messages what connotations are to words—the underlying associated part of meaning. Homologies, according to Brummett, serve as formal links across disparate categories of experience and function as lines of connection and influence (2, 154). For instance, buried in what outwardly appears to be an epic Western drama, we recognize the familiar form or pattern of a subtext about forbidden love stymied by social convention. We may even find the subtext proverbial, relevant, influential, reassuring, or applicable—in other words, homologous—to our own daily lives.

Homologies are rhetorical in that they carry the power to exercise influence between, among, and across seemingly dissimilar types of experiences or situations. A rhetorical homology according to Brummett refers to a "formal resemblance, grounded in discursive properties, that facilitates the work of political and social rhetoric, or influence" (3). A rhetorical homology buried in a love story that defies social conventions may implicitly confront our cultural values of class or gender, inspire us to rethink our definitions of love, or call into question the cultural politics we embrace. The more synonymous connections that are made between the story and our own experiences, or other texts, the more potent the homology.

The utility of homological analysis, as a method of rhetorical criticism, has to do with its capacity to reveal the rhetorical power of discourse formally concealed within a text. Here, discourse can be understood as the categories of belief, common sense, generally known statements, or acceptable accounts available about a topic to individuals in a particular historical moment. Discourse sets forth the conventional or institutional rules, knowledge, and power by which people are able to talk or write about something. In the introductory chapter of this book, Brummett stresses the heuristic power of homological analysis in unlocking the disguised thoughts, attitudes, and political and social convictions carried in texts. A homological analysis seeks to identify the taken-for-granted yet familiar forms of multilayered and polysemic meanings that are discretely hidden, coded, or disguised in the apparent order of a text or experience.

OUTING THE HOMOLOGICAL

Through a homological analysis of *Brokeback Mountain*, I hope to reveal the role that hidden rhetoric plays in texts, not only in this particular film, but also elsewhere in our lives. The social issues disguised in *Brokeback Mountain* may also be concealed in other popular films, in our favorite television sitcoms, in enduring literature, in memorable advertisements, in moving news stories, in compelling political campaigns, in online games, in cultural narratives, in our interpersonal discussions at home, work, and among friends. Exploring what lies beneath the surface of texts is crucial in guiding the critical thought needed to interpret and assess the power of persuasive efforts.

Knowing how others craft meaning at the implied formal level is instructive in our own rhetorical efforts. This is the case particularly when confronting critical social issues and seeking broad alliances among divergent groups. Whether you are trying to make sense of or promote a social movement, comprehend or produce a groundbreaking work of art, decide what candidate to support, affect positive social change, or create inclusion of difference, the capacity to read beyond surface messages as well as the ability to construct multilayered appeals contributes to a more comprehensive understanding of the power of rhetoric.

In this chapter, I contend that a homological analysis is particularly well suited to uncover the coded meanings and disguised social issues in a rhetorical text such as *Brokeback Mountain*. At first glance, *Brokeback Mountain* appears to be a dramatic film about gay cowboys in love; however, closeted in the rugged individualism and majestic landscape is formal rhetorical commentary about serious social issues and discursive convictions regarding the cultural constraints that idealizations of masculinity and class place on people and life situations.

I maintain that director Ang Lee's screen adaptation of author Annie Proulx's short story is steeped in numerous conflicting and disguised social issues. As Lee readily admits, "I always like making dramas, . . . which is about conflict. . . . You put different ingredients in conflict with each other, through which you examine humanity" (Lee). Furthermore, I argue that it is through its hidden rhetorical form that *Brokeback Mountain* is able to motivate audiences to reflect beyond the film's storyline about sexuality or sexual identity and to consider how underlying factors such as gender and class determine the ways in which people manage the constraints and opportunities posed in their everyday lives. The film is thus much more than a movie about gay cowboys; it is really about the constraints of masculinity, socioeconomic status, and cultural hegemony on our individual and collective being.

MASCULINITY AND CLASS

Masculinity and class are complex social issues that often work together behind the scenes of many cultural and public controversies. To examine how these social factors are operating beneath the plotline of *Brokeback Mountain,* it is necessary to review important developments and establish some working definitions. Once these basic concepts have been introduced, I will demonstrate the ways in which each operates through surreptitious rhetoric presented in key scenes and how they come together to complicate what ostensibly is a love story between two cowboys struggling with issues of sexuality and sexual identity.

Masculinity is most commonly misunderstood as the defining qualities, behaviors, and expectations that make up a normal, typical, or exemplary man. Such a definition is deceptively simple, however. Gender theorist Judith Butler argues that gender is not a quality with which we are born. Rather, she proposes the concept of performativity to explain that we perform gender via the cultural discourse that repetitively defines expected social norms. Philosopher Michel Foucault's scholarship suggests that masculinity and femininity, and for that matter sexuality, are the products of the discourse that regulates our being.

Over the last two decades, building on the works of Foucault and Butler, rhetoricians and other communication scholars working in the areas of feminism, performance studies, and cultural studies have increasingly begun to theorize and critique the normative power of masculinity in American culture. Scholars have examined the cultural, historical, mediated, and political representations of men, the performative aspects of masculinity in everyday life, and the social, economic, and health consequences posed by maintaining rigid notions of masculinity (e.g., Delgado; Ashcraft and Flores; Parry-Giles; Malin; Hanke; Palmer-Mehta; Clarkson; Baglia). Much of this current scholarship recognizes masculinity as a discursive, performative, cultural gender construction that describes and regulates the meaning of what it is to be a man or to be manly.

Basic definitions of class usually involve the categorization of people into groups based on shared socioeconomic status. In the United States, the conventional wisdom that America is a predominantly middle-class egalitarian society makes open discussion of class an uncomfortable subject, especially for those whose economic standing falls below or exceeds the assumed middle-class standard. As bell hooks, author of *Where We Stand: Class Matters*, writes, "It's the subject that makes us all tense, nervous, uncertain about where we stand" (vii).

Philosopher and historian Karl Marx argued that class designation (i.e., proletariat, petit-bourgeois, bourgeois) is related to the means of production (i.e., capitalism). In a society such as the United States, capitalism is the means of production around which social relations based on power and privilege are organized. Owners profiting from their industry are classified as the bourgeois, whereas the workers who labor in industry for low wages are designated members of the proletariat. Marx maintained that in a capitalist society the ruling bourgeois classes not only control the means and relations of production but also political, cultural, and intellectual life (Marx and Engels). In *Capital*, Marx critically analyzed capitalist production and examined the material inequities between classes, which he theorized would give rise to unified class-consciousness among the proletariat and result in antagonisms that would eventually lead the proletariat to overthrow capitalism and end class division.

Drawing from the work of Antonio Gramsci, post-Marxist theorists Ernesto LaClau and Chantal Mouffe offer an alternative to Marx's fixed notion of class and unified class-consciousness. As they explain in *Hegemony and Socialist Strategy: Towards a Radical Democratic Politics*, class is not tied to the means of production or to socioeconomic conditions but, rather, is the result of discourse and hegemonic practice. In other words, people are not fixed into particular designations of subordination at the hands of one particular social group; instead, people participate in the discursive ideological construction—"definition and articulation"—of their social, political, economic, religious, and historical identities and relations (153). In addition, LaClau and Mouffe claim that it is possible for individuals to hold multiple subject positions, or social identities, and to collectively maintain a "plurality of diverse and frequently contradictory positions" (84). LaClau and Mouffe argue that resistance or struggle against inequality does not result from a unified class-consciousness but becomes possible in the moment that democratic discourse makes available an alternative imaginary (155).

Yet, they also recognize that eradication of one inequality does not ensure the elimination of other inequalities (192). They thus advance an understanding of class particularly relevant to comprehending the ways in which class can remain hidden in discourse. For instance, a gay man or a woman of color who rises from poverty to wealth must still contend with discursive inequalities constructed around his sexuality or her race. Class, then, involves discursive assumptions and expressions of what it means to be homeless, poor, working class, middle class, upper class, prosperous, rich, well off, affluent, or wealthy in relation to contending subject positions of race, ethnicity, nationality, gender, age, sexuality, ability, and so on.

Exposing Masculinity and Class Matters in a Poor Man's West

THE MARLBORO MEN LOOK FOR WORK

Masculinity and class are masked from the onset of this seemingly classic Western. The film opens with a standard panoramic view of a sunrise breaking through the silhouetted peaks of a Western mountain range. The title, *Brokeback Mountain*, appears in white text, and the faint sounds of chirping birds along a desolate road become audible. As the title fades away, however, instead of the expected horse and rider featured in most Western epics, we see in their place the faint headlights of a semitruck. The theme song begins to play deliberately, note by note, as the camera follows the truck from the bottom right to the left side of the screen along a winding, open road. As dawn breaks, the truck stops, the passenger door opens, and out steps one of the main characters, Ennis Del Mar.

Ennis Del Mar's arrival in town by way of the passenger seat of a semitruck is an unexpected mode of transportation for a cowboy. A faithful horse or, in more contemporary settings, a pickup truck is the expected means of transport for a "real" Western cowboy. At the formal level, his arrival works to establish Ennis as a man of meager financial means and alerts the audience that this is not a typical Western. As the semitruck pulls away, a subtitle appears, informing us that the year is 1963 and the place is Signal, Wyoming. The camera follows Ennis, clad in jeans and other Western wear reminiscent of the Marlboro man, as he walks toward a group of buildings in what appears to be a small rural town. The town is set under fleecy cumulus clouds bearing the subtle yet visible signs of stormy weather ahead.

The scene cuts to Ennis leaning against the green, wood-paneled wall of a trailer. He waits silently, just to the left of the main door. His rolled-up brown paper grocery sack, containing a change of clothes, is perched within arms reach on the top step of the stairs leading to the trailer door. A train passes by, obstructing our full view of Ennis; we see his lower extremities and catch occasional glimpses of his body between the moving train cars. Finally, the train nears its end, and a medium shot shows Ennis smoking a cigarette, which he puts out halfway through and saves. This scene again stresses Ennis's working-class identity. His frugality is symbolized by the brown paper grocery sack serving as his luggage and by his cigarette rationing. His need for work signifies his working-class status.

A black, backfiring 1950s GMC pickup truck enters the scene and sputters to a stop near the trailer where Ennis waits. The driver, Jack Twist, gets out of the truck and gives the pickup's fender a swift kick, followed by a curse word and look of consternation. The fact that Jack arrives in a pickup truck, albeit old and in disrepair, signifies Jack's economic privilege over Ennis. Once Jack cools down and realizes he has an audience, he calmly places his hands on his hips and, in a John Wayne pose, turns slowly and walks a few steps toward Ennis. Ennis avoids eye contact and shuffles awkwardly as Jack looks toward him. Seeing Ennis's discomfort, Jack turns away and gazes out toward the horizon. While Jack's back is turned, Ennis cautiously surveys the situation before resetting his sight to the ground at his feet. Jack turns and stares back at an unresponsive Ennis. Jack pauses, places an out-stretched arm on the side of his truck, and reposes momentarily. The scene cuts to Jack's driver-side mirror, which reflects an image of Ennis, apparently sometime later, now seated on the stairs. Jack secretly observes Ennis in his side-view mirror as he gives himself a shave.

These early scenes establish class and masculinity in the subtext of *Brokeback Mountain*. Beneath the Marlboro man exterior projected by Ennis and Jack's John Wayne posturing are incongruent understandings of what being a man means, particularly as presumed in rural Western culture. The discourse and discursive practices in place during Ennis and Jack's time prefigure their possibilities. Rural masculinity in the 1960s came with very specific traditional convictions and expectations. Traditional views of masculinity and manhood placed value on whiteness, independence, power, control, reason, able-bodied strength, hard work, self-reliance, stoicism, heterosexual prowess, and endurance of a hardscrabble life. Historically, women, children, and people of color held a place beneath white men on the social hierarchy. The characteristics prescribed to women and children such as communicative expression (verbal, artistic, interpersonal, etc.), domesticity, gentleness, kindness, tenderness, affection, emotion, and playfulness were devalued.

Thus, Ennis and Jack find themselves in a situation where they are compelled to express their manliness through stoic silence and disinterested posturing. To appear friendly or engage in verbal repartee would compromise their subject positions as "real" rural Western men. Ennis's resemblance to the Marlboro man and Jack's John Wayne kinesics are visual expressions of the characters' inner desire to fit the masculine standards of their time—at least in outward appearance. Figures like the Marlboro man and John Wayne were not only symbolic of Western men but were upheld as traditional and exemplary representations of masculinity for rural men during this time. In these emblems of manliness, "masculinity is figured as a storehouse of toughened warrior energy ready to be unleashed on any transgressive character" (Malin 26). The romanticized ideal of Western manhood made no other allowances, especially for working-class men living in rural America. The material conditions of rural poverty and the history of culturally sanctioned violence in the West work in consort with these traditional ideas of masculinity to keep the culture in check.

We are now over 4 full minutes into the film and not a single word of dialogue has been spoken. Suddenly, a speeding station wagon, symbolic of family virtue, approaches and pulls up so close to where Ennis is seated that it startles him to his feet. Joe Aguirre, the foreman and a toughened warrior for whom Ennis and Jack have been waiting, has just arrived. Without acknowledging either Jack or Ennis, Aguirre (donning dark sunglasses, wearing a classic Western wrangler hat, and carrying a large silver thermos) enters the trailer and promptly shuts the door behind him. Aguirre abruptly breaks the excruciating silence by flinging open the trailer door and shouting, "If you pair a deuces are looking for work I suggest you get your scrawny asses in here pronto!"

Ennis and Jack take their cue and quickly enter the trailer. Inside, seated behind his metal desk, Aguirre enacts his position of overseer by delivering the work detail in a rapid-fire series of surly commands:

> Up on Brokeback, the Forest Service got designated campsites on the allotments. Them camps can be three, four miles from where we pasture the woollies. Bad predator loss if there's nobody lookin' after 'em at night. Now, what I want is a camp tender to stay in the main camp, where Forest Service says. But the herder, he's gonna pitch a pup tent on the q.t. with the sheep and he's gonna sleep there. You eat your supper and breakfast in the camp, but you sleep with the sheep, 100%. No fire, don't leave no sign. You roll up that tent every mornin' case the Forest Service snoops around.

The phone rings; Aguirre answers the call, curtly responds to the caller, hangs up, and then continues:

> You got the dogs, your .30–30. You [pointing at Jack] sleep there. Last summer I had goddamn near 25% loss. I don't want that again. You [now pointing at Ennis and standing to retrieve a watch from atop a gray file cabinet], Fridays at noon be down at the bridge with your grocery list and mules. Somebody with supplies will be there with a pickup [he stands up and tosses Ennis a watch]. Tomorrow morning we'll truck you up the jump-off.

Aguirre concludes by lighting a cigarette and returning to his chair. He tosses his silver lighter on the desk, picks up the phone, and gives Jack and Ennis a cold, steely stare. Aguirre's display of authoritative, hardnosed, no nonsense masculinity obscures an ideological assumption about class. He is the top dog in the superior position of foreman presumably because the best always rises to the top. Ennis, Jack, and others like them find themselves in lowly positions because of their own incompetence or lack of work ethic. The fact that Ennis and Jack are white, young, able-bodied men makes them suspect in the eyes of this weathered veteran. Either a lack of intelligence, poor work ethic, or some sort of deviance has landed them in their desperate situation. As far as Aguirre is concerned, they cannot be trusted and will require stern supervision and constant surveillance.

Jack and Ennis are intimidated by Aguirre's terseness, and without any further exchanges they quickly vacate the trailer. Once outside and away from the tough guy vim and vigor, Jack lights a cigarette while Ennis fumbles with the watch Aguirre had tossed at him. Jack extends a hand and introduces himself to Ennis. Ennis shakes Jack's hand and says, "Ennis." Jack, joking but mindful of proper manners, inquires, "Your folks just stop at Ennis?" Ennis adds, "Del Mar." "Well, nice to know you, Ennis Del Mar," intones Jack. With minimal introductions out of the way, the two make their way to a local bar.

At the bar, Jack tells Ennis that this is his second year at this job and that, last year during a storm, lightning killed 42 sheep. He remarks that he thought he'd asphyxiate from the smell and that Aguirre got "all over my ass, like I was suppose to control the weather." He admits to Ennis that it "beats working for my old man. Can't please my old man, no way. That's why I took to rodeoin'." Jack asks Ennis if he ever "rodeos," and Ennis answers, "You know, I mean, once in a while. When I got the entry fee in my pocket. Yeah." Jack asks Ennis if he's "from ranch people." Ennis replies, "Yeah, I was." Jack wonders out loud, "your folks run you off?" Ennis coyly explains, "No, they run themselves off. There was one curve in the road in 43 miles, and they missed it. So the bank took the ranch, and my brother and sister, they raised me, mostly." Jack responds, "shit, that's hard!" Ennis pulls out the half-smoked cigarette he had stored away earlier, and Jack hands him a lighter.

This exchange of self-disclosure not only establishes their common family dysfunction but also hints at shared class experience. Shrouded in Jack's comparison between Aguirre the boss and his own overbearing father are implications regarding the oppressive power wrought by the old guard of masculinity. For Jack the rodeo may have been an escape from his father's arrogance and dominance; however, it did not provide any class liberation. The poor compensation and dangerous work conditions were inescapable. Yet, Jack's struggles pale in comparison to the curve of misfortune and hardship Ennis faced when he and his siblings were orphaned.

HERDING SHEEP AND SHEPHERDING ONE ANOTHER

The next day Jack and Ennis gather their supplies along with the livestock and begin heading up Brokeback Mountain. As we watch the sheep being herded, we are vividly reminded that Jack and Ennis are not the legendary cowboys depicted in Western lore; they are, in fact, shepherds. The class rank of sheep tenders in the Western hierarchy couldn't be much lower. In an essay titled "Getting Movied," the author of the original "Brokeback Mountain" short story, Annie Proulx, writes about the lowly stature of herding sheep in places like Wyoming. She explains that "real cowpokes" despised sheep and that in previous decades Basques (ethnic peoples from the Pyrenees of northeastern Spain and southwestern France) were hired as flock herders (130). We are left to wonder whether any of those early headers might have shared the Spanish surnames of Aguirre or Del Mar. Regardless of ethnicity, Proulx's research confirms that "jobs were scarce in Wyoming in that period," that is, the early 1960s, and not only were "white ranch kids" hired as sheep tenders, "even married couples with children got hired to herd sheep" (133).

Ennis and Jack trek their flock past rolling rivers, through evergreen-filled valleys, over low-lying streams, and up to the mountainside meadow. Together, up on Brokeback, the two men build camp near a rushing river and settle into a daily rhythm, Jack tending the sheep, Ennis preparing meals. The natural terrain surrounding them is awesomely spectacular. The cycling sunsets, moonlight, and sunrises over the mountain views are strikingly magnificent. However, shadowed in this picturesque splendor are the irony and contradiction of a difficult life replete with unseen perils, such as monotony, isolation, loneliness, and ever-present physical danger.

AGAINST THE RULES AND FORMS OF RESISTANCE

Early one morning, as Ennis prepares yet another round of eggs, potatoes, and beans for breakfast, Jack registers his grievance. Drowsily he complains, "Oh, shit. Can't wait till I get my own spread and I won't have to put up with Joe Aguirre's crap no more." In a sympathetic attempt, Ennis interjects, "I'm savin' for a place myself. Alma and me, we're gonna get married when I come down off this mountain." Jack ignores Ennis's comment and continues with his grievance: "Shit, that stay with the sheep, no fire bullshit. Aguirre got no right makin' us do somethin' against rules." As Ennis cleans up the morning meal, Jack mounts his uncooperative horse and leaves in a frustrated huff to go tend the sheep. Another day passes, and Jack adamantly says to Ennis, "no more beans."

Jack's verbal tirades about Joe Aguirre and beans are more than what they appear on the surface. They are roundabout objections to the oppressive conditions wrought by masculine dominance and the poverty he is forced to contend with in his daily life. Unable or unwilling to articulate the pain and suffering caused by his subjugation, Jack channels his defiance by vilifying Aguirre as a tyrant and by protesting beans for what they represent: the food-stuff of poor peasantry.

As the week rolls on, Jack attempts to shoot a coyote and misses. The implied meaning of Jack's missed shot is significant. His inability to shoot a coyote in broad daylight makes his already enigmatic masculinity even more problematic. After all, what kind of a Western man can't shoot a coyote in plain sight? The patriarchs of traditional Western rural culture would likely regard Jack's poor mastery of weaponry and futile command over nature as a sign of weakness.

Friday arrives, and Ennis must submit his grocery list to their supplier for the following week. As a favor to Jack, Ennis puts in a special request for soup (a middle-class commodity) instead of beans. Ennis's gesture signals his will-ingness to accommodate Jack's desires. On his way back to camp with the week's supplies, Ennis unexpectedly comes across a bear. The bear frightens Ennis's horse, which throws him to the ground. Alarmed, his horse and the pack mules run away, leaving Ennis trailing in their tracks. Ennis finds himself at the mercy of nature. His lack of control over the unruly animals signals a deficiency of manly power by Western rural standards. A "real" Western man would have exerted his dominance accordingly by tying the mules securely, managing the reins effectively, and promptly shooting the bear.

GENDERED ROLES AND TRADING PLACES

Later that day, Jack arrives in camp, and Ennis is nowhere to be found. Late into the evening, Ennis enters the camp with his horse and mules in tow. Angry at having had no supper, Jack yells out, "Where the hell you been? Been up with the sheep all day, I get down here hungry as hell and all I find is beans." Jack's vehement outburst is the sort of classic gender entitlement acted out in many a familiar domestic scene. We've seen it played out in American television sitcoms, films, commercials, and in actual households. As the story goes, the famished, breadwinning patriarch arrives home, expecting his wife, domestic partner, or housekeeper to have a delicious and impeccably prepared meal ready for his immediate consumption. When the reality proves otherwise, the male figurehead becomes enraged, as though his masculine honor and privilege have been unduly affronted, and he unleashes his fury in words or action upon those closest to him.

Undaunted, Ennis storms past Jack and takes a seat beside the campfire. In the firelight, Jack catches a glimpse of blood on Ennis's face. In a more subdued voice, Jack asks, "What in the hell happened, Ennis?" Still reeling from the inci-dent, Ennis describes his encounter with the bear. Jack removes a bandanna from his neck, dips it in the hot water boiling on the campfire, and begins to wipe blood from the fresh wound on the side of Ennis's face. Ennis takes over, tending to his own wound. Jack sits on the ground next to Ennis and says, "Well we gotta do something about this food situation. Maybe I'll shoot one of the sheep." Annoyed, Ennis admonishes Jack by reminding him that they are supposed to "guard the sheep, not eat 'em." The next day, to appease Jack and in an effort to reclaim his superiority over nature, Ennis shoots an elk. That night he and Jack feast on elk meat.

Still discontent with his sheep-guarding duties, Jack repeats a now familiar refrain, "Aguirre got no right to make me do this." In yet another attempt to pacify Jack, Ennis suggests that they switch places: "I won't mind bein' out there." Jack stubbornly argues, "That ain't the point. The point is we both ought to be in this camp." Ennis repeats his suggestion: "I won't mind bein' out there."

At this stage in their partnership, Jack has been quite demanding. His complaints are unrelenting. Ennis, on the other hand, has made do with what little they have and with the difficulties presented. He has even gone out of his way to ensure Jack's contentment. They finally come to an agreement, and that night they reverse their roles: Ennis becomes the herder, and Jack, the camp tender. This role reversal carries significantly more meaning than a simple transposition of duties, however. For Jack the reversal becomes an act of defiance, a break from the rules imposed by Aguirre's patriarchal power. For Ennis it becomes a defining moment of empowerment.

FORTY WINKS AND BREAKING MORE RULES

Up on Brokeback, Ennis and Jack endure the hardships and isolation brought by unrelenting tasks, mundane food, treacherous weather, and cold nights. Though separated during the day by the compulsory tasks of herder and camp tender, at night they bond over whiskey, cigarettes, and campfire talk of horses, rodeos, recollections, daily events, and future prospects. Late one evening, after too much whiskey, Ennis is too drunk to return to his mandatory post with the sheep. He stays in camp and sleeps near the fire. Jack offers to share the tent with Ennis, but he refuses. After awakening to the sound of Ennis's clattering teeth, Jack demands that Ennis quit his "hammering" and get in the tent. That night, huddled together in the cold, Jack initiates sex, and Ennis takes control by brusquely obliging.

FIRST LIGHT AND A NEW DAY

Ennis and Jack greet the next day and their newfound intimacy with awkward silence followed by prolonged avoidance. The day almost passes before Ennis finally speaks to Jack. "This is a one-shot thing we got goin' on here," he murmurs. "Nobody's business but ours," agrees Jack. Ennis, as though addressing an unseen phantom from his past, insists, "You know I ain't queer." Jack, a bit reticent, affirms, "me neither." The denial of their feelings and their sexuality is staunchly informed by their internalized conceptions of masculinity and class. The rules of traditional masculinity mandate heterosexuality. Western rural ranching culture equated heterosexual courtship with entrance into manhood. High value was placed on young men finding a wife and procreating. Typically, a ranch family was large to help distribute the workload. The venerated family structure consisted of a father, a mother, and a half-dozen children or more. The more sons a man had, the more prized the family. The discursive possibilities were very strict. Any variance from the expectation was deemed problematic, even deviant, and was not beyond harsh reprimand or violent reprisal.

BAD NEWS AND LESS PAY

Despite their obstinate avowal, Ennis and Jack continue their relationship. Their one-shot, one-night stand develops into a bond of loving and tender affection. Before the summer's end, an early snowstorm and Joe Aguirre—citing predictions of an impending early winter—prematurely force Ennis and Jack off the mountain. By this point, the audience is aware that Joe Aguirre has been watching the pair from afar through a set of high-powered binoculars. He has witnessed the attention they've given each other at the expense of the sheep and finds it necessary to restore order. Jack informs Ennis that Aguirre has visited and instructed them to "bring 'em down." Ennis takes issue with the demand, arguing that the snow "barely stuck" and that Aguirre "is cutting us out of a whole month's pay." Borrowing one of Jack's phrases, Ennis grumbles, "it ain't right!" Jack offers to lend Ennis some money. Unhappy at Jack's charity-case insinuation, Ennis rails, "I don't need your money; I ain't in the poorhouse."

During their last moments on the mountain, Jack playfully ropes Ennis with a lariat and lassos him to the ground. Ennis pulls Jack down with him, and the two begin wrestling for dominance as they roll downhill. Soon the playful romp erupts into a fierce struggle. Jack unleashes a blow drawing blood from Ennis's nose. Remorseful at the sight, Jack attempts to stop Ennis's bleeding with his shirtsleeve; Ennis retaliates with a surprise punch, landing it squarely on Jack's jaw.

Ennis and Jack's scuffle seems an immature response to their conflicted feelings for each other and their impending separation, a type of schoolyard altercation between young boys with something to prove. Their fistfight, however, hides their fear of and disillusionment with traditional manhood. In the world they are about to reenter—where the only acceptable physical contact between men is in sports and violence—their hyper-masculine brawl is a thinly veiled attempt to assure themselves and those they are about to encounter of their manliness.

GOING SEPARATE WAYS

Eventually, the two descend from the mountain, collect their pay, and reluctantly exchange final farewells. Ennis scoffs, "I can't believe I left my damn shirt up there." "Yeah," replies Jack. Jack asks, "You gonna do this again next summer?" "Well, maybe not," answers Ennis. He reminds Jack, "Like I said, me and Alma is gettin' married in November. So, ah, I'll try to get somethin' on the ranch, I guess. And you?" Jack replies, "Might go up to my daddy's place and give him a hand through the winter. I might be back. If the Army don't get me." Ennis responds, "Well, I guess I'll see you around, huh?" "Right," says Jack. With no further discussion and without as much as a handshake, the two depart—Jack in his truck; Ennis on foot.

Their casual departure falls within the unspoken rules of working-class rural men's expected behavior in two major ways. First, showing any emotion, embracing, or prolonging goodbyes are acceptable behaviors for women and children but not for real men. Even to drive away together would have been questionable. Second, they had each given their word. To go back on their promise that this was a "one-shot thing" would have compromised their integrity. As an out-of-work ranch hand and aspiring bull rider, the only real assets they possess are their word and reputation.

As Jack drives away, he watches regretfully in his side-view mirror as the distance between Ennis and him grows. The reality of their separation hits Ennis so hard that he's completely overcome by emotion. Despondent, he ducks between two buildings and breaks down—gasping, retching, and cursing uncontrollably.

ROUGH TIMES

That December Ennis marries Alma. Though they have little money, they spend time together tobogganing in the snow and going to movies at the drive-in theater. Ennis temporarily takes a job shoveling hot asphalt as a highway construction laborer. Soon Alma is pregnant. While Ennis takes on the role of family man, Jack returns to Brokeback Mountain. He asks Joe Aguirre about a job on Brokeback and inquires about whether Ennis has been around. Aguirre throws Jack an accusatory glare and sharply responds, "You boys sure found a way to make the time pass up there." Just about then Jack notices the binoculars hanging on the wall. Aguirre continues, "Twist, you guys wasn't gettin' paid to leave the dogs babysit the sheep while you stemmed the rose. Get the hell out of my trailer." Jack promptly leaves the trailer.

Though Ennis appears to fulfill the requisites of manhood, he struggles to measure up to particular standards. His income as a ranch hand constantly puts his role of provider in jeopardy. His insufficient wage barely pays the rent, and the work offers little job security. He and Alma have children, neither of whom are boys. They name their daughters Alma Jr. and Jenny. By giving the eldest the moniker of Alma Jr., Ennis symbolically fulfills the expectation of fathering a "Junior" offspring.

ROPED IN BY A RODEO QUEEN

Unable to secure further employment on Brokeback Mountain, Jack returns to the rodeo circuit. Jack also struggles to meet the demands of manhood. Though the calf ropers and rodeo clowns enjoy admiration and respect, Jack struggles for attention as a mediocre bull rider.

During a rodeo, Jack meets Lureen, a rodeo queen barrel racer whose wealthy father runs a successful farm equipment business. After a whirlwind night together, during which Lureen initiates sex in the back of her new convertible, she and Jack begin a relationship. Eventually, they marry and settle in Texas, and Lureen gives birth to a baby boy they name Bobby. Lureen's pompous father, L. D. Newsome, believes his daughter has married beneath her class and takes sadistic joy in emasculating Jack at every opportunity. He insists on calling Jack "rodeo" instead of using his given name. This is L. D.'s way of constantly reminding Jack of his humble origins and undeserved privilege.

Ennis and Jack try to live straight, heterosexual lives. They fulfill the roles of husbands and fathers to the best of their abilities. Ennis, however, finds Alma's desire to have a social life and live in town stressful and at odds with his preference for isolation and rural living. Jack finds his domineering father-in-law's constant presence in his family life suffocating. Both Ennis and Jack long for the unconditional love and freedom from the constraints of manhood that they experienced together that summer on Brokeback Mountain.

DROPPING A LINE

After a 4-year lapse in contact, Ennis receives a postcard sent via general delivery by Jack. The postcard reads, "Friend, this letter is long overdue. Hope you get it. Heard you was in Riverton. I'm coming through on the 24th, thought I'd stop and buy you a beer. Drop me a line if you can, say you're there." Ennis makes his way to the post office to send his reply to Jack. He addresses a postcard to Jack in Texas and writes, "You bet." He signs the postcard, adds his address, and sends it on its way.

The day of Jack's arrival, Ennis is nervous with anticipation. Alma suggests they get a babysitter and take Jack to a restaurant. Ennis insists that "Jack ain't the restaurant type" and that they'll probably go out drinking if he even shows. Buried in this seemingly innocuous comment is a contradiction that reveals a rift in Ennis and Alma's class interests. For Alma, social activities represent an escape from the isolated, self-sustaining rural life that Ennis seeks. Even something as simple as going to a restaurant is a luxury she desires. Though Ennis still regards Jack as a struggling bull rider, Jack's marriage to Lureen now affords him the comforts that come with material wealth and convenience.

When Jack finally arrives, Ennis cannot contain his excitement. He dashes out of his apartment, races down the stairs, and greets Jack with a heaving embrace. Ennis pulls Jack up against a wall, and they kiss passionately. Alma is heading out the front door to greet Ennis's friend when she sees Ennis and Jack kissing. Shaken by what she sees, she cautiously retreats back inside. She struggles to make sense of what she saw and to decide how to proceed, for Alma, too, has been raised to value the same traditional ideas of masculinity and family. This is the second time in their marriage that she has witnessed a side of Ennis that she did not know existed. Ennis's response to Jack is similar in intensity yet opposite the fury he had unleashed one Fourth of July when he assaulted two disrespectful bikers. She is unsure what to make of Ennis's capacity for such reckless abandon and violent passion.

By now Ennis and Jack have made their way up the stairs and into the hallway near the kitchen, where Alma is standing numb in disbelief. Ennis introduces Jack, and Alma responds with a barely audible "hello." The men go on chattering about their children as Alma tries to remain calm and collected. Ennis announces that they're "goin' out drinking and might not get back tonight." As the two leave, Jack politely turns to Alma and says, "pleased to meet you, ma'am."

Jack and Ennis are eager to rekindle their relationship. They check into an old rundown motel and spend the evening together. They talk as they lie awake in bed, catching up on their lives. Jack says to Ennis, "Old Brokeback got us good, didn't it? So what're we gonna do now?" Ennis's financial situation does not afford him the luxury to think about anything else but his family's basic survival. Ennis reasons that there's nothing they can do, that he's "stuck" with the life he has and all he has time for is making a living.

The very next day, Jack and Ennis head to the mountains for their first so-called "fishing trip," despite Alma's concern that Ennis's foreman might fire him for his absence. That night around the campfire, Ennis and Jack quickly fall back into their old Brokeback Mountain rhythm. Jack reflects, "You know, it could be this way. Just like this, always." Ennis retorts, "Yeah? How you figure that?" Jack brings up the idea that they could have "a little ranch together somewhere, little cow and calf operation; it be some sweet life. Hell, Lureen's old man, you bet he'd give me a down payment if I'd get lost. Already more less said it."

Ennis reiterates, "Told you, ain't goin' to be that way. What I'm sayin', you got your wife and baby down in Texas; I got my life in Riverton." With some resentment in his voice, Jack barks, "Is that so? You and Alma, that's a life?" Ennis curtly admonishes Jack, "Shut up about Alma. This ain't her fault." Ennis continues, "Bottom line, we're around each other and this thing grabs on to us again in the wrong place, wrong time, we'll be dead."

In a flashback, we are transported to 1952, where Ennis as a child is seen standing with his father and brother looking at a mutilated corpse. Ennis explains that there were two old guys, named Earl and Rich, who ranched together back in his hometown. He describes them as "a joke in town, even though they was pretty tough old birds." One day Earl was found dead in a ditch. Ennis goes on, "They'd took a tire iron to him, spurred him up, drug him around by his dick till it pulled off." Jack is horrified. "You seen that?" he asks. Ennis affirms, "I was, what, 9 years old? My daddy, he made sure me and my brother seen it. Hell, for all I know, he done the job. Two guys livin' together? No way. We can get together once in awhile way the hell out in the back of nowhere, but . . . ." Jack interrupts with a protest about having waited 4 years already. Ennis retorts, "If you can't fix it, Jack, you gotta stand it." Jack wants to know, however, how long he must endure. "Long as we can ride it," remarks Ennis. " Ain't no reins on this one." Ennis's rodeo reference is not lost on Jack.

For the first time in the film, we understand the depth of Ennis's internalized fear and self-hatred. For a father to attempt to instill such a distorted lesson at such a formative age is cruelty beyond reproach. The homophobia imparted to Ennis left him permanently scarred, making it nearly impossible for him to communicate or convey emotion. Yet, it's not his sexuality that Ennis fears but rather what it can bring. The ruthless and destructive power wrought up by hate-filled patriarchs is what makes him cower. His suspicion that his father "done the deed" taught Ennis two things: no one can be trusted, and a love affair between two men is best kept a quiet tryst.

DIVORCE GRANTED AND THANKSGIVING

Ennis and Alma's poverty and conflicting class aspirations begin to drive them further and further apart. One night in bed, their relationship reaches a critical turning point. Concerned about their ability to support any additional children (and troubled by Ennis's aversion to sex in the missionary position), Alma insists that Ennis take precautions. Insulted by Alma's intimation that he's not measuring up as head of household, Ennis coldly remarks, "If you don't want no more my kids, I'll be happy to leave you alone." Alma meekly replies under her breath, "I'd have 'em, if you'd support 'em." This conversation marks the beginning of the end. Eventually, Alma and Ennis divorce.

Jack remains hopeful that Ennis's divorce will give them the opportunity to finally join their lives together. Jack makes the long drive to Wyoming to be with Ennis. When Ennis turns him away, he is devastated. His eternal optimism is crushed under the weight of Ennis's conformity. On the drive home, still hurting from Ennis's rejection, Jack undergoes a change of heart. From then on, he becomes a bit more jaded about love and a bit more resolute about his desires. Rather than face his family, he takes a detour to Mexico in search of a one-night stand.

Jack's father-in-law becomes more insufferable with each passing day. The relationship between Jack and L. D. moves beyond the antagonistic. During

Thanksgiving dinner, L. D. contradicts both Lureen and Jack's authority by encouraging Bobby to view the football game during their meal. L. D. says to Lureen, "You want your son to grow up to be a man don't you, daughter?" The comment infuriates Jack. He musters his new resolve to confront L. D.'s macho arrogance once and for all. "This is my house! This is my child! And you are my guest!" insists Jack. "So sit the hell down, or I'll knock your ignorant ass into next week." L. D. complies, and Bobby minds his dad.

Thanksgiving Day proves challenging for Ennis, as well. Single now, he spends Thanksgiving with his girls, Alma, and her new husband. That evening, alone in the kitchen with Ennis, Alma confronts him about his relationship with Jack. Ennis tries to reassure her that it meant nothing, until she calls Jack "Jack Nasty." Ennis becomes enraged, threatens Alma, and storms out of the house. Unable to cope with what has transpired Ennis, heads to a bar, and, in yet another attempt to regain control over his threatened masculinity, he starts a fight. Though he loses the brawl, his show of hyper-masculinity provides him with some reassurance.

LET IT BE

Over the span of 20 years, Ennis and Jack rely on their "fishing trips" as a way to reconnect and enjoy a respite from the trials and tribulations of manly life. They plan their rendezvous in the isolated mountain ranges surrounding Wyoming in places reminiscent of Brokeback Mountain. Their time together is often bittersweet. In lighter moments, they tease one another or trade stories about the woman Ennis is seeing and the rancher's wife Jack is pursuing. Their boasting, though jocular, masks their continued need to engage the expectations of heterosexuality. Their more serious discussions often center on what could have been. Departures are still particularly painful triggers.

On one occasion as they are preparing to part company, Jack and Ennis reopen longstanding wounds. The argument begins when Ennis informs Jack that he won't be able to meet up with him again in August and that they'll need to wait until November. An intense argument ensues in which Jack registers his complaints about their infrequent meetings, which always take place in the cold. He suggests Mexico as an alternative. Ennis objects because he prefers not to travel and he really can't afford to leave his job now that he has child support to pay. Their quarrel escalates, leading Jack to exclaim, "I wish I knew how to quit you!" Ennis fumes back, "Then why don't you! Why don't you let me be. It's because of you, Jack, that I'm like this. I'm nothin'. I'm nowhere." At that point there's nowhere for them to turn but to one another. They fall to the ground in a repentant, sorrowful embrace.

At this point in the film, the audience is moved beyond empathy. Ennis and Jack are no longer young men, and their situation grows more desperate as the years pass. Though the world around them is changing, Jack and Ennis are constrained by their lack of education and financial circumstances. Jack's financial stability is tied to his marriage, and Ennis is encumbered by debt and child support. There's no guarantee that, even if they rode off together into the sunset, they could support their already battered bodies through old age doing the work they did as young men. Issues of masculinity and class still plague them.

RETURN TO SENDER AND THE FINAL EXIT

Ennis learns of Jack's unexpected death through a returned postcard marked DECEASED. Shaken and distraught, he decides to call Lureen to find out what happened. She explains the freak tire accident in which Jack ended up drowned in his own blood. Ennis can't help but wonder if this was really an accident. In a brief flash onscreen, we see a man beaten savagely by three men; one swings a tire iron. Perhaps, strangers took Jack's life, or perhaps L. D. ordered the beating as retribution for Jack humiliating him on Thanksgiving Day. Ennis is paralyzed in thought. We are left to wonder who would commit such a heinous act. Lureen suggests that Ennis contact Jack's parents about scattering Jack's ashes on Brokeback Mountain. Ennis drives to see Jack's parents.

Jack's mother politely welcomes Ennis. Jack's father, John, is a hardened, unabashed character who lets Ennis know in so many words that he's aware of his relationship with Jack. He tells Ennis of Jack's incessant talk of bringing Ennis Del Mar up to the ranch to work it together. He also callously reveals that Jack had similar intentions for his Texas ranch neighbor. Ennis is visibly stunned. Jack's mother intervenes and asks Ennis if he would like to go up to Jack's room to see if there's something he'd like for a keepsake.

Ennis proceeds upstairs to the stark room Jack occupied as a child. Hidden away in Jack's closet, Ennis finds the old blood-stained shirt that he thought he had left on Brokeback. It is lovingly tucked inside of Jack's own Brokeback shirt. With a heavy heart, Ennis removes the shirts from the hanger, rolls them up together, and returns downstairs. Jack's mother takes the shirts from Ennis and puts them in a paper bag. As Ennis prepares to take his leave, John gruffly tells Ennis, "We got a family plot, and he's goin' in it." Ennis resigns himself to the Twist patriarch, a tough-hewn masculine force he knows he cannot fight. Jack's mother gives Ennis the paper bag containing the shirts and invites him to come back and visit again. Ennis thanks her for the mementos and leaves. The two shirts, one enveloping the other, a postcard of Brokeback Mountain, and memories are all that remain of a nearly 20-year struggle for love.

Conclusion: *Brokeback Mountain* on Higher Ground

Brokeback Mountain is no fairy tale love story. There is no happy ending, and we are left to ponder unanswered questions. Yet, by decoding issues of masculinity and class hidden in *Brokeback Mountain,* we see how it becomes a cautionary tale. The disguised social issue is not Ennis and Jack's sexuality but, rather, the cultural convictions that restrict their love. The film attempts to guide us, as audience members, through an examination of our own discursive options. It urges us to intervene in what matters most: the longstanding discursive conventions of masculinity and class that all too often go unspoken and uncontested in mainstream culture. In the case of this fictional yet homological text, outing the tacit arguments regarding masculinity and class is necessary not only for understanding what is discursively permissible in a given historical social context but for gauging the effectiveness of hidden rhetoric and its potential for resisting cultural hegemony and its destructive power.

By formally featuring masculinity and class as the source of conflict and contradiction, *Brokeback Mountain* offers us what author and critic Kenneth Burke describes in *Permanence and Change* as "perspective by incongruity." Through a homological analysis, we are able to see common connections in seemingly disparate issues that we may not have previously considered. For instance, we see how rigid concepts of masculinity and class can function to destroy family life and human potential.

Whether or not we've been presented with Jack and Ennis's exact circumstances, the hidden rhetoric provides the argument that we, too, have been constrained in ways not always immediately apparent. As we see Jack and Ennis struggling with their sexual identity, compounded by societal norms regulating masculinity and class in rural Western culture, common patterns begin to emerge. We, too, have sought affection, desired respect, felt the pain of lost or unrequited love, struggled to make ends meet, been bullied, or felt the weight of gender or cultural expectations. *Brokeback Mountain* is powerful because it is homologous. We find ourselves contemplating the social issues presented in the film long afterward, prompted perhaps by conversations with others, by news of a hate crime, by hyper-masculinity enacted in action films, or by allusions in hip hop lyrics.

The context may differ, but the forms repeat themselves in other texts: the Marlboro symbol of masculinity shows up in a Country Western music video, a sitcom articulates family expectations, an advertisement beckons class desire, and so forth. As audience members, we gain an understanding of the complexities and implications that such unyielding forms and categories pose for us and our ability to live contented lives. By uncovering the underlying social issues and contradictions in rhetorical texts, we are opened to the possibilities of alternative views and new discursive potentials that we might have initially missed.

11

Making Gay
Sense of the X-Men

William Earnest

M idway through *X2: X-Men United*, young Bobby Drake and his fellow mutants pay a surprise visit to his conservative, upper middle-class family. The scene depicts a rite of passage for many teenagers living in the mutant-fearing America of the film, announcing to your family that you're one of "those" people—special, different, mutated. Because mutation is a pressing social issue in the X-Men's world, the disclosure of one's "mutancy" is not to be taken lightly. After all, it's a condition that is misunderstood and feared by the general population. Mutants who go public risk everything from being rejected by family to political and social marginalization to physical violence.

This scene will seem familiar to many audience members, particularly those who have been in such "guess-what?" meetings before. These moments happen all the time in our world and play out much like the Drake family's drama. *Our* pressing social issue isn't mutation, of course, but sexual difference. The rhetorical setting, however—the situation, the characters, and so on—is the same in the film as it is for us; it's the rhetorical equivalent of a gay, lesbian, or bisexual teenager's "coming out" ritual.[1]

Like most rhetorical genres, the coming out ritual tends to follow certain conventions, to look and to sound a certain way, and this one goes by the book (Hart 121–22). Bobby kicks things off with the standard opener, "There's something I need to tell you," and what follows is a volley of real-world coming out dialogue. In the family's exchange, the most predictable lines go to Bobby's mother, Madeline, including:

So, when did you first know you were a . . . a . . . ?
We still love you, Bobby. It's just . . . this mutant problem is a little . . .
complicated.
Have you tried not being a mutant?
This is all my fault.

In response to this last line, a member of Bobby's entourage sardonically points out that the gene is inherited from males. "So it's *his* fault," he says with a glib nod of the head to Bobby's father.

As rhetorical disguises go, this scene is a bit of a Rorschach test for audiences. Some viewers will see the gay metaphor while others will not. In his NPR review of the film, for example, *Los Angeles Times* film critic Kenneth Turan plays excerpts from this very scene while observing, "One of the film's virtues is its matter-of-fact storytelling style. This film doesn't wink at us." Hence it seems that gay screenwriters Dan Harris and Michael Dougherty infused the scene with enough good-natured humor to prevent it from becoming maudlin, heavy handed, or over-obvious (Chaw; Vary 45).

Still, there may be just a little rhetorical winking going on, for director Bryan Singer has been forthright about touting the gay subtext of *X-Men* and *X2* in the press (Applebaum). And actor Ian McKellen told *The Advocate* that Singer *explicitly* invoked an analogy to gay rights issues when he first pitched the role of Magneto to him, suggesting that mutants were a perfect symbol for the social struggles of lesbians and gays (Vary 44). Despite (or perhaps because of) this intentional framing of the films as a metaphor for homosexuality and gay rights, Singer and his screenwriters equipped *X-Men* and *X2* with the rhetorical stealth needed to fly below the gaydar of many critics and audience members. Nevertheless, such external commentary by those involved with the films can serve as a "Psssst! Over here!" sign for anyone interested in sniffing out social issues in disguise. For the critic hunting rhetorical prey, it's a lucky break. Hidden rhetorics are usually not as intentional as they seem to be in this case. Besides, whether they're intentional or not, there is no guarantee that they will be easy to recognize. Indeed, some hidden rhetorics may remain hidden even from those who created them.

Although Bobby's coming out is the most apparent manifestation (at least for some) of Singer's metaphoric moral vision for the films, it is hardly the only one. Only a few scenes later in *X2*, Nightcrawler meets Mystique and is intrigued by the unique implications of her shape-shifting ability—implications that, from the perspective of our present analysis, represent the rhetorical strategy of "passing" (Blackmer; Shugart). "Why not stay in disguise all the time, you know—look like everyone else?" he inquires. "Because," she replies in sermonic deadpan, "we shouldn't have to."

Aside from these scenes in *X2*, the very premise of *The Last Stand*[2] seems to push the sexual difference metaphor even further (despite the departure of *X2*'s gay director and two gay screenwriters [Vary 45]). Though many mainstream moviegoers may not see the parallels, it seems hard to deny that the X-gene discovered in the third film is analogous to real-world speculation about the existence of a "gay" gene.[3] To be sure, *Variety*'s Justin Chang only slightly overstates the case when he says that this central conceit of *X3* makes *explicit* *X2*'s equating of mutation and homosexuality (41).

With vignettes and plotlines such as these thoroughly integrated into all three films, it seems unlikely that the hidden rhetoric at work here is primarily about, for example, class difference (though such a reading may be possible, as Wolf-Meyer has done with Batman and Robin).[4] In this chapter, I argue instead that, throughout all three films, the premise of "mutation" is *best* understood as a metaphor for non-mainstream sexualities, for doing so unlocks a wide variety of critical (and, one hopes, meaningful) observations. Indeed, the superhero genre itself seems particularly ready for such discursive mining these days. After all, 20th-century comic books are enjoying an unprecedented worldwide audience thanks to the technological advances that have made it possible to bring these stories to the big screen in believable ways that honor the spectacle of the original material (Coogan 2). Despite the fact that superheroes don't really exist (as far as we know), the remarkable popularity of the film versions of these stories suggests that *other factors* may be responsible for their deep resonance with audiences. Perhaps it's time to get out the rhetorical calculator and start punching in some equations.

And this thought leads me to conclude these opening paragraphs with a note about method. For the present analysis, metaphor is my critical tool of choice—the case for a couple of reasons. First, in my view, metaphor criticism is where all form criticism begins. If enough metaphors turn up in enough artifacts, then one is justified in suspecting that a full formal critique might be the way to go. But we are dealing here with only three texts, all of which derive from a single narrative. We may suspect that the *X-Men* films are *formally* about, for example, what it means to be different, but by concentrating on the simple critical equation of mutant = gay, we can pay homage to form while getting as much mileage as possible out of one particular metaphor—which segues to the second reason for choosing metaphor criticism as my basis: As metaphors go, we will see in the following pages that this one is *highly systematic*. In other words, our mutant = gay equation turns out to be the key that unlocks not only Bobby's coming out scene but also numerous other scenes, plotlines, and characters in each of the three films. Once transformed in this way, the films can be read productively as ways of thinking about (and making sense of) the social issues that alternative sexuality presents in early 21st-century America.

Background: Percival Pinkerton's Shadow

As comic-book sagas created by Marvel's Stan Lee in the 1960s, *X-Men, Spider-Man, Fantastic Four,* and others often featured narratives that sought to defend the American way of life against fascist ideology (Schmitt 155; Trushell 151). A brief examination of Lee's background makes his motivation for writing the stories in this way even clearer.[5]

The son of Jewish immigrants,[6] Lee came of age during the Great Depression and in his late teens went to work for Marvel forerunner Timely Comics. There his writing skills were discovered accidentally but put to good use nonetheless. Among other things, he wrote two of the early *Captain America* stories. Then in 1942, Lee enlisted in the U.S. Army, serving 3 years in the Signal Corps as a writer for training films and instructional manuals. Hardworking and patriotic, Lee's post-army career kicked into high gear just as the nuclear age dawned and the Cold War turned hot in Korea—more fuel for the fires of imagination.

His career then took a most unexpected turn—it almost ended. The cause of this near-demise was a McCarthy-era moral crusade against comic books that severely depressed product sales and tarnished the industry's reputation (Brown 18). In 1954, U.S. Senators Estes Kefauver and Robert Hendrickson launched a formal committee investigation into organized crime. A sidelight of this highly publicized hearing process included looking at how comic books might be responsible for violent or criminal behavior among young people. To help "answer" these questions, a German-born psychiatrist named Frederic Wertham was invited to testify. He used the televised hearings to gain popular support for his ongoing crusade against the comic-book industry for, as fate would have it, the press coverage of his appearance coincided perfectly with the publication of his book *Seduction of the Innocent.* These efforts led to the subsequent creation of the Comics Magazine Association of America and the Comic Book Code—"voluntary" efforts by comic-book publishers that amounted to de facto censorship (Park 276).

Wertham charged that comic books were leading America's children astray, encouraging crime, licentiousness, and violent behavior. Of particular note was his conclusion that the standard-issue superhero-sidekick pairing (most notably Batman, Robin, and Robin's bare legs) represented a homosexual fantasy relationship (Lee and Mair 90–91; Terrill 493).[7] Brown summarizes it this way: "Wertham accused the most traditional of superhero comics of instigating . . . homosexuality. . . . [S]uperheroes, those handsome muscle-bound men running around in tights, were obviously gay" (20). Such pseudo-scientific charges today would likely draw as much fire as support, but they were utterly incendiary in the 1950s (homosexuality would not even be declassified as a mental illness until the 1970s [Thompson 85]). The effect of Wertham's "moral entrepreneurship" was singular—comic books, their publishers, and (presumably) their readers were henceforth framed as deviant (Beggan 810; Brown 28–29).

Emerging from and informed by this background of economic, technological, political, and cultural upheaval, Lee helped create *The Fantastic Four* in 1961, *Spider-Man* in 1962, and *X-Men* in 1963—superheroes all, a bunch of troubled, gifted outsiders "burdened with self-doubt and existential angst" ("Comic Book"). But it is important to note that 4 months before the first *X-Men* hit the stands, Lee took a chance (to win a bet) on a World War II story with a ridiculous title that featured human rather than superhuman heroes—*Sgt. Fury and His Howling Commandos* (Lee and Mair 161–62). He won his bet. The *Fury* stories sold well despite their World War II setting (considered hackneyed according to the conventional wisdom) and despite the fact that they featured a far more diverse cast than had ever been seen before in comic books, including Americans of African, Italian, Irish, and Jewish descent—not to mention a *gay* character. The latter was English rather than American (perhaps casting him as a foreigner made it easier to get away with) and went by the somewhat foppish—and quite possibly coded—name of Percival Pinkerton. According to Lee, Pinkerton's sexual orientation was never explicitly revealed, only implied (it was 1963 after all). "I didn't play up the gay part," he told NPR, "but somehow you could assume he was gay in reading the stories. But he was brave and nice and friendly and everybody liked him and he was [just] one of the guys" ("Comic Book").

As for the *X-Men*, whose initial publication followed quickly on *Fury*'s heels, Lee claims to have had no specific cultural group in mind other than teenagers, and that genetic mutation provided a much-needed new plot device for the conferring of superpowers (other than, for example, exposure to cosmic rays). "It dawned on me," he writes, "that mutations often appear in nature, for no apparent reason. . . . Why couldn't I create a group of teenagers who had simply mutated and therefore gained some varied and extraordinary powers?" (Lee and Mair 165). Yet he has also made clear that he intended for *X-Men* to be an indictment of discrimination generally, to "make it a story against bigotry of all sorts" ("Superheroes" para. 3).

On balance, it seems unlikely that Lee created his mutation saga without at least a subconscious appreciation of the potential for reading it through the lens of alternative sexuality. After all, here was a man: (1) who was a patriotic, Jewish World War II veteran, (2) whose professional livelihood had been demonized by cultural conservatives, and (3) who had only months earlier created a hidden gay character in another comic-book series. In other words, he may have had a few cultural scores to settle. And as Schmitt has noted, Marvel and other 1960s-era comics publishers were characterized by their radical willingness to engage social issues that were often seen as unacceptable in the eyes of older generations (155).

Or maybe it was only about acne and angst after all. "It's funny how people will always read more into what you write than you ever put in there," Lee told NPR ("Comic Book"). Either way, he had developed an almost ideal cultural metaphor for gay experience and the persecution of sexual difference. And though it was apt in the 1960s, the metaphor has truly come into its own today, nearly four decades after the dawn of the gay liberation movement. As metaphors go, this one has aged well.

The Films

Whether consciously working with a gay subtext or not when he was writing the comic books in the 1960s, as executive producer of all three of the films, Lee had the benefit of 40 years of hindsight to guide him. As he himself said in an October 2006 newswire release (the telling title of which was "Superheroes Born Out of Discrimination"), "as so often happens in real life, if you have a different religion, a different country, a different sexual orientation, whatever the difference is, people—not all people, but it happens—are going to dislike you, distrust you, fear you." Director Bryan Singer, moreover, told PBS interviewer Charlie Rose[8] that he frequently sought Lee's input on the project. And in a special "making of" segment on the *X-Men* DVD, he further observed that the original story "was sort of Stan Lee's and Jack Kirby's way of commenting on prejudice."

So what was originally a general metaphor for civil rights appears to have evolved into a very specific, 21st-century incarnation of the issue. Cultural artifacts like *Crash* (2005) notwithstanding, the difference *du jour* in Hollywood seems to be focused as much or more on sexuality as ethnicity. In an interview with Filmfreakcentral.net critic Walter Chaw, *X2* screenwriter Dan Harris explained this cultural shift vis-à-vis the *X-Men* saga:

> [A] lot of it in the books started out as a race issue, in the last fifteen or twenty years—not only in the movies but in the books, as well, it's become more a metaphor for sexual identity and orientation because it's more appropriate to look at a person and have to say, "Are you a mutant?" It's the best metaphor for a hidden minority, you know, you can't always look at a person and know that they're a mutant just like you can't look at a person and know that they're gay. (Chaw)

A hidden rhetoric for a hidden minority—indeed, as Professor Xavier tells Logan shortly after meeting him, "anonymity is a mutant's first defense against the world's hostility."

I turn now to a brief analysis of the three feature films, discussing them in the order of their release: *X-Men* (2000), *X2: X-Men United* (2003), and *X-Men: The Last Stand* (2006). Though each film is rich enough to merit its own analysis, I recognize that there is a dearth of scholarly research to date in this area and invite others to investigate in more detail the initial survey offered here. As with previous high-profile cultural phenomena (*The X-Files,* for example), the *X-Men* films may merit "a thorough rhetorical investigation" solely on the basis of their enormous popularity and potential for widespread influence (Bellon 136).[9] But the prospect of unpacking discourse about significant and timely social issues from such popular culture artifacts is justification enough to proceed. And in the case of the present study, the rhetorical "backstory" we have sketched to this point suggests that our journey will be rife with useful discoveries. In the end, if franchises like the *X-Men* are in fact doing important social and political work on contemporary controversies such as the treatment of gay and lesbian Americans, a little scholarly attention can help provide a fitting forum for discussion and debate.

X-MEN

From the outset of the first film, mutation is framed as a social issue—and a particularly controversial one at that (Smith and Windes). "Are mutants dangerous?" is the shrill, staccato refrain of McCarthy-esque Senator Robert Kelly at a hearing to determine if mutants should be required to register with the government. Both the premise and the lines in the scene recall statements made by former U.S. Senator Jesse Helms, who in 1987 advocated not only mandatory HIV testing but also the quarantining of AIDS patients ("Senator Helms").

The congressional hearing is an extended scene, and one in which the rhetoric clearly mirrors that of other "family values" debates (Blain). Substitute the word "homosexual" or its equivalents for "mutant" in this scene—as in virtually every scene wherein the merits of mutancy are being debated—and the lines work just as well (a telltale sign that a metaphor is nearby). For example, making the substitution in the following observation by Jean Grey produces a seamless result for modeling the plight of gays and lesbians who face discrimination: "Mutants who have come forward and revealed themselves publicly have been met with fear, hostility, even violence."

"What is it the mutant community has to *hide* I wonder that makes them so afraid to identify themselves?" retorts Kelly. "There are even rumors," he continues, ". . . of mutants so powerful that they can enter our minds and control our thoughts, taking away our God-given free will." He then concludes to thunderous applause and a standing ovation as he shouts, "I think the American people deserve the right to decide whether they want their children to be in school with mutants—to be *taught by* mutants!"

At that line, diligent students of 20th-century American history ought to prick up their ears, for it evokes the rhetoric of anti-gay crusader Anita Bryant and others (Blain 34; Brummett 260; Medhurst 4). Bryant's "Save Our Children" campaign was inspired by a Baptist minister who declared that he would burn down his church before letting a homosexual teach there. The Bryant campaign was successful in getting the gay rights ordinance in Dade County, Florida, overturned and went on to help other cities do the same (Moser).

More specifically, Kelly's attack on mutant educators recalls the debate over California's Proposition 6—better known as the Briggs Initiative—which voters defeated in 1978. Had it passed, the initiative would have permitted local school districts to dismiss or deny employment to gay teachers. The film's parallels to Proposition 6 and similar historical proposals shows up again, but this time near the end—suggesting that its creators thought the point important enough to use as rhetorical bookends. As Senator Kelly's doppelgänger (Mystique in drag) appears on television to announce that he's dropping his support for the Mutant Registration Act, the announcer's voiceover—shown in subtitles on the television the X-Men are watching at the mansion—reports that the legislation "continues to draw support from many parents' rights groups who feel threatened by unidentified mutants in their school systems."

The character of Senator Kelly figures prominently in *X-Men*, and given what we know of Stan Lee's past, it is not hard to recognize Kelly as an amalgam of the various moral crusaders that Lee has come up against or observed over the years. Kelly is certainly equal parts Estes Kefauver and Frederic Wertham of the 1950s witch-hunts, with dashes of Anita Bryant and Jesse Helms thrown in to round out the specific demands of the gay subtext (and its accompanying rhetoric of "moral panic"). What we have in this scene is, in fact, a condensed re-creation of the Senate's Kefauver hearings, featuring a kind of discourse that researcher David Park, like his colleague Cindy Griffin, describes in highly rhetorical terms when he notes that the senator's 1954 subcommittee "was primarily a symbolic display, a show trial, where the questions asked were prompted more by the practical concerns of the Senators . . . than by the analyses of the scientists involved" (261).

This description exactly matches the Kelly Senate hearing in the film. It's clear in the scene that, even though he is supposed to be questioning Dr. Grey, the senator is doing little more than grandstanding. Rather than use the forum for true dialogue, Kelly speaks in a one-sided way and frequently turns to address the chamber's standing-room-only audience rather than his supposed interlocutor. In Griffin's view, these are the rhetorical fingerprints of ideology—dialogue that is little more than monologue and the creation of one view of reality at the expense of another (308).

In private, Robert Kelly's rhetoric is even more vitriolic. "If it were up to me, I'd lock 'em all away. It's a war. It's the reason people like me exist," he confides to an aide—an aide, it turns out, who was killed by Magneto's forces and replaced by a perfect replica (a la Mystique) to effect Kelly's kidnapping. At this point, Mystique reveals her true identity to a very surprised senator and, turning his own words against him, issues a rebuke that every sexually "different" child and teen who has ever experienced harassment knows by heart: "*People like you* were the reason I was afraid to go to school as a child!" She then proceeds to karate-kick the horrified man into unconsciousness, but even as she does so, it is hard to feel anything but empathy toward her and to smile at the senator's comeuppance.

Robert Kelly's next scene is one of the most remarkable in the film, but this time the dialogue is not the rhetorical artifact of interest; that honor goes instead to the scene's staging, which is set in Magneto's cliff-top headquarters. As the scene opens, we find Kelly bound to a chair. What he doesn't know is that he's about to become the test subject for Magneto's energy device, a mutation accelerator to be unleashed on world leaders at the upcoming UN summit on Ellis Island.

After some chit-chat and the ominous line, "God works too slowly," we watch Magneto ascend a tall, narrow, metal shaft that has rounded, circular shapes at the top. He clamps down on the controls and begins to use his own magnetic power to activate the device. As he does so, the circular head begins to spin faster and faster. As it builds toward its climax, we see Magneto nearly faint in what looks like a combination of ecstasy and pain. At the point where his eyes roll into the back of his head, a shower of wavelike white energy erupts from the very top of the platform and cascades out and down until it washes over the senator. The gay (and in this case homoerotic) subtext seems hard to ignore on a close visual inspection of the scene—a tall shaft with a round head, a massive buildup of energy, and an explosion of white, liquid-like "essence."

Cigarette, anyone?

At all events, it turns out that this "exposure" to Magneto's energy wave does *not* accelerate the evolutionary process and realize his dream of turning the world's leaders into fellow *Homo superiors*. Instead, it's fatal to humans. Kelly temporarily gains a great deal of plasticity, but it's simply a side effect of his degenerating cellular structure (which makes him literally what he no doubt considered all mutants to be figuratively—a degenerate). On the examination table at Xavier's school, he deteriorates into a mound (and then puddle) of water (a veiled reference, perhaps, to the Wicked Witch of the West; after all, the senator was from Kansas).

Unintended allusions to Judy Garland films notwithstanding, the hidden rhetoric here is rich in possibility. Senator Kelly experiences the mutant/homo-phobe's worst nightmare, which reads like a Who's Who of gay stereotypes: He is abducted by mentally unstable criminals and then forced into a sex act that exposes him to an infectious, deadly substance—normally a life-giving force of nature that, with a handful of people, has not only gone wrong but is being misused (after all, to be a "practicing" mutant is a choice).

This rhetorical emphasis on the unnatural, unhealthy aspects of mutancy is echoed elsewhere. "We should love the mutant but hate the mutation," Kelly tells his fellow senators, not in the film itself but in a 30-minute mockumentary called the "Mutant Watch," aired by the FOX network to promote the film's release.[10] This reimagining of the familiar evangelical Christian trope "love the sinner, hate the sin"—so frequently applied to alternative sexualities (Blain 44; Lynch 383)—seems a clear and obvious choice by the film's promoters to analogize mutancy and homosexuality.

Elsewhere in the "Mutant Watch," when asked to explain his view that muta-tion doesn't represent a perfectly natural phenomenon, Kelly responds Socrati-cally by positing "Evolution? Or *Aberration?*" In this way, mutancy represents a real threat to the survival of *Homo sapiens* as a species. But even if Magneto's acceleration device had worked as planned and advanced the species, no doubt detractors would still manage to accuse mutantkind of engaging in forced "recruitment," an idea that Anita Bryant helped to popularize (Moser).

Robert Kelly's nightmare represents a subtext that runs throughout all three films, namely, that mutancy represents unrestrained, undisciplined, unhealthy sexuality. He sees mutancy as many see AIDS—as a threat to the survival of the human species—a view that makes it possible to declare war against mutant-kind.[11] But whereas mutantphobes like Kelly do not distinguish "good" mutants from "bad," Xavier's X-Men do. The mutant community is thus divided about what is and is not proper behavior; some mutants, explains Xavier, have gifts "so extreme that they've become a danger to themselves and those around them." It is also possible that these "dangerous" mutants are a separate metaphor for HIV/AIDS. To be sure, the question of a "cure" (and the rhetorical choice to label it as such) drives the plot of *X3*. After all, if someone has AIDS, why wouldn't they choose to be cured?

We find licentiousness coded into many of the trilogy's characters, but most often in the female characters and particularly in Jean Grey, Rogue, and Mystique. When Wolverine asks Jean if she's ever used Cerebro, for example, her reply is telling: "It takes a degree of control, and, uh, for someone like me. . . ." She trails off, but Cyclops finishes the sentence for her: ". . . it's dangerous." Indeed, Cyclops himself will learn this truth the hard way in *X3* when Jean's lack of self-control hands her over to the ultimate metaphor for sexual addic-tion and depravity—the Phoenix Force.

Then there's Rogue, who is essentially a black widow in waiting. "The first boy I ever kissed ended up in a coma for three weeks," she tells Logan. As with most mutants, her power first manifested itself in adolescence during a stolen kiss—drawing a parallel between the awakening of sexual desire (and, in gen-eral, the discovery of one's orientation) and the emergence of mutant powers, since both occur during puberty. As a sexual being, Rogue's very touch can be deadly, which makes her doubly useful as a gay metaphor. First, she represents "strange flesh"—part of a biblical injunction against same-sex relations still used in some circles.[12] Reinforcing the idea of aberration over evolution (an argument levied against mutation in the films and homosexuality in real life), and not unlike bygone warnings against interracial marriage, the central trans-gression that drives these prohibitions is the idea of a perversion of the natural order or divine law.

A second interpretation of Rogue's condition is more straightforward. Because physical contact with her can kill, she is the single best metaphor for *disease* of any character in the films. If we accept this premise, then it is easy to draw parallels to HIV/AIDS. Not all mutants are "infectious" in this way, but as one of the characters whose sexual side is presented more often than most, the conclusion is hard to miss: Not all mutants/gays are deadly, but just one exposure to someone who is "infected" is enough to seal your doom.

For her part, Mystique is a rhetorical analysis unto herself. She is portrayed as overtly sexual and exhibitionist (hence the lack of clothes), and her ability to shape-shift could be read as a metaphor for bisexuality. But for our purposes, what's just as interesting is that she appears to represent sadomasochism, deriving pleasure from giving and receiving physical pain. The best example of this is a deliberate visual aside during her fight scene with Wolverine at the Statue of Liberty. In the middle of an extended volley of kicks, head butts, and body slams, she gets knocked to the floor in a move that catches her off guard. As the camera zooms in and the action catches its breath, she flashes an "I like it" expression of surprised pleasure followed by a quick and suggestive licking of her lips. If Wolverine is any indication, Mystique seems to like her men rough and her sex rougher. More to the point, her predilection for non-vanilla sex recalls anti-gay stereotypes about sadomasochism, leather, orgies, and other "unusual" or "unhealthy" sex acts that are supposedly common among homosexuals.

X2: X-MEN UNITED

At the beginning of this chapter, Bobby's coming out scene was offered as the primary example of *X2*'s gay subtext. Picking up where we left off, it's worth revisiting the Drake home to examine the second half of the scene, in which things go from bad to worse for everyone. The tongue-in-cheek, almost playful dialogue between the X-Men and the Drakes is quickly replaced by a violent confrontation with a battalion of police. In a way, the scene in its entirety represents the hypocrisy of American "tolerance"—guarded rhetorical acceptance contradicted by material discrimination; to be sure, this is the very critique commonly levied at U.S. Vice President Dick Cheney, who publicly declares his love for and acceptance of his lesbian daughter Mary while simultaneously endorsing the Bush administration's push for a constitutional amendment banning gay marriage.

The more or less civil debate of the scene's first part quickly escalates into a material threat to life, limb, and property. Bobby's younger brother storms out of the family meeting and places a call to 911 to tell the police that the family is being held hostage in their own home (a formal metaphor for homosexuality's perceived threat to the nuclear family). As the X-Men attempt to take their leave, the police surround the house. When a trigger-happy officer tells Wolverine to put his "knives" away, he misinterprets the superhero's attempt to explain why he can't and fires a slug squarely into his forehead, dropping him on the spot.

As X-Man apprentice Pyro looks around at the persecution they're being unfairly subjected to, he has what can best be described as a Rosa Parks moment. The officers ask the X-Men to lie down, and he alone refuses to comply. "We don't wanna hurt ya, kid," pleads one of the officers.

But Pyro will have none of it. "You know all those 'dangerous' mutants you hear about on the news?" he taunts. "I'm the worst one." He then proceeds to shoot fireballs at the nice suburban police officers and torch their cars. As more police units arrive, Pyro takes them out one by one, evincing as he does so an expression that is part surprise, part joy, and part rapturous rage. Rogue manages to disrupt him by temporarily draining his life force, which she does by grabbing his ankle. At the same time, she uses her other hand to wave out the burning fires. This internal conflict among the X-Men is part of the ongoing game of "good mutant/bad mutant" that will erupt into outright mutant-on-mutant violence in X3.

It's probably a stretch to suggest that Pyro's great balls of fire make him a flamer of sorts, but it's too tempting an interpretation not to at least mention. A more productive reading, however, is derived from the scene's formal elements—white, heterosexual, suburban sensibilities are threatened by mutancy/homosexuality. This perfectly manicured house and its beautiful nuclear family are torn apart, both figuratively vis-à-vis Bobby's prodigal choices and literally thanks to Pyro (at the very least, the house will need a facelift and a new lawn). It would seem that mutancy and humanity are fundamentally incompatible—mix the two, and the best you can hope for is debris.

The mutant lifestyle presents still other dilemmas for the Drakes. From their perspective, mutants seem to live communally, generally eschew the heterosexual institution of marriage, and subvert middle-class values by relabeling complicated moral "problems" like mutation as *gifts* ("You have to understand," says Mr. Drake in defense of his family's disappointed reaction, "we thought Bobby was going to a school for the gifted." "He *is* gifted," counters Rogue).

Thanks to his own gift of self-healing, meanwhile, Wolverine's bullet extracts itself from his forehead, and the X-Jet arrives, Harrier-style, to ferry the team away. As they make their way to the plane, the camera goes to great lengths to show that none of the humans involved in the melee was killed or even seriously injured (which has to be seen to be believed). As they hurry across the wrecked lawn, Bobby stops and glances longingly back at his family, who are looking down upon the whole scene from an upstairs window. Madeline Drake's arms are wrapped tightly around her "good" son's shoulders. She means well, this suburban mom. As she said, this whole mutant problem is complicated. After all, Bobby and his kind have "forced" the Drakes into making this difficult choice.

Someone in the film who clearly does not mean well, however, is Colonel William Stryker. In symbolic terms, Stryker is a perfect Nazi, an amoral scientist and military officer bent on genocide. In true Mengele style, he had previously taken advantage of Logan's natural gift of rapid healing and grafted the inde-structible metal adamantium onto the mutant's skeleton. And at the Alkali Lake facility, he has a holding cell full of mutant children that he tortures and, we learn, plans to exterminate as test subjects when his genocide device is ready for trial runs. "I'm a scientist," he explains when one of his lieutenants questions the ethics of this aspect of his operation.

The character of Stryker is worth mentioning for at least two reasons. First, coded as a Nazi, it's not unreasonable to link him to the Third Reich's use of pink triangles and criminalization of homosexuals under the German statute known as Paragraph 175. Second, like the elder Warren Worthington in *X3*, Stryker is deeply ashamed and resentful of his own mutant son. Years earlier, Stryker had brought his son Jason to Xavier's school, but he did so for correc-tion rather than development. "You wanted me to cure your son, but mutation is not a disease," Xavier reminds him at Alkali Lake—a line that foreshadows the plot of the third film.

It is Stryker, moreover, the genocidal, mutant-killing Nazi, who brings Xavier's and Magneto's factions together. To him, as with Senator Kelly, mutation repre-sents a genetic aberration rather than a natural function of evolution. To counter such anti-mutant rhetoric, as well as Magneto's equally genocidal anti-human rhetoric, the film goes out of its way to advocate a Rodney King "can't we all just get along" discourse, and it does so in two ways. It grounds itself, first, in a nor-malizing scientific discourse, and, second, in the rationalist discourse of American liberalism. In fact, the film wastes no time in making these points, for they are lit-erally the first words to fall on the ears of audience members and are intended to frame everything that follows. As the opening-sequence animation and main title fade, we see star fields and hear Patrick Stewart's soothing, paternal voice engaging us in an internal monologue (in which, once again, terms denoting sexual difference can be readily substituted):

> Mutants. Since the discovery of their existence they have been regarded with fear, suspicion, often hatred. Across the planet, debate rages: Are mutants the next link in the evolutionary chain or simply a new species of humanity fight-ing for their share of the world?

As this prologue concludes, the first scene begins with a close-up of a famil-iar sign with three words: THE WHITE HOUSE. While the imagery of the very epicen-ter of American liberal power is suggestive enough, lest anyone miss the point we immediately hear a White House tour guide reciting the following excerpt from Lincoln's first inaugural address: "We are not enemies, but friends. We must not be enemies. Though passion may have strained, it must not break, the bonds of our affection." In these general discourses about science, tolerance, and under-standing, it is hard not to think of any repressed group in American society, past or present, and hear in particular the echoes of contemporary political, religious, and cultural debates over the proper status of gays and lesbians, even the nature of homosexuality. The message is clear: Whether we be *Homo sapiens* or *Homo superior*, at the end of the day, we're all *Homos* together.

Finally, another clue to the gay subtext at work—not just in *X2* but all three films—is the fact that almost every mutant has two names, their human birth name and their mutant "code" name. It is this exchange of both sets of names that helps Logan/Wolverine and Marie/Rogue identify (literally "come out") to each other as mutants during their first meeting. This convention is reminiscent of the stage names taken by drag queens and code names (such as "Mary") commonly used by gay men to label each other, often in jest.

In *X2* specifically there is another variation on this name game that's worth noting, a scene in which using his code name literally helps John/Pyro come to terms with both his mutant identity and his apparent destiny. On the X-Jet when they first meet, Magneto and John speak slowly and quietly in a scene that director Singer shoots in close-up, as if to highlight its emotional and psychological importance:

> "What's your name?" asks Magneto.
> "John," he replies.
> "What's your *real* name?" purrs the elder mutant.

After a knowing pause, John replies in a voice that is equal parts defiance and resignation: "Pyro." As Kachgal pointed out in her analysis of MTV's *The Real World*, this represents a kind of "confessional" rhetoric in the Foucauldian sense, whereby John is claiming his true identity and ridding himself of shame and guilt (over the fiasco chez Drake, perhaps) (363). But such confession can come at a price, depending on who actually benefits from it. In this case, Magneto self-servingly manufactures the confession to seduce John into joining the Brotherhood. "You're a god among insects," exhorts Magneto. "Never let anyone tell you different," he adds, the irony of which seems lost on the conflicted teenager. By film's end, Magneto's recruitment effort is successful, and a disciple is born.

X-MEN: THE LAST STAND

The genocidal threat posed by Colonel Stryker having been safely abated in *X2*, by the time of *X3*, mutants have become more mainstream than ever. There's even a cabinet-level Department of Mutant Affairs run by none other than Dr. Hank McCoy, the once and future X-Man known as Beast. Mutants now seem fully integrated into the dream of American liberalism, with all the rights and privileges pertaining thereto.[13]

But all hell breaks loose when pharmaceutical company Worthington Labs discovers a young mutant named Leech who produces an antibody that can permanently suppress the X-gene (the factor responsible for the mutation phenomenon). The company's obsessed founder goes all out to develop and promote the antibody as a "cure"—for his own son, future X-Man Angel, as much as for anyone else.

Worthington, like Colonel Stryker before him, regards mutancy as abnormal—something to be dreaded and an evolutionary threat to be avoided. Confirming one of Kenneth Burke's great fears, this Man of Science is presumed to be acting in the best interests of liberal society but, in fact, is engaging in nothing less than Hitlerism. In developing the cure, apparently neither he nor the administration in Washington thinks to question the morality (or even the meaning) of their actions. Burke describes how these missteps can occur, even accurately predicting the film's climactic showdown between Magneto's Brotherhood and the U.S. military:

> If the technical expert, as such, is assigned the task of perfecting new powers of chemical, bacteriological, or atomic destruction, his morality *as technical expert* requires only that he apply himself to his task as effectively as possible. The question of what the new force might mean, as released into a social texture emotionally and intellectually unfit to control it, or as surrendered to men whose *specialty* is *professional killing*—well, that is simply "none of his business." (30, italics in original)

And so goes the plot of the third film. The cure is a "new force" that is released into a society, mutant and nonmutant alike, that does not know what to do with it—other than to load it into Magneto-proof plastic guns and give it to the army.

How did it come to this? The genesis of the cure is revealed in the film's second scene, another "coming out" moment the dialogue of which could be lifted verbatim and applied to any young gay son who gets "caught in the act" by his disapproving, disappointed straight father. In this case, the act is self-mutilation. A distraught Warren Worthington III tries desperately to hide his "thorn in the flesh"—a lovely pair of mutant wings—by sawing them off. Standing in the bathroom and covered in blood and feathers, the boy sobs "I'm sorry" after his suspicious father bursts in on him. "Oh, God!" recoils the dad in horror and disgust. "Not you." Fast-forward 10 years and we find that Worthington Labs has perfected a cure for young Warren's condition—at a now-converted prison complex on Alcatraz Island. But once a prison, always a prison, at least metaphorically—or so the filmmakers seem to be suggesting based on their choices. That's no cure, boys and girls. *Caveat mutantus*—let the mutant beware.

And let the viewer beware of some very telling formal elements in the composition of *The Last Stand*. There's Alcatraz, of course, but that's just for starters.

There's also the small matter of where Alcatraz happens to be located—in San Francisco, America's unofficial gay capital. When juxtaposed with the story's other major city, Washington DC, the true nature of the film's hidden rhetoric becomes clearer; like Martin Luther King, Jr., in the "I Have a Dream" speech, mutants/gays are staking a claim on their piece of the American Dream (Vail 58–59). It is a piece long denied them, and when it is almost within reach, the majority suddenly changes the rules of the game. In King's time, it would have been paramount to the Johnson administration announcing a "cure" for being black. The assumption of course is that it's for the recipients' own good, that is, that they're better off being white/nonmutant/straight.

"It's a better life. It's what we all want," explains the elder Worthington as Angel, realizing what he's being forced to give up to acquire mainstream status, begins to resist the assimilation procedure he "volunteered" for.

"No," counters his son. "It's what *you* want."

At that, Angel hurtles himself through the plateglass window of his father's high-rise office, spreads his wings (both literally and figuratively), and begins to soar triumphantly across the city. After a moment, he is directly over the bay and in full view of the Alcatraz facility, where the very source of the mutation cure, Leech himself, gazes up at him in envious wonder. For the first time, we see Leech's otherwise spacious quarters as a prison cell (it *is* Alcatraz), trapping him behind a window barely larger than his face. The composition of Angel's escape scene is no accident. After all, he could have just flapped away down a side street. Instead, the filmmakers seem to have carefully constructed a visual tableau rife with symbols of oppression and liberation. As an anti-cure protestor's placard declares elsewhere in the film, ONLY GOD CAN CHANGE DNA.

But not every mutant is convinced that the mainstream American Dream, a house with a white picket fence, and 2.5 mixed-mutant kids, is the way to go. Malcolm X to Charles Xavier's Martin Luther King, Magneto advocates reversal rather than reconciliation. "We are the cure, the cure for their infirm, imperfect condition called *Homo sapiens!*" he shouts to the delight of his gathered minions. After a terrorist-style attack on a government-run cure distribution center, Magneto broadcasts a taped ultimatum to the human population. "Your streets are not safe," he warns them. "*You* are not safe." It is every suburban soccer mom's nightmare, the mutant version of the "homosexual agenda" writ large (Lens 327).

In the end, American liberal democracy prevails by extending full citizenship to its mutant population. Along the way, high-profile nonmutants like the president and Warren Worthington learn a thing or two, as much about themselves as about mutants (the latter when his son swoops in to save him from execution at the hands of the Brotherhood). And with Dr. McCoy's help, the president's chief political conundrum is resolved (at least for now), namely, "how democracy survives when one man can move cities with his mind." As a reward for his service, the president appoints Dr. McCoy the nation's ambassador to the United Nations. It all makes for a tidy little civics lesson.

Speaking of tidy, the most dangerous mutants in the film—metaphors for HIV/AIDS brought on by "promiscuity" among some homosexuals—are effectively neutralized. Magneto, Mystique, and Rogue all receive the cure, though only Rogue does so willingly. Sadly, Jean Grey has to be sacrificed lest the world be destroyed by the Phoenix Force's uncontrolled surges of power (which, it should be noted, appear to be entwined with sexual desire, first for Cyclops and then for Wolverine). Depicted as a mutant with unlimited power, unlimited sexual energy, yet very limited self-discipline, she represents the ultimate virus.

On the other hand, perhaps Jean Grey represents American patriarchy's continuing struggle to come to terms with strong women—as do Rogue and Mystique in this regard (Johnston 382). All are depicted as "too" sexual, and therefore all must be made to "behave" if society is to go on. Equal rights for mutants/gays in the eyes of the law is one thing, but redefining the standards of what it means to be (homo)sexual is one bridge the hetero-normative mainstream just isn't willing to build (Lucaites and Condit 19–20). At this point, at least, it remains a bridge too far.

Conclusion

The method used here to unpack the hidden rhetoric of these three films is easily applied to other science fiction and/or fantasy artifacts. As I said in the introduction, such genres, particularly as they are brought to life on the big screen, may be especially ripe for rhetorical picking given that they ostensibly feature people, plots, and processes that do not exist in our world.

Or do they? After all, *we* wrote them. *We* filmed them. At some level, therefore, they will always be *about us*. The job of the popular culture critic is to find the rhetorical equation that unlocks the code. Cracking that code will always be more art than science, but sometimes a good place to start is by looking and listening for the "surprise of the familiar"—that is, spotting something that is *almost* (but not quite) the same as something we recognize. In the case of the present critique, the original clue was the composition and dialogue of the Drake family meeting. It caught my attention because it looked and sounded so familiar. My curiosity thus piqued, I made a quick inventory of the scene's elements:

A tension-filled family meeting? *Check.*

A prodigal teenaged son? *Check.*

Guilty, disappointed parents? *Check.*

Making an announcement about one's sexuality? *Nope.*

Bingo. There it was, the only thing absent from an otherwise well-known, predictable list. At this point, the critic's next move is to assign a variable to the missing piece (*x* has always been a favorite) and try to solve for it, starting with the very thing thought to be missing (sexuality in this case). Sometimes one's initial hunch will be confirmed, sometimes not. If not, keep going. Try more values for *x*, or try different methods (such as the ones described in the other chapters of this book). In the end, no matter the approach taken, keep an eye on the prize—there is important work to be done when it comes to social issues. Because they can be sensitive, complex subjects, often the best way—sometimes the *only* way—for them to enter the public's imagination is to do so in disguise, where they wait patiently for discerning, imaginative critics to properly introduce them.

Notes

1. A similar moment occurs in the third *X-Men* film when Warren Worthington discovers that his young son is a mutant. This scene is discussed in detail later in this chapter.

2. For simplicity's sake, the second and third films will frequently be referred to as *X2* and *X3* rather than their longer, formal titles of *X2: X-Men United* and *X-Men: The Last Stand*.

3. A scientific thesis that remains unproven despite the preliminary findings of some studies reported in the mid-1990s (Hamer et al.; Toufexis 95).

4. Note the word *primarily*. It is possible to interpret the films through the lens of class difference, especially if one uses species as the metaphor. In *X-Men*, we see this when Magneto mocks the capabilities of the merely human police force arrayed before him. "You *Homo sapiens* and your *guns*," he scoffs.

5. The background narrative summarized here is drawn from *Excelsior! The Amazing Life of Stan Lee* by Stan Lee and George Mair.

6. Erik Lehnsherr/Magneto was a Jewish immigrant to America.

7. And let's not forget that Robin's name was "Dick" Grayson.

8. The Charlie Rose interview is included as a special feature on the DVD release of *X-Men*.

9. And as Stanley has pointed out, far more people consume their comic-book rhetoric from movie adaptations than from the printed versions of the stories (143).

10. Both the "Mutant Watch" special and the Web site of the same name were clearly intended by the studio as an unflattering send-up of Kelly's McCarthy-esque rhetoric. The former was reissued as part of the DVD release of the film.

11. Alex de Waal (2004) uses such metaphors when describing the status of AIDS in Africa.

12. The terminology appears in some translations of Jude 1:6–7.

13. Urban has astutely pointed out that, as secretary of mutant affairs, Dr. Hank McCoy is the film's equivalent of Barney Frank, calling him "a politician who looks out for his mutant brethren" (para. 5).

References

Adelson, Betty M. *The Lives of Dwarfs: Their Journey From Public Curiosity Toward Social Liberation.* New Brunswick: Rutgers University Press, 2005.

Alexenberg, Menahem. "New Islamic Map for Peace." *Meru Foundation eTORUS Newsletter* 12 June 2003. 3 Apr. 2007 <http://www.meru.org/Newsletter/SpecialNotice Alexenberg.html>.

Altschiller, Donald. *Hate Crimes: A Reference Handbook.* Santa Barbara, CA: ABC-CLIO, 1999.

Anderson, Benedict. *Imagined Communities.* New York: Verso, 1983.

Anderson, David C. *Crime and the Politics of Hysteria: How the Willie Horton Story Changed American Politics.* New York: Crown, 1995.

Anderson, Terry. *The Movement and the Sixties.* Oxford: Oxford University Press, 1995.

Appiah, K. Anthony. "'No Bad Nigger': Blacks as the Ethical Principle in the Movies." *Media Spectacle.* Eds. Marjorie Garber, John Matlock, and Rebecca L. Walkowitz. New York: Routledge, 1993.

Applebaum, Stephen. "Interviews/Movies/Bryan Singer/*X-Men 2.*" bbc.co.uk 25 April 2003. 2 Jan. 2007 <http://www.bbc.co.uk/films/2003/04/25/bryan_singer_x_men_2_ interview.shtml>.

Aristotle. *The Art of Rhetoric.* Trans. J. H. Freese. Cambridge, MA: Harvard University Press, 1926.

Arkow, Phil. "The Relationships Between Animal Abuse and Other Forms of Family Violence." *Family Violence and Sexual Assault Bulletin* 12 (1996): 29–34.

Arnold, Thomas K. "Home Video Spending Falls in Q1." Lexis Nexis. Lexis Nexis Academic Universe. Scarborough-Phillips Library, Austin, Texas. 9 September 2006 <http://web.lexis-nexis.com>.

Ascione, Frank R. "The Abuse of Animals and Human Interpersonal Violence: Making the Connection." *Child Abuse, Domestic Violence, and Animal Abuse: Linking the Circles of Compassion for Prevention and Intervention.* Eds. Frank R. Ascione and Phil Arkow. West Lafayette, IN: Purdue University Press, 1999. 50–61.

———. "Battered Women's Reports of Their Partners' and Their Children's Cruelty to Animals." *Journal of Emotional Abuse* 1 (1998): 119–33.

———. "Children Who Are Cruel to Animals: A Review of Research and Implications for Developmental Psychopathology." *Anthrozoos* 6 (1993): 226–47.

Ascione, Frank R., and Phil Arkow, eds. *Child Abuse, Domestic Violence, and Animal Abuse: Linking the Circles of Compassion for Prevention and Intervention.* West Lafayette, IN: Purdue University Press, 1999.

Ascione, Frank R., Claudia V. Weber, and David S. Wood. "The Abuse of Animals and Domestic Violence: A National Survey of Shelters for Women Who Are Battered." *Society and Animals* 5 (1997): 205–18.

Ashcraft, Karen Lee, and Lisa Flores. "'Slaves With White Collars': Persistent Performances of Masculinity in Crisis." *Text and Performance Quarterly* 23 (2003): 1–29.

Austin Powers: Goldmember. Dir. Jay Roach. Perf. Mike Meyers, Beyoncé Knowles, and Seth Green. New Line Cinema, 2002.

Austin Powers: The Spy Who Shagged Me. Dir. Jay Roach. Perf. Mike Meyers and Heather Graham. New Line Cinema, 1998.

Bacciocco, Edward J., Jr. *The New Left in America: Reform to Revolution, 1956–1970.* Stanford, CA: Hoover Institution, 1974.

Baglia, Jay. *The Viagra Adventure: Masculinity, Media, and the Performance of Sexual Health.* New York: Peter Lang, 2005.

Beggan, James K. "Labeling Theory." *Encyclopedia of Leadership.* Vol. 2. Thousand Oaks, CA: Sage, 2004.

Bellon, Joe. "The Strange Discourse of *The X-Files*: What It Is, What It Does, and What Is at Stake." *Critical Studies in Mass Communication* 16 (1999): 136–54.

Beneke, Timothy. *Men on Rape.* New York: St. Martin's, 1982.

Biesecker, Barbara A. "Remembering World War II: The Rhetoric and Politics of National Commemoration at the Turn of the 21st Century." *Quarterly Journal of Speech* 88 (2002): 393–409.

Black, Edwin. *Rhetorical Criticism: A Study in Method.* Madison: University of Wisconsin Press, 1978.

Blackmer, Corinne E. "The Veils of the Law: Race and Sexuality in Nella Larsen's Passing." *College Literature* 22.3 (1995): 50–67.

Blackstock, Nathan. *Cointelpro: The FBI's Secret War on Political Freedom.* New York: Pathfinder, 1988.

Blain, Michael. "The Politics of Victimage: Power and Subjection in a US Anti-Gay Campaign." *Critical Discourse Studies* 2 (2005): 31–50.

Blair, Carole, Marsha S. Jeppeson, and Enrico Pucci, Jr. "Public Memorializing in Postmodernity: The Vietnam Veterans Memorial as Prototype." *Quarterly Journal of Speech* 77 (1991): 263–88.

Blum, Harold P. "Sanctified Aggression, Hate, and the Alteration of Standards and Values." *The Birth of Hatred: Developmental, Clinical, and Technical Aspects of Intense Aggression.* Eds. Salman Akhtar, Selma Kramer, and Henri Parens. Northvale, NJ: Jason Aronson, 1995. 15–37.

Boddington, Craig. "So You Want a Bigger Gun?" *Guns and Ammo* Mar. 1999: 74–80.

The Bodyguard. Dir. Mick Jackson. Perf. Whitney Houston and Kevin Costner. Warner Brothers, 1992.

Bogle, Donald. *Toms, Coons, Mulattoes, Mammies, and Bucks: An Interpretive History of Blacks in American Films.* 4th ed. New York: Continuum, 2002.

Bouse, Derek. "Are Wildlife Films Really 'Nature Documentaries'?" *Critical Studies in Mass Communication* 15 (1998): 116–40.

Bowman, Michael S. "Looking for Stonewall's Arm: Tourist Performance as Research Method." *Opening Acts: Performance in/as Communication and Cultural Studies.* Ed. Judith Hamera. Thousand Oaks: Sage, 2006. 102–33.

Boyer, Paul, and Stephen Nissenbaum. *Salem Possessed: The Social Origins of Witchcraft.* Cambridge, MA: Harvard University Press, 1974.

Breznican, Anthony. "Penguins' Progress." *USA Today* 29 Nov. 2005: 6.

Briggs, Robin. *Witches and Neighbors: The Social and Cultural Context of European Witchcraft.* New York: Viking, 1996.

Brinson, Susan. "The Myth of White Superiority in *Mississippi Burning.*" *Southern Communication Journal* 60 (1995): 211–21.

Brokeback Mountain. Dir. Ang Lee. Perf. Heath Ledger, Jake Gyllenhaal, Linda Cardellini, Anna Faris, Anne Hathaway, Michelle Williams, and Randy Quaid. Focus Features, 2005.

"Brokeback Mountain." Internet Movie Database. 1 Sept. 2006 <http://www.imdb.com/title/tt0388795/business>.

Brown, Bruce D. "A Cauldron of Controversy." *Washington Post* 13 Sept. 1992: F1.

Brown, Dan. *The Da Vinci Code.* New York: Doubleday, 2003.

Brown, Jeffrey A. "Comic Book Fandom and Cultural Capital." *Journal of Popular Culture* 30.4 (1997): 13–32.

Brummett, Barry. "Burkean Scapegoating, Mortification, and Transcendence in Presidential Campaign Rhetoric." *Central States Speech Journal* 32 (1981): 254–64.

———. "Electric Literature as Equipment for Living: Haunted House Films." *Critical Studies in Mass Communication* 2 (1985): 247–61.

———. "The Homology Hypothesis: Pornography on the VCR." *Critical Studies in Mass Communication* 5 (1988): 202–16.

———. "A Pentadic Analysis of Ideologies in Two Gay Rights Controversies." *Central States Speech Journal* 30 (1979): 250–61.

———. *Rhetorical Dimensions of Popular Culture.* Tuscaloosa: University of Alabama Press, 1991.

———. *Rhetorical Homologies: Form, Culture, Experience.* Tuscaloosa: University of Alabama Press, 2004.

Brummett, Barry, and Si-Ye Nam. "Korean Apocalyptic Discourse, October, 1992: A Speculative Explanation." *Howard Journal of Communications* 6 (1995): 306–23.

Bureau of Labor Statistics. "Women's Share of Labor Force to Edge Higher by 2008." *Occupational Outlook Quarterly* 6 Feb. 2001. U.S. Department of Labor. 20 Jan. 2007 <http://www.bls.gov/opub/ted/2000/feb/wk3/art01.htm>.

Burke, Kenneth. *Attitudes Toward History.* 3rd ed. Berkeley: University of California Press, 1984.

———. *Counter-Statement.* Berkeley: University of California Press, 1968.

———. *A Grammar of Motives.* 1945. Berkeley: University of California Press, 1969.

———. *Language as Symbolic Action.* Berkeley: University of California Press, 1966.

———. *Permanence and Change: An Anatomy of Purpose.* 3rd ed. Berkeley: University of California Press, 1984.

———. *The Philosophy of Literary Form: Studies in Symbolic Action.* 3rd ed. Berkeley: University of California Press, 1973.

———. *A Rhetoric of Motives.* 1950. Berkeley: University of California Press, 1969.

———. *The Rhetoric of Religion: Studies in Logology.* 1961. Berkeley: University of California Press, 1970.

"The Burning." *Seinfeld.* Dir. Andy Ackerman. Perf. Jerry Seinfeld, Jason Alexander, Julia Louis-Dreyfus, and Michael Richards. NBC. New York City. 19 Mar. 1998.

Bush, George W. "President Delivers State of the Union Address." *The White House Online* 29 Jan. 2002. 3 Apr. 2007 <http://www.whitehouse.gov/news/releases/2002/01/20020129-11.html>.

"Business Data for *Mississippi Burning.*" 15 Jan. 2005. Internet Movie Database. 3 Apr. 2007 <http://www.imdb.com/title/tt0095647/business>.

Butler, Judith. *Bodies That Matter: On the Discursive Limits of Sex.* London: Routledge, 1993.

———. *Gender Trouble.* London: Routledge, 1990.

Bynum, Bill. "Lessons From the Varmint Masters." *Mossy Oak Hunting the Country* Winter 1999: 54–59.

Byrne, Eleanor, and Martin McQuillan. *Deconstructing Disney.* London: Pluto, 1999.

Cagin, Seth, and Philip Dray. *We Are Not Afraid: The Story of Goodman, Schwerner, and Chaney and the Civil Rights Campaign for Mississippi.* New York: Macmillan, 1988.

Campbell, Karlyn Kors, and Kathleen Hall Jamieson. "Form and Genre in Rhetorical Criticism: An Introduction." *Form and Genre: Shaping Rhetorical Action.* Eds. Karlyn Kors Campbell and Kathleen Hall Jamieson. Falls Church, VA: Speech Communication Association, 1978. 9–32.

Carlson, A. Cheree, and John E. Hocking. "Strategies of Redemption at the Vietnam Veterans' Memorial." *Western Journal of Speech Communication* 52 (1988): 203–15.

Carmichael, Stokely. (untitled speech). 19 Apr. 1967. Instructional Resources Center. University of Washington. 5 May 2006 <courses.washington.edu/spcmu/carmichael/>.

———. "Black Power." 29 Oct. 1966. *American Rhetoric.* 5 May 2006 <www.american rhetoric.com/speeches/stokelycarmichaelblackpower.html>.

Cartmill, Matt. *A View to a Death in the Morning: Hunting and Nature Through History.* Cambridge, MA: Harvard University Press, 1993.

Chang, Justin. "Mutants Miss the Mark." *Variety* 29 May 2006: 31, 41.

Chaw, Walter. "The Hero's Ambassador." Filmfreakcentral.net 6 Feb. 2005. 6 Jan. 2007 <http://www.filmfreakcentral.net/notes/dharrisinterview.htm>.

Cialdini, Robert B. *Influence: The Psychology of Influence.* New York: Quill, 1993.

Clarkson, Jay. "Contesting Masculinity's Makeover: Queer Eye, Consumer Masculinity, and 'Straight-Acting' Gays." *Journal of Communication Inquiry* 29 (2005): 235–55.

Cloud, Dana L. *Control and Consolation in American Culture and Politics: Rhetorics of Therapy.* Thousand Oaks, CA: Sage, 1998.

———. "The Limits of Interpretation: Ambivalence and the Stereotype in *Spenser: For Hire.*" *Critical Studies in Mass Communication* 9 (1992): 311–24.

Cold Mountain. Dir. Anthony Minghella. Perf. Nicole Kidman, Jude Law, and Renee Zellweger. Miramax, 2003.

Coleman, Robin R. Means. *African American Viewers and the Black Situation Comedy: Situating Racial Humor.* New York: Garland, 2000.

"Comic Book Writer Stan Lee." *Fresh Air.* NPR. WHYY, Philadelphia. 4 June 2002.

Coogan, Peter. *Superhero: The Secret Origin of a Genre.* Austin, TX: MonkeyBrain, 2006.

Cooper, Brenda. "'The White-Black Fault Line': Relevancy of Race and Racism in Spectator's Experiences of Spike Lee's *Do the Right Thing.*" *Howard Journal of Communications* 9 (1998): 205–28.

"Cruelty to Animals and Human Violence." *Training Key.* Arlington, VA: International Association of Chiefs of Police, 1989. 392.

Curry, Jack. "*Mississippi* Wins 4 Critics' Board Awards." *USA Today* 14 Dec. 1988: D1.

Curtis, Christopher. "States Consider Restricting Gay Adoption." *PlanetOut News* 21 Feb. 2006. 6 Apr. 2007 <http://www.planetout.com/news/article-print.html?2006/02/21/1>.

The Da Vinci Code. Dir. Ron Howard. Perf. Tom Hanks and Audrey Tatou. Columbia Pictures, 2006.

Dan Brown Official Web Site. 28 Oct. 2005. <http://www.danbrown.com/>.

De Waal, Alex. "Everything You Ever Wanted to Know. . . ." *Index on Censorship* 33.1 (2004): 27–37.

Dees, Morris. "Hate Crimes: Our Nation Is Greater Because of Our Diversity." *Vital Speeches of the Day* 66 (2000): 247–52.

Delgado, Fernando. "All Along the Border: Kid Frost and the Performance of Brown Masculinity." *Text and Performance Quarterly* 20 (2000): 388–401.

Denby, David. "Partners." *New Yorker* 12 Sept. 2005: 58.

Diller, Christopher. "Sentimental Types and Social Reform in *Uncle Tom's Cabin*." *Studies in American Fiction* 32 (2004): 21–48.

Drinnon, Richard. *Facing West: The Metaphysics of Indian-Hating and Empire-Building.* Minneapolis: University of Minnesota Press, 1980.

Driscoll, Kimberley. "Haunted Happenings." Salem.com. 8 Nov. 2006 <http://www.salem.com/Pages/SalemMA_WebDocs/S00A87F79>.

Dworkin, Andrea. "Pornography Happens to Women." *The Price We Pay: The Case Against Racist Speech, Hate Propaganda, and Pornography.* Eds. Laura J. Lederer and Richard Delgado. New York: Hill, 1995. 181–90.

Dyer, Richard. *White.* New York: Routledge, 1997.

Edelman, Murray. *Politics as Symbolic Action: Mass Arousal and Quiescence.* New York: Academic Press, 1971.

Elf. Dir. Jon Favreau. Perf. Will Ferrell and James Caan. New Line Cinema, 2003.

Eliot, T. S. *The Idea of a Christian Society.* London: Faber, 1939.

Elsworth, Catherine. "Stop Making Us Out as Mystical Freaks and Unconscionable Assassins, Albinos Complain." *Telegraph.co.uk* 18 May 2006. 6 Apr. 2007 <http://www.telegraph.co.uk/news/main.jhtml?xml=/news/2006/05/18/wcannes118.xml>.

Etchingham, Julie. "Hate.com Expands on the Net." *BBC News* 12 Jan. 2000. 4 Apr. 2000 <http://news.bbc.co.uk/hi/english/world/americas/newsid_600000/600876.stm>.

Evans, Nicholas. *The Horse Whisperer.* New York: Dell, 1996.

Farley, John C. "That Old Black Magic." *Time* 27 Nov. 2000: 14.

Felthous, Alan R. "Aggression Against Cats, Dogs and People." *Child Psychiatry and Human Development* 10 (1980): 169–77.

Felthous, Alan R., and Stephen R. Kellert. "Childhood Cruelty to Animals and Later Aggression Against People: A Review." *American Journal of Psychiatry* 144 (1987): 710–17.

Festinger, Leon. *A Theory of Cognitive Dissonance.* Stanford: Stanford University Press, 1957.

The Firm. Dir. Sydney Pollack. Perf. Tom Cruise and Jeanne Tripplehorn. Paramount, 1993.

Foss, Sonja K. "Ambiguity as Persuasion: The Vietnam Veterans Memorial." *Communication Quarterly* 34 (1986): 326–40.

Foucault, Michel. *Discipline and Punish.* New York: Vintage, 1977.

———. *History of Sexuality.* New York: Pantheon, 1978.

Franklin, Adrian. *Animals and Modern Cultures: A Sociology of Human-Animal Relations in Modernity.* London: Sage, 1999.

Frederickson, George M. *The Black Image in the White Mind: The Debate on Afro-American Character and Destiny, 1817–1914.* New York: Harper, 1971.

Freedman, Monroe H., and Eric M. Freedman, eds. *Group Defamation and Freedom of Speech: The Relationship Between Language and Violence.* Westport, CT: Greenwood, 1995.

Freud, Sigmund. "A Neurosis of Demoniacal Possession in the Seventeenth Century." 1923. *Collected Papers.* Vol. 4. Ed. Ernest Jones. Trans. Joan Riviere. New York: Basic, 1959. 436–72.

Gabbard, Krin. "Black Angels." *Chronicle of Higher Education* 49 (2003): 22 pars. 16 Jan. 2007 <http://web.ebscohost.com>.

Gallagher, Victoria. "Black Power in Berkeley: Postmodern Constructions in the Rhetoric of Stokely Carmichael." *Quarterly Journal of Speech* 87 (2001): 144–57.

"Game Targets Hunters." *American Rifleman* July 1999: 147+.

Gates, Henry Louis, Jr. *The Signifying Monkey: A Theory of African-American Literary Criticism.* New York: Oxford University Press, 1988.

Geertz, Clifford. *The Interpretation of Cultures.* New York: Basic, 1973.

Giordano, Alice. "Reawakening of History." *Boston Globe* 15 Apr. 2001: G1.

Giroux, Henry. *The Mouse That Roared: Disney and the End of Innocence.* Lanham, MD: Rowman, 1999.

Gordon, Devin. "The 'Code' Breakers." *Newsweek* 2 Jan. 2005: 94–106.

Gourevitch, Philip. *We Wish to Inform You That Tomorrow We Will Be Killed With Our Families: Stories From Rwanda.* New York: Farrar, 1998.

Gray, Herman. *Watching Race: Television and the Struggle for Blackness.* Minneapolis: University of Minnesota Press, 1995.

Gresham, Tom. "Gresham on Guns: Power of the Net." *Petersen's Hunting* Feb. 2000: 51.

Griffin, Cindy L. "Rhetoricizing Alienation: Mary Wollstonecraft and the Rhetorical Construction of Women's Oppression." *Quarterly Journal of Speech* 80 (1994): 293–312.

Groth, A. Nicholas. *Men Who Rape: The Psychology of the Offender.* New York: Plenum, 1979.

Gunn, Joshua. *Modern Occult Rhetoric: Mass Media and the Drama of Secrecy in the Twentieth Century.* Tuscaloosa: University of Alabama Press, 2005.

Hahn, Steven. "Hunting, Fishing, and Foraging: Common Rights and Class Relations in the Postbellum South." *Radical History Review* 26 (1982): 37–64.

Hall, Carla. "Director Parker, Master Manipulator." *Washington Post* 9 Dec. 1988: C01.

Hamer, Dean, Stella Hu, Victoria A. Magnuson, Nan Hu, and Angela M. L. Pattatucci. "A Linkage Between DNA Markers on the X Chromosome and Male Sexual Orientation." *Science* 261 (1993): 321–27.

Hank the Angry Drunken Dwarf Official Website. 8 July 2006 <http://www.hankthed warf.com/flash_dynamic/frameset.html>.

Hanke, Robert. "Hegemonic Masculinity in *Thirtysomething*." *Critical Studies in Mass Communication* 7 (1990): 231–48.

Hart, Roderick. *Modern Rhetorical Criticism.* 2nd ed. Boston: Allyn, 1997.

Hasian, Marouf, and Cheree Carlson. "Revisionism and Collective Memory: The Struggle for Meaning in the *Amistad* Affair." *Communication Monographs* 67 (2000): 42–55.

Hazler, Richard J. *Breaking the Cycle of Violence: Interventions for Bullying and Victimization.* Washington, DC: Accelerated Development, 1996.

Heinemann, Evelyn. *Witches: A Psychoanalytic Exploration of the Killing of Women.* Trans. Donald Kiraly. London: Free Association, 2000.

"Hezbollah Sharply Rejects Cease-Fire, Say It Will Continue Rocket Strikes." *Foxnews.com* 17 July 2006. 3 Apr. 2007 <http://www.foxnews.com/story/0,2933,203908,00.html>.

Hicks, J. Heather. "Hoodoo Economics: White Men's Work and Black Men's Magic in Contemporary American Film." *Camera Obscura* 53 (2003): 27–55.

Hobsbawm, Eric. *Nations and Nationalism Since 1780.* Cambridge, UK: Cambridge University Press, 1990.

hooks, bell. *Where We Stand: Class Matters.* New York: Routledge, 2000.

The Horse Whisperer. Dir. Robert Redford. Perf. Robert Redford, Kristin Scott Thomas, Scarlett Johansson, Sam Neill, and Dianne Wiest. Buena Vista, 1998.

Iles, Jennifer. "Recalling the Ghosts of War: Performing Tourism on the Battlefields of the Western Front." *Text and Performance Quarterly* 26 (2006): 162–80.

Ingebretsen, Edward J. *At Stake: Monsters and the Rhetoric of Fear in Public Culture.* Chicago: University of Chicago Press, 2001.

Ingold, Tim. "From Trust to Domination: An Alternative History of Human-Animal Relations." *Animals and Human Society: Changing Perspectives.* Eds. Aubrey Manning and James Serpell. London: Routledge, 1994. 1–22.

Ivie, Robert L. "Literalizing the Metaphor of Soviet Savagery: President Truman's Plain Style." *Southern Speech Communication Journal* 51 (1986): 91–105.

———. "The Metaphor of Force in Prowar Discourse: The Case of 1812." *Quarterly Journal of Speech* 68 (1982): 240–53.

Jacobs, James B., and Kimberly Potter. *Hate Crimes: Criminal Law and Identity Politics.* New York: Oxford University Press, 1998.

Jameson, Fredric. "Reification and Utopia in Mass Culture." *Social Text* 1 (1979): 130–48.

JanMohamed, Abdul R. "The Economy of Manichean Allegory: The Function of Racial Difference in Colonialist Literature." *Critical Inquiry* 12 (1985): 59–87.

Jenness, Valerie, and Kendal Broad. *Hate Crimes: New Social Movements and the Politics of Violence.* New York: Aldine de Gruyter, 1997.

Johnston, Anne. "Mass Media and the Sexual Revolution." *History of the Mass Media in the United States: An Encyclopedia.* Ed. Margaret A. Blanchard. Chicago: Fitzroy Dearborn, 1998. 380–82.

Kachgal, Tara. "'Look at *The Real World.* There's Always a Gay Teen on There': Sexual Citizenship and Youth-Targeted Reality Television." *Feminist Media Studies* 4 (2004): 361–64.

Karlsen, Carol F. *The Devil in the Shape of a Woman: Witchcraft in Colonial New England.* New York: Norton, 1998.

Kellert, Stephen R. "American Attitudes Toward and Knowledge of Animals: An Update." *International Journal for the Study of Animal Problems* 1 (1980): 87–119.

———. "Perceptions of Animals in America." *Perceptions of Animals in American Culture.* Ed. R. J. Hoage. Washington, DC: Smithsonian, 1989. 5–24.

———. "Perceptions of Animals in American Society." *Transactions: Forty-First North American Wildlife and Natural Resources Conference.* Ed. Kenneth Sabol. Washington, DC: Wildlife Management Institute, 1976. 533–46.

———. *Policy Implications of a National Study of American Attitudes and Behavioral Relations to Animals.* Washington, DC: Government Printing Office, 1978.

Kellert, Stephen R., and Joyce K. Berry. *Phase III: Knowledge, Affection and Basic Attitudes Toward Animals in American Society.* Unpublished mss., 1980. Yale University, New Haven, CT.

Kellert, Stephen R., and Alan R. Felthous. "Childhood Cruelty Toward Animals Among Criminals and Noncriminals." *Human Relations* 38 (1985): 1113–129.

Kellett, Peter M. "Acts of Power, Control, and Resistance." *Hate Speech.* Eds. Rita Kirk Whillock and David Slayden. Thousand Oaks, CA: Sage, 1995. 142–62.

Kelly, Robert J. "Black Rage, Murder, Racism, and Madness: The Metamorphosis of Colin Ferguson." *Hate Crime: The Global Politics of Polarization.* Eds. Robert J. Kelly and Jess Maghan. Carbondale: Southern Illinois University Press, 1998. 22–36.

Kennedy, Dan. "Little People Big World: Will TLC's New Reality Show Really Change Our Perceptions of Dwarfs?" *Slate* 24 Mar. 2006. 6 Apr. 2007 <http://www.slate.com/id/2138626/>.

LaClau, Ernesto, and Chantal Mouffe. *Hegemony and Socialist Strategy: Towards a Radical Democratic Politics*, 2nd ed. New York: Verso, 1994.

Lakoff, George, and Mark Johnson. *Metaphors We Live By.* Chicago: University of Chicago Press, 1980.

Lakoff, Robin Tolmach. *The Language War.* Berkeley: University of California Press, 2000.

Lawrence, Bruce B. *Defenders of God: The Fundamentalist Revolt Against the Modern Age.* San Francisco: Harper, 1989.

Leach, Edmund. "Anthropological Aspects of Language: Animal Categories and Verbal Abuse." *New Directions in the Study of Language.* Ed. Eric Lenneberg. Cambridge, MA: MIT Press, 1964. 23–63.

Lee, Ang. "Directing From the Heart." *Brokeback Mountain* DVD Bonus Feature.

Lee, Stan, and George Mair. *Excelsior! The Amazing Life of Stan Lee.* New York: Fireside, 2002.

Lens, Vicki. "Social Work and the Supreme Court: A Clash of Values; A Time for Action." *Social Work* 49 (2004): 327–30.

Letellier, Patrick. "March of the Zealots: Penguins and America's Cultural Wars." *Lesbian News* Dec. 2005: 16.

Levack, Brian P. *The Witch-Hunt in Early Modern Europe.* 3rd ed. Harlow, UK: Pearson, 2006.

Levin, Jack, and Jack McDevitt. *Hate Crimes: The Rising Tide of Bigotry and Bloodshed.* New York: Plenum, 1993.

Lévi-Strauss, Claude. *The Raw and the Cooked.* Trans. J. Weightman and D. Weightman. New York: Harper, 1969.

Lippman, John. "In Hollywood, It's Penguin Season." *Wall Street Journal* 29 July 2005: W6.

Lipsitz, George. *Time Passages: Collective Memory and American Popular Culture.* Minneapolis: University of Minnesota Press, 1990.

Lockwood, Randall. "Animal Cruelty: No Small Matter." *Police* July 1987: 11+.

Lockwood, Randall, and Ann Church. "Deadly Serious: An FBI Perspective on Animal Cruelty." *Humane Society of the United States News* 41 (1996): 27–30.

Lockwood, Randall, and Guy R. Hodge. "The Tangled Web of Animal Abuse: The Links Between Cruelty to Animals and Human Violence." *Humane Society of the United States News* 31 (1986): 10–15.

The Lord of the Rings: The Fellowship of the Ring. Dir. Peter Jackson. Perf. Elijah Wood, Ian McKellen, and Viggo Mortenson. New Line Cinema, 2001.

The Lord of the Rings: The Two Towers. Dir. Peter Jackson. Perf. Elijah Wood, Ian McKellen, and Viggo Mortenson. New Line Cinema, 2002.

Lucaites, John L., and Celeste M. Condit. "Reconstructing <Equality>: Culturetypal and Counter-cultural Rhetorics in the Martyred Black Vision." *Communication Monographs* 57 (1990): 5–24.

Lynch, John. "Institution and Imprimatur: Institutional Rhetoric and the Failure of the Catholic Church's Pastoral Letter on Homosexuality." *Rhetoric and Public Affairs* 8 (2005): 383–403.

MacCannell, Dean. "Staged Authenticity: Arrangements of Social Space in Tourist Settings." *American Journal of Sociology* 79 (1973): 589–603.

MacDonald, Scott. "Up Close and Political: Three Short Ruminations on Ideology in the Nature Film." *Film Quarterly* 59.3 (2006): 4–21.

Mackey-Kallis, Susan, and Dan Hahn. "Who's to Blame for America's Drug Problem? The Search for Scapegoats in the 'War on Drugs.'" *Communication Quarterly* 42 (1994): 1–20.

Madison, Kelly. "Legitimation Crisis and Containment: The 'Anti-Racist-White-Hero' Film." *Critical Studies in Mass Communication* 16 (1999): 399–416.

Malin, Brenton J. *American Masculinity Under Clinton: Popular Media and the Nineties "Crisis of Masculinity."* New York: Peter Lang, 2005.

Marable, Manning. *Race, Reform, and Rebellion.* London: Macmillan, 1984.

March of the Penguin. Dir. Luc Jacquet. Warner, 2005.

Marcus, Laurence R. *Fighting Words: The Politics of Hateful Speech.* Westport, CT: Praeger, 1996.

Marden, Peter. *The Decline of Politics: Governance, Globalization and the Public Sphere.* Aldershot, UK: Ashgate, 2003.

Marks, Stuart A. *Southern Hunting in Black and White: Nature, History, and Ritual in a Carolina Community.* Princeton: Princeton University Press, 1991.

Marquand, Robert. "Feelings Smolder Over *Burning* Issue." *Christian Science Monitor* 24 Feb. 1989: 11.

Marx, Karl. *Capital.* Vol. 1: *The Process of Capitalist Production.* Ed. Fredrick Engels. New York: International, 1979.

Marx, Karl, and Frederick Engels. *The German Ideology.* Part 1. Ed. C. J. Arthur. New York: International, 1995.

Masson, Jeffrey Moussaieff, ed. and trans. *The Complete Letters of Sigmund Freud to Wilhelm Fliess 1887–1904.* Cambridge, MA: Harvard University Press, 1985.

Mather, Cotton. "A Discourse on Witches." 1689. *Witchcraft in Europe, 400–1700: A Documentary History.* Eds. Alan Charles Kors and Edward Peters. Philadelphia: University of Pennsylvania Press, 2001. 367–70.

———. "Memorable Providences Relating to Witchcrafts and Possessions." 1689. *The Witchcraft Sourcebook.* Ed. Brian P. Levack. New York: Routledge, 2004. 261–65.

The Matrix Reloaded. Dir. Andy Wachowski and Larry Wachowski. Perf. Keanu Reeves, Laurence Fishburn, Carie-Anne Moss, and Jada Pinkett Smith. Warner Brothers, 2003.

McCall, Nathan. *Makes Me Wanna Holler: A Young Black Man in America.* New York: Random, 1994.

Mechling, Jay, and Angus K. Gillespie. "Introduction." *American Wildlife in Symbol and Story.* Eds. Angus K. Gillespie and Jay Mechling. Knoxville: University of Tennessee Press, 1987. 1–14.

Medhurst, Martin. "The First Amendment vs. Human Rights: A Case Study in Community Sentiment and Argument From Definition." *Western Journal of Speech Communication* 46 (1982): 1–19.

Michaud, Chris. "GLAAD Honors *Brokeback Mountain.*" Advocate.com. 29 Mar. 2006. 1 Sept. 2006 <http://www.advocate.com/news_detail_ektid28367.asp>.

Miller, Andrew. "Clowning Around in a Tuxedo at 50 Below." *Times Higher Education Supplement* 16 Dec. 2005: 13.

Miller, Jonathan. "March of the Conservatives: Penguin Film as Political Fodder." *New York Times* 13 Sept. 2005: 2.

Milloy, Courtland. "We Need Black Historians." *Washington Post* 15 Jan. 1989: B03.

Mississippi Burning. Dir. Alan Parker. Orion Pictures, 1988.

Miyoshi, Masao. "A Borderless World? From Colonialism to Transnationalism and the Decline of the Nation-State." *Critical Inquiry* 19 (1993): 726–51.

Morrison, Toni. *Playing in the Dark: Whiteness and the Literary Imagination.* Cambridge, MA: Harvard University Press, 1992.

Moser, Bob. "Holy War: The Religious Crusade Against Gays Has Been Building for 30 Years. Now the Movement Is Reaching Truly Biblical Proportions." *Intelligence Report* (Spring 2005). 9 Jan. 2007 <http://www.splcenter.org/intel/intelreport/article.jsp?aid=522>.

Murray, Sarah. "Digital Government: Public Service in the US." *Financial Times* 4 Oct. 2006.

Nakayama, Thomas K., and Robert L. Krizek. "Whiteness as a Strategic Rhetoric." *Whiteness: The Communication of Social Identity.* Eds. Thomas K. Nakayama and Judith N. Martin. Thousand Oaks, CA: Sage, 1999: 87–106.

National Organization for Albinism and Hypopigmentation (NOAH) Web Site. 11 Nov. 2005 <http://www.albinism.org/>.

Nichols, Bill. *Ideology and the Image: Social Representation in the Cinema and Other Media.* Bloomington: Indiana University Press, 1981.

Noel, Josh. "A Fight Is on Over Dwarf-Wrestling Shows." *The Chicago Tribune* 27 Apr. 2006. 8 July 2006 <http://www.chicagotribune.com/news/local/chicago/chi-0604270040apr27,1,2000502.story>.

Norton, Mary Beth. *In the Devil's Snare: The Salem Witchcraft Crisis of 1692.* New York: Alfred A. Knopf, 2002.

Nossiter, Adam. *Of Long Memory: Mississippi and the Murder of Medgar Evers.* 2nd ed. Cambridge, MA: DeCapo Press, 2002.

O'Donnell, Lawrence, Flavis Colgan, Lisa Myers, and Joe Scarborough. "Scarborough Country for June 25, 2004." *Scarborough Country, MSNBC.* 25 June 2004. Transcript.

Ogbar, Jeffrey. *Black Power: Radical Politics and African American Identity.* Baltimore: Johns Hopkins University Press, 2004.

Okenfuss, Dan. "Officers' Monthly Message." Online posting. Sept. 2005. http://www.lpaonline.org/monthly_05_sep.doc.

Oliver, Mary Beth. "Portrayals of Crime, Race, and Aggression in 'Reality-Based' Police Shows: A Content Analysis." *Journal of Communication* 38 (1994): 179–93.

Olson, Kathryn M. "Detecting a Common Interpretive Framework for Impersonal Violence: The Homology in Participants' Rhetoric on Sport Hunting, 'Hate Crimes,' and Stranger Rape." *Southern Communication Journal* 67 (2002): 215–44.

———. "Expanding the Horizons of Justification: The Role of Myth in Cultural Transformation." *Argument in Controversy.* Ed. Donn W. Parson. Annandale, VA: Speech Communication Association, 1991. 46–52.

———. "The Function of Form in Newspapers' Political Conflict Coverage: The *New York Times'* Shaping of Expectations in the Bitburg Controversy." *Political Communication* 12 (1995): 43–64.

———. "The Role of Dissociation in Redeeming Knowledge Claims: Nineteenth-Century Shakers' Epistemological Resistance to Decline." *Philosophy and Rhetoric* 28 (1995): 45–68.

Osborn, Michael. "Archetypal Metaphor in Rhetoric: The Light-Dark Family." *Readings in Rhetorical Criticism.* 2nd ed. Ed. Carl R. Burgchardt. State College, PA: Strata, 2000: 456–70.

——. "The Evolution of the Archetypal Sea in Rhetoric and Poetic." *Quarterly Journal of Speech* 63 (1977): 347–63.

Osteen, Joel. *Your Best Life Now: 7 Steps to Living at Your Full Potential.* New York: Warner Faith, 2004.

Palmer-Mehta, Valerie. "The Wisdom of Folly: Disrupting Masculinity in *King of the Hill.*" *Text and Performance Quarterly* 26 (2006): 181–98.

Park, David. "The Kefauver Comic Book Hearings as Show Trial: Decency, Authority, and the Dominated Expert." *Cultural Studies* 16 (2002): 259–88.

Parry-Giles, Shawn. "Gendered Politics and Presidential Image Construction: A Reassessment of the 'Feminine Style.'" *Communication Monographs* 63 (1996): 337–53.

"Penguin Family Values." *New York Times* 18 Sept. 2005: 11.

Peniel, Joseph E. *The Black Power Movement: Rethinking the Civil Rights–Black Power Era.* New York: Taylor, 2006.

Porter, Pete. "Review Section." *Society and Animals* 14 (2006): 201–15.

Pounsett, Geoffrey. "Natural History: Going Wild for the Big Screen." *Realscreen* 1 Sept. 2005: 33.

Powder. Dir. Victor Salva. Perf. Mary Steenburgen, Jeff Goldblum, and Sean Patrick Flanery. Buena Vista Pictures, 1995.

"Pride and Prejudice." *Dharma and Greg.* FX. 21 June 2006.

The Princess Bride. Dir. Rob Reiner. Perf. Cary Elwes and Robin Wright Penn. Twentieth Century Fox, 1987.

Proulx, Annie. *Brokeback Mountain.* New York: Scribner, 2005.

——. "Getting Movied." *Brokeback Mountain: Story to Screenplay.* Annie Proulx, Larry McMurtry, and Diana Ossana. New York: Scribner, 2005. 129–38.

Proulx, Annie, Larry McMurtry, and Diana Ossana. *Brokeback Mountain: Story to Screenplay.* New York: Scribner, 2005.

Puig, Claudia. "March of the Penguins Is Generating Heat." *USA Today* 12 July 2005: 1.

Purkiss, Diane. *The Witch in History: Early Modern and Twentieth-century Representations.* London: Routledge, 1996.

Reyes, Damaso. "March of Penguins Into Hearts, Minds and Video Stores." *New York Amsterdam News* 8 Dec. 2005: 22.

Richards, I. A. *The Philosophy of Rhetoric.* Oxford, UK: Oxford University Press, 1936.

Richardson, John H. *In the Little World: A True Story of Dwarfs, Love, and Trouble.* New York: Harper, 2001.

Ringel, Eleanor. "Truth Isn't as Simple as Black, White in *Mississippi Burning.*" *Atlanta Journal and Constitution* 22 Jan. 1989: K01.

Roberts, Monty. *The Man Who Listens to Horses.* New York: Ballantine, 1998.

Rupp, J. Scott. "Recruiting Made Easy." *Petersen's Hunting* Feb. 2000: 28+.

Said, Edward W. *Culture and Imperialism.* New York: Vintage, 1993.

——. *Orientalism.* New York: Vintage, 1978.

Salem Office of Tourism and Cultural Affairs, Inc. "Early Salem." Destination Salem. 14 Dec. 2006 <http://salem.org/17th_Century.asp>.

——. "History." Destination Salem. 14 Dec. 2006 <http://www.salem.org/history.asp>.

——. "Salem Visitors Guide." Destination Salem. 12 Dec. 2006 <http://salem.org/visitors.asp>.

"Salem Wax Museum." Salemwaxmuseum.com. 8 Nov. 2006 <http://www.salemwaxmuseum.com/>.

"Salem Witch Village." Salemwitchvillage.net. 8 Nov. 2006 <http://www.salemwitchvillage.net/home.html>.

Schickel, Richard. "Love in a Very Cold Climate." *Time* 11 July 2005: 68.

Schmitt, Ronald. "Deconstructive Comics." *Journal of Popular Culture* 25.4 (1992): 153–61.

Scott, A. O. "The Hollywood-Style Documentary." *New York Times* 11 Dec. 2005: 74.

———. "Reading From Left to Right." *New York Times* 25 Sept. 2005: 1.

Scott, Robert L., and Wayne Brockriede. *The Rhetoric of Black Power*. New York: Harper, 1969.

"Senator Helms and the Guilty Victims." *New York Times* 17 June 1987: A30.

"Sharing the Story: The Making of *Brokeback Mountain*." Prod. Amy Beers. *Brokeback Mountain* DVD Bonus Feature. Logo Movie Special, 2005.

Shugart, Helene A. "Performing Ambiguity: The Passing of Ellen DeGeneres." *Text and Performance Quarterly* 23 (2003): 30–54.

Sievert, Suzanne. "It's Not Just How We Play That Matters." *Newsweek* 19 Mar. 2001: 137+.

Signorielli, Nancy, Ariana Horry, and Kristin Carlton. "Minorities in Prime Time: Is There Parity?" National Communication Association Convention. Chicago, IL. Nov. 2004.

Simon Birch. Dir. Mark Steven Johnson. Perf. Ian Michael Smith, Joseph Mazzello, and Ashley Judd. Disney, 1998.

"The 'Smartest' Whitetails." *North American Whitetail* Dec. 1999: 10+.

Smith, Cheryl. "Animal Cruelty and the Link to Other Violent Crimes." *Latham Letter* Winter 1995: 1+.

Smith, Ralph R., and Russel R. Windes. "The Progay and Antigay Issue Culture: Interpretation, Influence and Dissent." *Quarterly Journal of Speech* 83 (1997): 28–48.

Smith, Sean. "Baby Penguins = Big $." *Newsweek* 22 Aug. 2005: 12.

Spitz, David, and Starling Hunter. "Contested Codes: The Social Construction of Napster." *Information Society* 21 (2005): 169–80.

"The Stand In." *Seinfeld*. Dir. Tom Cherones. Perf. Jerry Seinfeld, Jason Alexander, Julia Louis-Dreyfus, and Michael Richards. NBC. New York City. 24 Feb. 1994.

Stanley, Kelli E. "'Suffering Sappho!': *Wonder Woman* and the (Re)Invention of the Feminine Ideal." *Helios* 32 (2005): 143–71.

"The State of Black America: Executive Summary 2007." National Urban League 2007. 12 June 2007 <http://www.nul.org/thestateofblackamerica.html>.

Stevens, Dennis J. *Inside the Mind of a Serial Rapist*. San Francisco: Austin, 1999.

Stewart, Charles. "The Evolution of a Revolution: Stokely Carmichael and the Rhetoric of Black Power." *Quarterly Journal of Speech* 83 (1997): 429–46.

Sullivan, Andrew. "What's So Bad About Hate?" *New York Times Magazine* 26 Sept. 1999: 50+.

"Superheroes Born Out of Discrimination." WENN Entertainment News Wire Service 17 Oct. 2006.

Sussman, Les, and Sally Bordwell. *The Rapist File*. New York: Chelsea House, 1981.

"Taiwan Cheers Lee's Oscar Win." *Los Angeles Times* 7 Mar. 2006: E3. Lexis Nexis. Lexis Nexis Academic Universe. Scarborough-Phillips Library, Austin, Texas. 9 Sept. 2006 <http://web.lexis-nexis.com>.

Taylor, Susan Lee. "Music Piracy: Differences in the Ethical Perceptions of Business Majors and Music Business Majors." *Journal of Education for Business* 79 (2004): 306–10.

Terrill, Robert E. "Spectacular Repression: Sanitizing the Batman." *Critical Studies in Mass Communication* 17 (2000): 493–509.

Thernstrom, Melanie. "The Crucifixion of Matthew Shepard." *Vanity Fair* Mar. 1999: 209+.

Thomas, Jo. "How White Supremacist Turned Promising Son Into Monster: Extreme Views, Strict Control Created Murderer." *San Francisco Chronicle* 31 Dec. 1999. 4 Apr. 2000 <http://www.sfgate.com/cgi-bin/article.cgi?file=/chronicle/archive/ 1999/12/31/MN6065.DTL>.

Thompson, Mark, ed. *Long Road to Freedom: The Advocate History of the Gay and Lesbian Movement.* New York: St. Martin's, 1994.

Thomson, Rosemarie Garland. *Extraordinary Bodies: Figuring Physical Disability in American Culture and Literature.* New York: Columbia University Press, 1997.

Toufexis, Anastasia. "New Evidence of a 'Gay Gene.'" *Time* 13 Nov. 1995: 95.

Trask, Richard. "Ask the Expert." Nationalgeographic.com. 14 Dec. 2006 <http://www3 .nationalgeographic.com/salem/>.

Trushell, John M. "American Dreams of Mutants: *The X-Men*—'Pulp' Fiction, Science Fiction, and Superheroes." *Journal of Popular Culture* 38 (2004): 149–68.

Turan, Kenneth. "*X2:* Many More Mutants." *Morning Edition.* NPR. 2 May 2003. 6 Jan. 2007 <http://www.npr.org/templates/story/story.php?storyId=1249629>.

Urban, Robert. "*X-Men:* The Last Stand as Gay Metaphor." Afterelton.com 26 May 2006. 3 Jan. 2007 <http://www.afterelton.com/movies/2006/5/xmenreview2.html>.

U.S. Department of Justice. *Hate Crimes Statistics, 1994.* Washington, DC: Federal Bureau of Investigation, Criminal Justice Information Services Division, 1995.

Vail, Mark. "The 'Integrative' Rhetoric of Martin Luther King, Jr.'s 'I Have a Dream' Speech." *Rhetoric and Public Affairs* 9 (2006): 51–78.

Vanden Brook, T. "Big Buck$: Deer Hunters Make Huge Impact on Wisconsin Economy." *Milwaukee Journal Sentinel* 20 Nov. 1999: 1A+.

———. "Deer Population Exploding Across the USA." *USA Today* 22 Dec. 2000: 17A+.

Vary, Adam B. "Mutant Is the New Gay." *The Advocate* 23 May 2006: 44–45.

Veith, Ilza. *Hysteria: The History of a Disease.* Chicago: University of Chicago Press, 1965.

Walker, Matt. "Bird-brained." *New Scientist* 188 (2005): 17.

Walters, Mark. "Opening Weekend One to Remember." *Oconomowoc Enterprise* 7 Dec. 2000: B6.

Watts, Eric K., and Mark P. Orbe. "The Spectacular Consumption of 'True' African American Culture: 'Whassup' with the Budweiser Guys?" *Critical Studies in Media Communication* 19 (2002): 1–20.

Webster, John. "The Displaying of Supposed Witchcraft." 1677. *The Witchcraft Sourcebook.* Ed. Brian P. Levack. New York: Routledge, 2004. 307–11.

Whillock, Rita Kirk, and David Slayden, eds. *Hate Speech.* Thousand Oaks, CA: Sage, 1995.

White, Ken, and Ken Shapiro. "The Animal Connection." *Animals' Agenda* Mar./Apr. 1994: 19+.

Wilkins, Roy, and Ron Clark. *Search and Destroy: A Report by the Commission of Inquiry into the Black Panthers and the Police.* New York: Metropolitan Applied Research Center, 1973.

Willow. Dir. Ron Howard. Perf. Warwick Davis, Val Kilmer, and Joanne Whalley. Twentieth Century Fox, 1988.

Witch City. Dir. Joe Cultrera and Henry Ferrini. DVD. Picture Business Productions, 1996.

Wolf-Meyer, Matthew J. "Batman and Robin in the Nude, or Class and Its Exceptions." *Extrapolation* 47 (2006): 187–206.

Worden, Amy. "Study: Hate Groups Merge, Get More Dangerous." *APBNews.com* 15 Mar. 2000. 4 Apr. 2000 <http://www.apbnews.com/newscenter/breakingnews/2000/03/15/hatecrimes0315_01.html>.

World Wrestling Entertainment Web Site. 19 July 2006. 16 Dec. 2006 <http://www.wwe.com/inside/news/juniors>.

X-Men. Dir. Bryan Singer. Perf. Patrick Stewart and Ian McKellen. 20th Century Fox, 2000.

X-Men: The Last Stand. Dir. Brett Ratner. Perf. Patrick Stewart and Ian McKellen. 20th Century Fox, 2006.

X2: X-Men United. Dir. Bryan Singer. Perf. Patrick Stewart and Ian McKellen. 20th Century Fox, 2003.

Yatzeck, Richard. *Hunting the Edges.* Madison: University of Wisconsin Press, 1999.

"The Year in Hate." *Southern Poverty Law Center* 2000. 5 May 2000 <http://www.splcenter.org/cgi-bin/p . . . e=/intelligenceproject/ip-4m2.html>.

Zavarzadeh, Mas'ud. *Seeing Films Politically.* Albany: State University of New York Press, 1991.

Index

About the Editor

Barry Brummett is Charles Sapp Centennial Professor of Communication at the University of Texas at Austin, where he is also Chair of the Department of Communication Studies. Brummett received his PhD from the University of Minnesota in 1978. He is the author of several articles and books including *Rhetorical Homologies: Form, Culture, Experience,* and *Rhetoric in Popular Culture.* His most recent research projects have to do with the rhetoric of style and its emergence as a global system of communication.

About the Contributors

Angela J. Aguayo is an Assistant Professor in the Department of Communication Studies at Eastern Illinois University. She is interested in the investigation of the media as a site of political communication, social contestation, protest, and social change. Aguayo's research program is specifically focused on the rhetorical history of documentary film and video as public argument and the use of this medium in the social change process. In addition to her primary research interests, Aguayo produces documentary video shorts and has screened them at several film festivals including the New York Underground Film Festival, the Cinematexas International Film Festival, and the Spark Student Film Festival.

Sharon Avital is a PhD student at the Department of Communication Studies at the University of Texas at Austin. She is interested in the intersection of rhetoric, religion, and aesthetics. Bodily cognition and transcendence of the body-mind duality are essential for her view of communication and human self-understanding. More specifically, Avital studies the relations between image and word in cultural texts and the ways in which perception and bodily sensations are played about in popular culture and the religious sphere. An Israeli who has traveled and lived in different places, Avital's work crosses different cultures and religions and is inspired by her experience as a yoga teacher and a therapist in alternative medicine.

William Earnest is an Assistant Professor of Communication at St. Edward's University in Austin, Texas. He holds PhD and masters degrees from the University of Texas at Austin, where he taught as an Assistant Instructor from 1997 until 2001. His doctoral work focused on communication issues unique to multimedia presentations. From 2002 to 2005, he was on the faculty of the University of Texas's prestigious McCombs School of Business, where he lectured in Business Communication and was nominated for a Texas Exes Outstanding Teaching Award. Earnest hails from Wichita Falls, Texas, home of his alma mater,

Midwestern State University. From 1990 to 1995, he was an Atlanta-based systems analyst, technical writer, and corporate trainer for Electronic Data Systems.

Teresita (Tere) Garza is Assistant Professor of Communication at St. Edward's University in Austin, Texas. Her teaching and research areas include rhetorical theory and criticism, popular culture, communication theory, cultural studies, Native American-Chicana/o film, and communication. Originally from Racine, Wisconsin, Garza received her BA from the University of Wisconsin–Parkside and her MA in Communication from the University of Wisconsin–Milwaukee. Prior to receiving her doctorate, she was the Assistant Director of the Interim Multicultural Center (now the Multicultural Student Center) and Multicultural Council (MCC) advisor at the University of Wisconsin–Madison. She received her PhD in Communication Studies from the University of Iowa.

Roger Gatchet earned his BA degree in speech communication from the California Polytechnic State University of San Luis Obispo in 2001 and his MA from the University of Texas at Austin in 2007. He is a doctoral student at the University of Texas at Austin in the Department of Communication Studies. Gatchet draws from a variety of critical-cultural theories, as well as psychoanalytic approaches to rhetorical criticism to investigate the power relations that structure and determine a variety of cultural texts and practices. Some of his research interests include witch-hunting as both a historical practice and a persecutory form, the intersections between rhetoric and tourism, and the rhetoric of popular music.

E. Johanna Hartelius is a doctoral candidate in the Communication Studies Department, University of Texas at Austin. Her previous publications include an article on rhetorical homologies and pedagogy in the winter issue of *Rhetoric Society Quarterly* (2006) and a co-authored chapter in Joseph Burke's (Ed.) *Fixing the Fragmented Public University: Decentralization with Direction* (Jossey-Bass, 2007). She is currently working on her dissertation on the rhetoric of expertise. Her other research foci include the functions of cynicism in American culture and politics, classical rhetorical theory and philosophy, and the rhetoric of digital and visual media. Hartelius directs the Pre-Graduate School Internship, part of the Intellectual Entrepreneurship Consortium at the University of Texas. She also teaches college-level courses in public speaking, rhetoric and popular culture, theories of persuasion, and interviewing.

Kristen Hoerl is Assistant Professor of Communication and Journalism at Auburn University in Auburn, Alabama, and the director of Auburn University's public speaking program. Her teaching and research areas include rhetorical criticism, critical theory, social movements, public memory, and popular culture. She is currently interested in popular media depictions of activism and dissent and their role in contemporary debates about the process of social change in the

United States. Originally from Denver, Colorado, she received her BA from the Pennsylvania State University at University Park. She received her PhD in Communication Studies from the University of Texas at Austin.

Kathryn M. Olson (PhD, Northwestern) is Professor of Communication at the University of Wisconsin–Milwaukee. Her research interests are in rhetoric and public argument. She directs the University of Wisconsin at Milwaukee's Rhetorical Leadership Graduate Certificate/Concentration Program, which is dedicated to empowering citizens. The chapter published in this collection previously appeared in the *Southern Communication Journal* and won the 2003 Southern Communication Association's Rose B. Johnson Award for the most outstanding article published in the journal in 2002. In 2006, the National Communication Association's Women's Caucus honored Professor Olson with the Francine Merritt Award, which annually recognizes one individual who has made "outstanding contributions to the lives of women in communication."

Lisa Glebatis Perks earned her MA at Pennsylvania State and is currently a doctoral candidate in the Department of Communication Studies at the University of Texas at Austin. Her scholarly interests revolve around the rhetoric of media, with particular attention to the ways in which mediated communication can empower or disempower people on the basis of race, gender, and class. She is currently writing her dissertation on the meanings television viewers co-create with stereotype-driven sketch comedy and how scholars can more thoroughly mine polysemic interpretations of humor. In her free time, Perks enjoys running, knitting, and watching reality television.

Luke Winslow is a doctoral student and Assistant Instructor at the University of Texas at Austin. He earned his BA from Azusa Pacific University and his MA from California State University at Fullerton before moving to Texas. His research interests include contemporary rhetorical criticism, the rhetoric of popular culture, and the theories and methods of Kenneth Burke. Past research has ranged from the rhetoric of Dr. Phil McGraw and the self-help movement to major league baseball's steroid controversy. Winslow is currently looking into masculinity as a rhetorical construct. He is fascinated by the way popular culture attempts to define what it means to be a "man" and the way those definitions empower some and disempower others. He is an active member of the National Communication Association and the Western States Communication Association.